LONG LIVE THE KING

LONG LIVE THE KING

THE MYSTERIOUS FATE OF EDWARD II

KATHRYN WARNER

This book is dedicated to John Alan Lamb, in memory
of sixteen years.

First published 2017

The History Press
The Mill, Brimscombe Port
Stroud, Gloucestershire, GL5 2QG
www.thehistorypress.co.uk

© Kathryn Warner, 2017

The right of Kathryn Warner to be identified as the Author
of this work has been asserted in accordance with the
Copyright, Designs and Patents Act 1988.

British Library Cataloguing in Publication Data.
A catalogue record for this book is available from the British Library.

ISBN 978 0 7509 7011 2

Typesetting and origination by The History Press
Printed in Malta by Melita Press

CONTENTS

ACKNOWLEDGEMENTS

I owe a huge debt of gratitude to Ian Mortimer, without whom it would not have been possible to write this book. His immense research on Edward II's survival after 1327 has blazed a trail for the rest of us, and his tireless dedication to uncovering the mysteries of what happened in and after 1327 has long been an inspiration to me.

I also owe a great debt to my friends of the Auramala Project in Italy, who are doing incredible research on the possibility of Edward II's survival in that country. In particular I wish to thank Ivan Fowler, MariaRosa Gatti, Elena Corbellini, Mario Traxino, Stefano Castagneto, Luciano Maffi, Elena Giacomotti, Simone Bertelegni and Alice Galbiati.

Thank you to my lovely talented friend Craig Robinson for taking superb photographs for me to use in the book, and to everyone at Berkeley Castle, especially Helen Berryman and Joshua Nash, for giving Craig access and for permission to use the photos here.

Thank you to the staff at Gloucester Cathedral, Bristol Cathedral, Cologne Cathedral (especially Christine Di Costanzo), St Mary's church in Berkeley, the church of Sant'Eustorgio and the office of cultural heritage in Milan, the cathedral archive of Genoa, the capitulary library in Vercelli, the hermitage of Sant'Alberto, Oramala Castle, the Archives départementales de l'Hérault, and the DGA Education, Culture, Jeunesse, Sport, Loisirs in Montpellier.

Thank you to the excellent genealogist and researcher Kevin McKenzie, who has helped me and the Auramala Project so much and given so generously of his time and expertise.

Thank you again to my wonderful friends in Italy, especially Gianna Baucero, Claudia Bergamini, Ezio Candellone, Maurizio Tarotti, Gabriela Grandi, Andrea Candellone, Angela Barbero Candellone, Claudia Candellone, Alberto Portalupi, Gaia Portalupi, Lorenzo Tarotti, Gian Luca Marino, Fabrizio Zerbin, Caterina Costanza, Massimo Greppi, Enza Battaglia, Monsignor Sergio Salvini, His Excellency the Archbishop of Vercelli Father Marco Arnolfo, Timoty Leonardi, and Margherita Grillo, with whom I spent a wonderful day exploring historic Milan.

Thank you to the staff at the seminary of Vercelli, the university library of Pavia, Original History Walks and the Chesterton Association, and all the others in Vercelli and Pavia who have been so incredibly generous, kind and welcoming.

Thank you to the Reverend Chris Harrington, Mary Cummins, Lesley Pinchbeck, Pete Banks, Sue Banks, Chris Cullen, Michael Cullen, Marilyn Scholefield and everyone at St Andrew's church, Heckington, Lincolnshire, for inviting me to speak there about Edward II and for their kind hospitality. Thank you to all the staff at the English Library Düsseldorf, a resource I have enjoyed for many years, and also for inviting me to speak there.

Thank you to Paul Dryburgh for giving me the opportunity to speak about Edward II at the International Medieval Congress, and to Professor Mark Ormrod of the University of York for moderating our session.

For all their support and help, thank you to my dear friends Laurel Albright, Juliana Brümmer, Rachel Fitzpatrick, Valentino Križanić Kovačić, Vishnu Nair, Jen Parcell, Sami Parkkonen, Joanne Renaud, Gillian Thomson, Julie Thomson, Sarah Ursell, Masud Vorajee and Kate Wingrove. Thank you to all my history friends on my blog and my social media, especially Bev Newman and Susan Wakefield for helping to suggest the book's title. Thank you to all of you who have been so kind to me during recent difficult times. Thank you to all my wonderful students in Düsseldorf.

Thank you always and forever to my mum Elaine, my dad Phil, my stepmum Betty and my father-in-law Alan for your endless love and support.

Without John Lamb, I would not have been able to write this book. I'm sorry that you never got to read it, my love.

Last but certainly not least, thank you to my editor Mark Beynon and everyone at The History Press for giving me the opportunity to write a book I've been desperate to write for years.

TIMELINE

25 April 1284	Birth of Edward II 'of Caernarfon', fourth son of Edward I and his first queen Leonor of Castile.
19 August 1284	Death of Edward's 10-year-old brother Alfonso of Bayonne, making Edward heir to the throne.
28 November 1290	Edward's mother Leonor of Castile dies; he inherits her county of Ponthieu in northern France.
c. late 1295	Birth of Isabella of France, daughter of Philip IV of France and Joan I of Navarre.
8 September 1299	Wedding of Edward I and his second wife Marguerite of France, half-sister of Philip IV.
1 June 1300 and 5 August 1301	Births of Edward of Caernarfon's half-brothers Thomas of Brotherton, Earl of Norfolk and Edmund of Woodstock, Earl of Kent.
7 February 1301	Edward made Prince of Wales and Earl of Chester.
7 July 1307	Edward I dies; Edward II becomes King of England and Lord of Ireland; he is already Duke of Aquitaine.
25 January 1308	Edward marries Isabella of France.
25 February 1308	Edward and Isabella's coronation as King and Queen of England.
19 June 1312	Execution of Edward's 'favourite', Piers Gaveston.

13 November 1312	Birth of Edward and Isabella's first child Edward of Windsor, later Edward III.
24 June 1314	Edward loses the Battle of Bannockburn to Robert Bruce.
15 August 1316	Birth of Edward and Isabella's second son John of Eltham, Earl of Cornwall.
18 June 1318	Birth of their third child Eleanor of Woodstock, duchess of Guelders.
c. 1319/20	Hugh Despenser the Younger becomes Edward's latest favourite.
5 July 1321	Birth of Edward and Isabella's youngest child Joan of the Tower, Queen of Scotland.
1321/22	'Contrariant' rebellion of a group of English barons against Edward and Hugh Despenser.
29 August 1321	Despenser and his father are exiled from England; they return in March 1322.
2 January 1322	Accession of Isabella's third and last brother Charles IV as King of France.
13 February 1322	Roger Mortimer imprisoned in the Tower of London during the rebellion against the king.
1 August 1323	Roger Mortimer escapes and flees to the Continent.
July 1324	Edward goes to war against his brother-in-law Charles IV of France (the War of Saint-Sardos).
18 September 1324	Edward confiscates Queen Isabella's lands.
9 March 1325	Queen Isabella leaves for France to negotiate peace between her husband and brother.
12 September 1325	Edward of Windsor, made Duke of Aquitaine and Count of Ponthieu, leaves for France; he pays homage to his uncle Charles IV on the 24th.

c. late October 1325	Isabella refuses to return to Edward unless he sends Hugh Despenser away from him.
1 December 1325	Edward writes to Isabella for the last time.
c. late 1325/early 1326	Isabella begins an association with Roger Mortimer.
5 February 1326	Isabella writes to the Archbishop of Canterbury explaining why she cannot return to Edward.
27 August 1326	Isabella betroths her son Edward of Windsor to a daughter of the Count of Hainault and Holland.
21 or 22 September 1326	Isabella's invasion force leaves Dordrecht; arrives in Suffolk on the 24th.
2 October 1326	Edward II flees from London to South Wales.
20–24 October 1326	Edward and others on the sea in South Wales.
27 October 1326	Execution of Hugh Despenser the Elder, Earl of Winchester, in Bristol.
16 November 1326	Capture of Edward II near Neath in South Wales; he is sent to Kenilworth Castle.
17 November 1326	Execution of Edmund Fitzalan, Earl of Arundel, in Hereford.
24 November 1326	Execution of Hugh Despenser the Younger in Hereford.
12 January 1327	Start of the Parliament in London which deposes Edward II.
20 January 1327	Last day of Edward II's reign.
25 January 1327	First day of Edward III's reign.
1 February 1327	Coronation of Edward III.
3 April 1327	Edward of Caernarfon moved from Kenilworth Castle to Berkeley Castle; is in Gloucester on 5 April and probably arrives at Berkeley on the 6th.

c. mid-June/mid-July 1327	The Dunheved group succeed in temporarily freeing Edward from Berkeley.
27 July 1327	Thomas, Lord Berkeley sends a second letter to the chancellor of England informing him about the attack on his castle and the Dunheveds' seizure of Edward.
14 September 1327	William Shalford, deputy justice of Wales, writes to Roger Mortimer about a Welsh plot to free Edward; Mortimer sends man-at-arms William Ockley with a message to Berkeley Castle.
21 September 1327	Official date of Edward II's death.
22 September–21 October 1327	Edward's body is guarded at Berkeley Castle by sergeant-at-arms William Beaukaire.
23/24 September 1327	Thomas Gurney informs Edward III of his father's death during the night at Lincoln.
Before 29 September 1327	Edward's joint custodian Sir John Maltravers is paid 'for services to the king's father' in Dorset and is at Corfe Castle, Dorset.
c. late September/October 1327	A group of knights, abbots and burgesses see Edward's body 'superficially' (according to one chronicler).
6 October 1327	An abbey is granted permission to keep the anniversary of Edward's death on 21 September every year.
21 October 1327	Edward II's body is moved from Berkeley Castle to St Peter's Abbey, Gloucester.
23 October 1327	The Archbishop of York asks for prayers for Edward's soul.
13 November 1327	Edward III's 15th birthday.

20 December 1327	Funeral of Edward II at St Peter's Abbey.
c. 22/24 December 1327	The woman who embalmed Edward's body is taken to Queen Isabella.
25 January 1328	Wedding of Edward III and Philippa of Hainault in York.
5 November 1328	Edward II's first cousin Henry, Earl of Lancaster tells the mayor and aldermen of London he has news from Edward's half-brother the Earl of Kent which he dare not write down.
8 March 1329	A group of men later associated with the Earl of Kent are ordered to be taken to Edward III.
24 March 1329	The Earl of Kent begins making preparations to visit Pope John XXII in Avignon; he leaves *c.* 11 June.
24 September 1329	John Maltravers named as constable of Corfe Castle, Dorset, apparently a confirmation of an appointment made on 17 November 1326.
10 October 1329	William Melton, Archbishop of York, is informed that Edward is alive; he sends a messenger to Donald, Earl of Mar in Scotland; Mar promises to bring an army to England to help release Edward.
Before 3 December 1329	The Earl of Kent returns to England.
7 December 1329	Sheriffs and justices warned about 'false rumours of the arrival of foreigners' in England, most probably with reference to Donald of Mar and his army.
14 January (almost certainly 1330)	The Archbishop of York sends a letter to his kinsman the mayor of London, Simon Swanland, telling him that Edward of Caernarfon is alive and well and in a safe place.

18 February 1330	Coronation of Philippa of Hainault, who is five months pregnant, as Queen of England; the Earl of Kent attends.
10 March 1330	Four of the Earl of Kent's adherents ordered to be arrested.
13 March 1330	Arrest of the Earl of Kent in Winchester.
14 March 1330	Order for the imprisonment of Kent's wife and children.
16 March 1330	Kent confesses to attempting to free his half-brother Edward of Caernarfon from captivity; he names some of his adherents.
19 March 1330	Execution of the Earl of Kent for treason.
31 March 1330	Order for the arrest of several dozen of Kent's adherents.
c. March/April 1330	According to the Fieschi Letter, Edward II makes his way from Corfe Castle to Ireland after hearing of the death of the Earl of Kent.
March–August 1330	Orders issued for the arrest of many more of Kent's adherents, and for inquisitions to be held across several English counties and Wales to discover the identity of others; many are imprisoned and their lands and goods seized; at least eighteen flee the country.
13 April 1330	All the sheriffs of England and the justice of Wales are told to arrest anyone who claims that Edward II is still alive; two chroniclers say that belief in Edward's survival is widespread at this time.
23 and 30 April 1330	The Archbishop of York appears before King's Bench.
15 June 1330	Birth of Edward III and Queen Philippa's first child Edward of Woodstock (later Prince of Wales and father of Richard II).

July/August 1330	Measures taken against an invasion of England from the Continent by former allies of the Earl of Kent.
8 August 1330	Justice of Wales ordered to arrest anyone supporting the Earl of Kent's adherent Sir Rhys ap Gruffudd, who in September 1327 had tried to free Edward of Caernarfon from Berkeley.
10 August 1330	Sir William Aune, constable of Caerphilly Castle, 'indicted for adhesion' to the Earl of Kent.
19 October 1330	Edward III arrests his mother Queen Isabella's favourite Roger Mortimer at Nottingham Castle; the king keeps his mother under temporary house arrest.
26 November 1330	Parliament opens at Westminster; Thomas, Lord Berkeley says that until now he had not known of Edward II's death; Thomas Gurney and William Ockley sentenced to death for Edward's murder; John Maltravers, John Deveril and Bogo Bayouse sentenced to death for the entrapment of the Earl of Kent.
29 November 1330	Execution of Roger Mortimer, Earl of March.
1 December 1330	Edward III appoints William Melton, Archbishop of York, as treasurer of England.
3 December 1330	Edward III orders the arrest of Thomas Gurney, William Ockley, John Deveril and Bogo Bayouse; Gurney, Bayouse and John Maltravers flee abroad; Ockley and Deveril disappear from history.

Early December 1330	Edward III pardons the late Earl of Kent and his adherents; restores their lands and goods; invites those who have fled to return to England.
24 December 1330	Execution of Mortimer's ally Sir Simon Bereford.
c. December 1330	According to the Fieschi Letter, Edward II leaves Ireland and travels via the port of Sandwich to Sluis in Flanders; he subsequently makes his way through France to the pope in Avignon, with whom he spends fifteen days.
20 May 1331	Edward III writes to Alfonso XI of Castile thanking him for arresting Thomas Gurney; Gurney later escapes and flees to Naples; John Maltravers evades capture in Spain and ends up in Flanders.
Early to mid-1330s	According to the Fieschi Letter, Edward II travels from Avignon to Paris, Brabant, Cologne, Milan, *Milascio* and Sant'Alberto di Butrio.
9–10 May 1332	Edward II's elder daughter Eleanor of Woodstock stays at the port of Sluis, Flanders.
26/27 May 1332	Wedding of Eleanor of Woodstock and Count Reinhoud II of Guelders in Nijmegen.
25 July 1332–31 January 1333	Giles of Spain, sent to Spain by Edward III to arrest Thomas Gurney, instead arrests several men accused of conspiring towards Edward II's death.
16 January 1333	Edward III learns that Gurney is now in Naples.
c. June 1333	Death of Thomas Gurney, arrested by Sir William Thweng, in Gascony on his way back to England.

c. summer 1332 or summer 1333	Edward of Caernarfon crosses the Alps into Italy?
Late 1333/early 1334	Edward of Caernarfon arrives in *Milascio*?
23 March 1334	Edward III sends his friend William Montacute to talk to John Maltravers, who is in exile in Flanders.
26 July 1334	Death of Bogo Bayouse in Rome.
4 December 1334	Death of Pope John XXII in Avignon; Benedict XII elected on 20 December.
29 March and 3 June 1335	Seven men in England, including Thomas, Lord Berkeley and his brother, pardoned for receiving John Maltravers.
31 January 1336	Death of Cardinal Luca Fieschi in Avignon.
13 June until late October 1336	Siege of Pontremoli, formerly a fief of Luca Fieschi and his brothers near Mulazzo, currently held by Luca's nephew-in-law; is this the 'war' which prompts Edward to move from *Milascio* to Sant'Alberto di Butrio?
16 March 1337	Thomas, Lord Berkeley cleared of all charges relating to Edward II's death and pardoned.
c. 1338	Manuele Fieschi, papal notary and future Bishop of Vercelli, writes (or completes) a letter telling Edward III that his father survived Berkeley Castle and ended up in Italy.
5 September 1338	Holy Roman Emperor Ludwig of Bavaria makes Edward III a vicar of the empire in Koblenz.
c. early September 1338	Edward III in Koblenz meets William the Welshman, 'who asserts that he is the king's father'.
13 September 1338	Pope Benedict XII appoints Arnaud Verdale as his envoy to Ludwig of Bavaria.

January 1339	Arnaud Verdale becomes Bishop of Maguelone; some years later he compiles the cartulary where the Fieschi Letter is found in the nineteenth century.
22 August 1358	Death of Isabella of France, dowager Queen of England, Edward II's widow.
27 October 1361	Death of Thomas, Lord Berkeley.
16 February 1364	Death of Sir John Maltravers.
21 June 1377	Death of Edward III, aged 64.
1877	The Fieschi Letter is discovered in a cartulary of Arnaud Verdale, and is presented in Paris on 21 September 1877, the 550th anniversary of Edward II's death.

Dramatis Personae

Royalty

Edward II, known as Edward of Caernarfon, b. 25 April 1284: son of Edward I, King of England (1239–1307; reigned 1272–1307) and his first wife Leonor of Castile (*c.* 1241–90); King of England July 1307–January 1327.

Isabella of France (*c.* 1295–22 August 1358): Queen of England; daughter of Philip IV, King of France, and Joan I, Queen of Navarre; marries Edward II on 25 January 1308.

Edward III (13 November 1312–21 June 1377): King of England; eldest child of Edward II and Isabella of France; succeeds his deposed father as king on 25 January 1327.

Philippa of Hainault (*c.* 1314–69): Queen of England; daughter of Willem, Count of Hainault and Holland, niece of Philip VI of France; marries Edward III on 25 January 1328.

John of Eltham (1316–36), **Eleanor of Woodstock** (1318–55) and **Joan of the Tower** (1321–62): the younger children of Edward II and Isabella of France.

Louis X (1289–1316), **Philip V** (*c.* 1291–1322) and **Charles IV** (1294–1328): Kings of France and Navarre; Queen Isabella's brothers.

Philip VI or Philip de Valois (1293–1350): King of France; son of Philip IV's brother Charles de Valois; Queen Isabella's first cousin and, via his sister **Jeanne de Valois**, Queen Philippa's uncle.

Edmund of Woodstock (5 August 1301–executed 19 March 1330): Earl of Kent; son of Edward I and his second queen **Marguerite of France** (1278/79–1318), the half-sister of Philip IV of France; half-brother of Edward II, uncle of Edward III and grandfather of Richard II; first cousin of Queen Isabella; his older brother is **Thomas of Brotherton**, Earl of Norfolk and Earl Marshal of England (1300–38).

Eleanor Despenser née de Clare (1292–1337): Edward II's eldest and favourite niece; second child of his second-eldest sister Joan of Acre, Countess of Gloucester (1272–1307); marries Hugh Despenser the Younger in 1306.

Thomas of Lancaster (*c.* 1278–1322): Earl of Lancaster, Leicester and Derby; grandson of Henry III, nephew of Edward I and first cousin of Edward II; half-brother of Joan I of Navarre and uncle of Queen Isabella.

Henry of Lancaster (*c.* 1281–1345): Earl of Lancaster, Leicester and Derby; brother and heir of Thomas; guardian of the former King Edward II in early 1327.

Margaret (1275–*c.* early 1330s), Duchess of Brabant and **Mary** (1279–1332), a nun at Amesbury Priory: the only two of Edward II's sisters alive after 1316.

NOBILITY

Hugh Despenser the Younger (*c.* 1288–24 November 1326): Lord of Glamorgan; appointed Edward II's chamberlain in 1318 and his 'favourite' from about 1319; marries Eleanor de Clare in 1306; Edward's nephew by marriage; his eldest son is Hugh or Huchon, born *c.* 1309.

Hugh Despenser the Elder (1261–27 October 1326): Earl of Winchester; father of Hugh Despenser the Younger; a loyal supporter of Edward II throughout his reign.

Roger Mortimer (1287–29 November 1330): Lord of Wigmore; appoints himself first Earl of March in 1328; imprisoned by Edward II in 1322, and later Isabella of France's 'favourite' and probably her co-ruler of England during Edward III's minority.

Edmund Fitzalan (1285–17 November 1326): Earl of Arundel; at first an enemy and later a close ally of Edward II; cousin and enemy of Roger Mortimer; his son and heir is **Richard**, b. *c.* 1313, who marries Hugh Despenser the Younger's eldest daughter Isabella (b. *c.* 1312) in 1321 and who joins the Earl of Kent's plot in 1330.

Donald (*c.* 1290s/early 1300s–11 August 1332): Earl of Mar; nephew of Edward II's great enemy Robert Bruce, King of Scotland, imprisoned in England as a child in 1306 by Edward I, but becomes a long-term friend and ally of Edward II.

Humphrey de Bohun (*c.* 1276–16 March 1322): Earl of Hereford; marries Edward II's fifth sister Elizabeth (d. 1316) in 1302; dies in rebellion against the king.

John de Bohun (1305–36): Earl of Hereford; eldest son of Humphrey and Elizabeth; nephew of Edward II and first cousin of Edward III.

Bishops

William Melton: elected Archbishop of York in late 1315; friend and ally of Edward II; dies April 1340; writes the Melton Letter in January 1330.

John Stratford: Bishop of Winchester 1323–33, Archbishop of Canterbury 1333–48; persecuted by Edward II in 1323.

Adam Orleton: Bishop of Hereford 1317–27, Bishop of Worcester 1327–33, Bishop of Winchester 1333–45; persecuted by Edward II in the 1320s; Stratford and Orleton play significant roles in Edward's deposition in 1326/27.

Hamo Hethe: Bishop of Rochester 1317–52; supports Edward II in 1326/27.

Stephen Gravesend: Bishop of London 1318–38; joins the Earl of Kent's plot to free Edward in 1330.

Walter Stapledon: Bishop of Exeter 1308–26; murdered in London in October 1326 after the queen's invasion.

Robert Wyvill: Bishop of Salisbury 1330–75; previously parson of Kingsclere, Hampshire, and succeeded there by his brother Walter in 1330; secretary of Queen Isabella.

Popes (in Avignon, not Rome)

Clement V: born Bertrand Got; Archbishop of Bordeaux; Pope June 1305–April 1314.

John XXII: born Jacques Duèse; Cardinal-bishop of Porto; Pope August 1316–December 1334, following a period of *Sede vacante* of over two years.

Benedict XII: born Jacques Fournier; Cardinal-bishop of Mirepoix; Pope December 1334–April 1342.

Clement VI: born Pierre Roger; Archbishop of Rouen; Pope May 1342–December 1352.

BERKELEY CASTLE, 1327 / CORFE CASTLE, 1330

Thomas, Lord Berkeley (*c*. mid-1290s–1361): Lord of Berkeley in Gloucestershire; married to Roger Mortimer's eldest daughter Margaret; imprisoned by Edward II in 1322; Edward's custodian in 1327.

Sir John Maltravers (*c*. 1290 or earlier–1364): brother-in-law of Thomas Berkeley, and a knight of Dorset; flees from England in 1322 and with Roger Mortimer on the Continent between 1323 and 1326; Edward of Caernarfon's other official custodian in 1327; constable of Corfe Castle, Dorset.

Sir Thomas Gurney: a knight of Somerset, also an enemy of the king in 1321/22; appointed by Thomas Berkeley to share custody of Edward in 1327; convicted in 1330 of Edward's murder; dies in Gascony in 1333, having fled to Spain and then Italy.

William Ockley: a man-at-arms and adherent of Roger Mortimer sent to Berkeley Castle in September 1327, and convicted in 1330 of Edward II's murder; disappears.

William Beaukaire: a royal sergeant-at-arms, probably French; seemingly an adherent of Edward II and Hugh Despenser the Younger in 1326; guards Edward's body for a month in 1327; in Edward III's household in 1328 then no longer appears on record in England.

Thomas Dunheved: a Dominican friar, and his brother **Stephen**, formerly Lord of Dunchurch in Warwickshire: leaders of a group who temporarily free Edward from Berkeley Castle in 1327.

William Shalford: Roger Mortimer's deputy justice of Wales; sends a letter to Mortimer which prompts Mortimer to send William Ockley to Berkeley Castle in September 1327.

John Deveril: Probably the acting constable of Corfe Castle under John Maltravers in 1329/30; sentenced to death in 1330 for entrapping the Earl of Kent into believing that Edward of Caernarfon was still alive; disappears.

Sir Bogo Bayouse: a knight of Yorkshire and supporter of Roger Mortimer, at Corfe Castle in 1329/30; also sentenced to death for entrapping the Earl of Kent; dies in Rome in 1334.

OTHERS

Sir Rhys ap Gruffudd (b. *c.* 1280s): a knight of South Wales and a loyal supporter of Edward II; flees to Scotland after trying to free Edward from captivity in September 1327, and involved in the Earl of Kent's plot in 1330.

Sir Gruffudd Llwyd (b. *c.* 1260s): a knight of North Wales, also a loyal supporter of Edward II; imprisoned in September 1327 for taking part in the plot to free Edward; his son is **Ieuan**.

Simon Swanland: mayor of London 1329/30; a draper, knighted 1337; kinsman of William Melton, Archbishop of York.

Thomas, Lord Wake (b.1297/98): brother-in-law of Edmund of Woodstock, Earl of Kent; first cousin of Roger Mortimer; son-in-law of Edward II's first cousin Henry, Earl of Lancaster.

Margaret Wake, Countess of Kent (b. *c.* late 1290s): sister of Thomas; marries Edward II's half-brother Edmund of Woodstock, Earl of Kent, in late 1325; grandmother of Richard II.

Sir Ingelram Berenger (b. 1271 or earlier): a knight of Wiltshire; a long-term adherent of Hugh Despenser the Elder, Earl of Winchester; joins the conspiracy of the Earl of Kent in 1329/30.

William la Zouche: Lord of Ashby, Leicestershire; captures Edward II and Hugh Despenser the Younger in November 1326; marries Despenser's widow Eleanor de Clare in early 1329; joins the conspiracy of the Earl of Kent in 1329/30.

ITALY, FRANCE, THE LOW COUNTRIES AND GERMANY, 1330S

Luca Fieschi (b. *c.* 1270/03): appointed cardinal in March 1300; dies in January 1336; born into a noble Italian family and a kinsman of Edward I and Edward II via his mother; nephew of Pope Adrian V (born Ottobuono Fieschi) and great-nephew of Pope Innocent IV (born Sinibaldo Fieschi).

Manuele Fieschi: a second cousin once removed of Luca; Bishop of Vercelli 1343–48; notary of Pope John XXII then Benedict XII from 1327; author of the Fieschi Letter.

Percivalle Fieschi: a first cousin of Manuele; appointed Bishop of Brescia in 1317 and Bishop of Tortona in 1325.

Bernabo Malaspina: nephew of Cardinal Luca Fieschi; appointed Bishop of Luni in 1321; brother of Niccolo Malaspina.

Niccolo Malaspina: nephew of Cardinal Luca; Marquis of Oramala in the Staffora valley near the hermitage of Sant'Alberto di Butrio.

Pietro Rossi: marries Cardinal Luca's niece Ginetta Fieschi in October 1328; Lord of Pontremoli.

Luchino Visconti: marries Cardinal Luca's niece Isabella Fieschi in 1331; Lord of Milan; his brother **Giovanni Visconti** is made Lord and Bishop of Novara in 1331 and Archbishop of Milan in 1342, and is Luchino's co-ruler of the city.

Antonio Fieschi: brother of Ginetta and Isabella, Cardinal Luca's nephew; succeeds his cousin Bernabo Malaspina as Bishop of Luni in 1338.

Carlo Fieschi: brother of Cardinal Luca and father of Ginetta, Isabella and Antonio; 'captain of the people' of Genoa; appointed as a member of Edward II's council in August 1315 and often acknowledged as his kinsman.

Guillaume Laudun: Archbishop of Vienne 1321–7, Archbishop of Toulouse 1327–45; dies 1352; an envoy of John XXII to Edward II several times, the last time in May/June 1326; a Dominican.

Edouard I (1294/95–1336): Count of Bar in eastern France; Edward II's nephew, son of his eldest sister Eleanor (1269–98).

John II (1275–1312): Duke of Brabant; Edward II's brother-in-law and father of John III.

John III (1300–55): Duke of Brabant; Edward II's nephew, only child of his third sister **Margaret** (1275–*c*. early 1330s).

Margareta of Brabant (1276–1311): sister of Duke John II and aunt of John III; marries **Henry of Luxembourg**, Holy Roman Emperor (*c.* 1275–1313) and is the mother of John 'the Blind', King of Bohemia (d. 1346) and Marie of Luxembourg, Queen of France (d. 1324).

Balduin of Luxembourg (*c.* 1285–1354): Archbishop of Trier from December 1307 and ruler of the town of Koblenz; brother of Henry of Luxembourg, Holy Roman Emperor, and brother-in-law of Margareta of Brabant; one of the seven electors (the men who elect the Kings of Germany).

Ludwig of Bavaria (1282–1347): also sometimes called Louis the Bavarian or *Ludwig der Bayer* in German; Holy Roman Emperor, King of Germany and Italy, Duke of Bavaria; married to Margareta of Hainault (b. 1311), sister of Philippa, Queen of Edward III of England.

Wilhelm (*c.* 1299–1361): Count, then Margrave and later Duke of Jülich; married to Johanna of Hainault, Queen Philippa's other sister; his brother **Walram von Jülich** is appointed Archbishop of Cologne in January 1332 and is one of the seven electors.

Arnaud Verdale: Bishop of Maguelone (near Montpellier in the south of France) 1339–52; Pope Benedict XII's envoy to Ludwig of Bavaria in 1338/39; the Fieschi Letter is copied into his cartulary.

William le Galeys ('the Welshman'): taken to Koblenz in *c.* early September 1338 when Edward III is meeting Ludwig of Bavaria; claims to be Edward III's father.

INTRODUCTION

It was the night of Monday 21 September 1327. King Edward III of England, not yet 15 years old, was holding Parliament at Lincoln. Also present in Lincoln was the young king's mother Queen Isabella, the real ruler of the country during her son's minority. Meanwhile, 160 miles away, Edward III's father Sir Edward of Caernarfon, formerly King Edward II, who had been forced to abdicate in favour of his teenage son nine months earlier, lay in misery at Berkeley Castle in Gloucestershire. Abandoned by everyone, detested by his wife, tormented, starved and abused, the former king was kept in a tiny cell, with decaying animal corpses deliberately disposed of nearby in the hope that the foul stench would kill him. On the night of 21 September, a group of murderers slipped into his room. They turned him on to his stomach and held him down, and inserted a drenching-horn inside his anus. A poker, heated in a fire until it was red-hot, was slid inside the horn and up into the man's intestines. His agonising screams as he died slowly could be heard miles away, and drove many of the inhabitants of Berkeley village to their knees in horror, to pray for the soul of a human dying in such torment. This method of foul murder was chosen so that no one would see marks on Edward's dead body and realise that he had been murdered, and as a punishment for his being the passive partner in sexual acts with men. Even to this day, a story goes, ghostly echoes of Edward's dying screams can still be heard at Berkeley.

If this is the tale you have always heard about Edward II's death, you are far from alone. The lurid and disgusting story of the deposed king's murder by red-hot poker at Berkeley Castle in September 1327, and the abuse and mistreatment inflicted on him beforehand by his jailers, has become part of popular culture. It appears in Christopher Marlowe's play about Edward (c. 1592) and is repeated ad nauseam online; a Google search for 'Edward II poker' brings up hundreds of thousands of hits, and the number increases all the time. The story is also still often told as though it is certainly true, and arouses considerable public interest, as grotesque torture/murders often do: in November 2015, the Yesterday channel's Medieval Murder Mysteries series featured the story, with one guest claiming that the story of the poker is true.

It is not. Edward of Caernarfon, formerly King Edward II of England, was well treated at Berkeley Castle and had servants, access to a chapel, good food, wine and wax candles, and if he was murdered there at all, it was far more likely to have been done by suffocation or smothering. The notion that he was tormented and abused and kept in a cell next to animal corpses was invented twenty-five years later by the chronicler Geoffrey le Baker, who was promoting Edward's candidacy as a saint and therefore grossly exaggerating his woes and the patience with which he suffered them; it is disproved by evidence from Berkeley Castle records and the chancery rolls issued at the time by the English government. The majority of chroniclers from the late 1320s until the 1360s do not mention a red-hot poker as the cause of Edward's death; this tale was a minority opinion first related by chroniclers far in time and place from Berkeley Castle which much later became the 'accepted' story, while the evidence from other chronicles stating that Edward was suffocated or strangled or died of illness or even natural causes was – and still is – mostly ignored. Christopher Marlowe's play about Edward in the late sixteenth century also went a long way to popularising the story. Finally, late in the twentieth century, historians began to question the red-hot poker narrative and to look at other possibilities. Most historians of the fourteenth century now reject the tale, but still assume that Edward II died at Berkeley Castle on or around 21 September 1327, most probably murdered.

Ian Mortimer is the main exception, and discusses Edward's survival past 1327 at length in his books *The Greatest Traitor*, *The Perfect King* and *Medieval Intrigue*, and also in academic articles and in essays on his website; he is the 'public face' of the notion that Edward II lived past 1327. I also argue for Edward's survival in my biographies of him and his wife Isabella, *The Unconventional King* and *The Rebel Queen*, and in my *English Historical Review* article about the plot of Edward's half-brother the Earl of Kent to free him from captivity in 1330, years after Kent attended his funeral. Although in 1978 the red-hot poker story was described as 'one of the worst *soi-disant* [so-called] histories ever to be foisted on an unsuspecting public', it is often repeated in books written about the era by non-experts as though it is certain fact, even well into the twenty-first century.[1]

For five and a half centuries, few people ever questioned the idea that Edward II died at Berkeley Castle in September 1327. In 1877, however, a remarkable document called the Fieschi Letter was discovered in an archive in Montpellier in the south of France; it was discussed by the great historian T. F. Tout at the beginning of the 1920s and published in the third volume of his Collected Papers in 1934. The Fieschi Letter describes in detail how Edward II escaped from Berkeley Castle in 1327 and made his way to Ireland, to the pope in Avignon and through Brabant, Cologne and Milan to an Italian hermitage. For all the drama and excitement of this tale, it was an entire century after the letter's discovery before Edward II's fate and possible survival really began to be examined by English-speaking historians, in a groundbreaking article entitled 'Where is Edward II?' by George Peddy Cuttino and Thomas W. Lyman in 1978. This was followed eighteen years later in 1996 by Edward II specialist Professor Roy Martin Haines' article 'Edwardus Redivivus' in the *Transactions of the Bristol and Gloucestershire Archaeological Society*, and in 2003 by Haines' long academic biography of Edward II published by a Canadian university press; he had also written a short book in 2002 about Edward's death and possible survival past 1327, aimed at the popular market.

Professor Haines is a firm believer in the idea that Edward II died at Berkeley Castle in 1327, as are Edward's other academic biographer Professor Seymour Phillips and most other historians of the period. For example, there is J. S. Hamilton's 2008 article 'The Uncertain Death of Edward II' for *History Compass*, and Nicholas Vincent's debate on the subject with Ian Mortimer in the January 2016 edition of *BBC History Magazine*. Andy King's article 'The Death of Edward II Revisited' was published in the ninth volume of *Fourteenth Century England* in June 2016, and also comes down in favour of Edward's death in September 1327. In 2003, Ian Mortimer entered the fray and first expressed his belief that Edward II did survive past 1327 in his biography of Edward's nemesis Roger Mortimer (no relation), first Earl of March, *The Greatest Traitor*; he expanded at length on his ideas in his 2005 *English Historical Review* article 'The Death of Edward II in Berkeley Castle', his 2006 biography of Edward's son Edward III, *The Perfect King*, and his 2010 collection of academic essays, *Medieval Intrigue*. In 2003 and 2005, the writers Paul Doherty and Alison Weir also discussed Edward II's potential survival in their books about Edward's queen, Isabella of France, and decided in favour of it.[2]

Paul Doherty's 1985 novel *Death of a King* is an early exploration of the possibility that Edward II survived past 1327. Written in the form of a report by a clerk of Edward III whom the king appoints to investigate his father's death, it follows the Fieschi Letter and has Edward II surviving as a hermit in Italy, but unfortunately the novel is hopelessly historically inaccurate and can hardly be taken seriously. To date, no other historian has publicly accepted the notion that Edward survived after 1327, preferring the traditional narrative that he died at Berkeley Castle that year. This is a perfectly reasonable stand to take, but the standard of debate has often been poor, with historians preferring to wield the words 'unconvincing' and 'implausible' in lieu of actual arguments when dismissing the notion that Edward II might have lived beyond his official death. A particular low point was reached in the discussion between Nicholas Vincent and Ian Mortimer about the matter in *BBC History Magazine* in January 2016, when Vincent dismissed the idea that a man who met Edward III eleven years after Edward II's death and claimed to be his father might really have been Edward II on the grounds that Vincent himself often sees a homeless man claiming to be the King of Poland on the streets of Paris in the twenty-first century and does not execute him as a royal pretender.

Yet there is considerable evidence that Edward II did indeed live past 1327, or at least that many influential people of the era believed that he did. In January 1330, the former king's close friend and ally William Melton, the Archbishop of York, told the mayor of London in a letter that Edward was then alive and in good bodily health, and asked the mayor (a wealthy draper) to provide money, clothes, shoes and other items for the supposedly dead man. In March 1330, Edward II's half-brother the Earl of Kent was beheaded after trying to free Edward from captivity. Contrary to the claims of some historians, Kent did not act alone or with a mere handful of clerics; he was supported by hundreds of people. Two contemporary chroniclers both state that a belief that Edward II was not dead was widespread in England in the late 1320s. Some years after this, probably in the late 1330s, an Italian nobleman and papal notary who later became a bishop wrote a detailed letter explaining to Edward III how his father had escaped from Berkeley Castle and had subsequently travelled to Ireland, to the pope in Avignon, and to Brabant, Germany and Italy. In Koblenz, Germany in September 1338, one of Edward III's household officials recorded that a man 'who asserts that he is the king's father' was taken to the king. And as Ian Mortimer has pointed out, the whole narrative of Edward II's death in September 1327 was set in motion by the former king's legal guardian Thomas, Lord Berkeley, who sent a letter to Edward III telling him that his father was dead. Berkeley rather curiously told Parliament three years later that he had, in fact, not heard of Edward's death until he arrived at this present Parliament. Puzzlingly, though, there is also considerable plausible evidence that Edward did die in 1327, even if the manner in which he died is not (and almost certainly never will be) clear.

Until now, there has been no book dedicated solely to exploring the mystery of the death and/or survival of Edward II, with the exception of Roy Martin Haines' *Death of a King*, a rather peculiar little book published by an obscure press in 2002, which is only 155 pages long with numerous illustrations and quotations from literature but with no footnotes, source citations or index, and which is now very difficult to find. I have decided therefore to write a book of my own on the topic, with as much detail as possible, setting out the evidence both for

Edward's death in 1327 and his survival after this date. I have divided the book into several sections. Part I contains four chapters on Edward II and his reign, the vital years of his downfall and deposition in the years 1325–27, and his imprisonment in 1327, to set the scene for readers unfamiliar with the general background. Part II looks at all the evidence for Edward's death in 1327 and its aftermath; the men charged with his murder and their fate; what fourteenth-century chronicles say about it; and so on. Part III covers the evidence for Edward's survival after 1327, including the Melton Letter, the Fieschi Letter and the Earl of Kent's plot to free him. Part IV is entitled 'Arguments For and Against Edward's Death and Survival'. There is also an afterword by Ivan Fowler of the Auramala Project (a team researching Edward's possible survival in Italy), an introduction and a conclusion, appendices containing some of the most important sources in both English and the original Latin or French, a timeline, short biographies of the main characters and photos. My aim is to introduce the reader to the debate and all the evidence both for Edward II's death in 1327 and his survival after this date, to show that there is vastly more to his story than the mythical red-hot poker.

PART I

THE RELUCTANT KING

1

THE MAKING OF THE
RELUCTANT KING, 1284–1314

Edward II was born in Caernarfon, North Wales on 25 April 1284, the feast day of St Mark the Evangelist, in the twelfth year of his father's reign as King of England. His parents were both in their 40s at the time of his birth, and in April 1284 had been married six months short of thirty years. They were Edward I, King of England, Lord of Ireland and Duke of Aquitaine, born in June 1239 and then almost 45 years old, and his Spanish queen Leonor of Castile, who was probably born in late 1241 and was thus 42 when she gave birth to Edward, her youngest child. Edward I had recently conquered North Wales, and had just begun building the magnificent and massive stone castle which still stands in Caernarfon. Edward II was therefore probably born in the middle of a muddy building site, unless Queen Leonor had decided to take more comfortable lodgings in the town itself. Edward II has always been strongly associated with his birthplace, and in his own lifetime and ever since has generally been known as Edward of Caernarfon. He was the first of three Kings of England born in Wales (the others are Henry V, born in 1386, and Henry VII, born in 1457) and the first of two English monarchs with a Spanish parent (the other is Mary I, born in 1516 as the daughter of Henry VIII and Katherine of Aragon).

Edward I had succeeded his father Henry III as King of England in November 1272. He and Queen Leonor were on crusade in the Holy Land at this time, where Edward survived an assassination attempt by Sultan Baibars on his 33rd birthday in June 1272, and returned to England in August 1274. Queen Leonor was the twelfth of the fifteen children of a great warrior-king: Fernando or Ferdinand III, King of Castile and Leon (two of the four kingdoms of medieval Spain), who died in May 1252 in Seville, where his tomb still exists in the cathedral. Fernando had recaptured much of southern Spain from its Muslim rulers the Almohad dynasty in the 1230s and 1240s, and was canonised as St Fernando four centuries after his death in 1671; his feast day is 30 May, the date of his death in 1252, and he is the patron saint of the city of Seville. Edward II's grandfather was a Spanish warrior-saint, and his many Spanish uncles included the Archbishops of Seville and Toledo, a senator of Rome, and King Alfonso X, known to history as 'the Wise' or 'the Learned' and a lawmaker, musician and astrologer; the Alphonsus crater on the Moon is named after him. The 15-year-old Lord Edward, elder son and heir of Henry III of England, married Alfonso X's much younger half-sister Doña Leonor in Burgos, northern Spain, on 1 November 1254, when she was 13 or shortly to turn 13. Over the next thirty years the couple had at least fourteen children together and perhaps as many as sixteen, though more than half of them died in childhood. By the time their fourth son and youngest child Edward of Caernarfon was born in April 1284, only six of his thirteen or more older siblings still lived: Eleanor, Joan of Acre (who was born in the Holy Land in 1272), Margaret, Mary, Elizabeth, and the only surviving boy, Alfonso.

Alfonso, named after his uncle and godfather Alfonso X of Castile, was born in Bayonne, southern France in November 1273 and had been heir to the English throne since the death of his 6-year-old brother Henry in October 1274. Edward I and Queen Leonor's first son John had died at the age of 5 in 1271 during the lifetime of his grandfather Henry III. Edward of Caernarfon was not born next in line to his father's throne, but in August 1284, four months after his birth, his brother Alfonso of Bayonne died suddenly at the age of 10. The three elder brothers he never knew having all died young, Edward of Caernarfon became heir to the throne, and luckily for his father was a healthy boy who survived childhood. His mother Queen Leonor died in November 1290 when he was only 6, and nine years later his father married a second wife, Marguerite of France, daughter of King Philip III (who was Edward I's first cousin) and half-sister of Philip IV. With Marguerite, Edward I had two more sons, Edward of Caernarfon's half-brothers: Thomas of Brotherton, Earl of Norfolk, born in June 1300, and Edmund of Woodstock, Earl of Kent, born in August 1301 and seventeen years Edward's junior. Only six of Edward I's seventeen or nineteen children outlived him: Margaret, Mary, Elizabeth and Edward II from his first marriage, and Thomas and Edmund from his second.[1]

Edward I died on 7 July 1307 at the age of 68, in the village of Burgh-by-Sands near Carlisle in the far north-west of his kingdom, on his way to yet another military campaign in Scotland. Edward's brother-in-law King Alexander III of Scotland had died in 1286, having outlived all three of his children and leaving as his sole heir his 3-year-old granddaughter Margaret 'the Maid' of Norway, daughter of King Erik II of Norway and Alexander's daughter Margaret. Margaret the Maid, Queen of Scotland in her own right, was betrothed in 1289 to her cousin Edward of Caernarfon, but she died the following year without ever setting foot in her kingdom. In 1292 the Guardians of Scotland, who had asked Edward I for his aid and counsel, chose John Balliol as their king, but in 1296 Balliol allied with Philip IV in his war against Edward I. Edward thus invaded Scotland and removed Balliol from the throne. The candidate with the second-best claim to the throne in 1292 had been Robert Bruce, and Bruce's grandson of the same name had himself crowned King of Scots in March 1306 following a ten-year interregnum. Edward I, whose counsel to the Scottish Guardians had come with a price attached – that the kings of Scotland thereafter would acknowledge him and his successors as their overlords for the kingdom – set out on a campaign against Robert Bruce, but died before he reached Scotland. His son and successor Edward II was a very different kind of man to his father, and although he had been raised to believe that he was the rightful overlord of Scotland, he was never able to impose the slightest authority on Bruce. Indeed, his merely sporadic and always unsuccessful forays into the northern kingdom allowed Bruce to entrench his position, defeat his enemies and gain numerous new allies.

Edward II was 23 years old when he became King of England and Lord of Ireland in July 1307. He already held several titles: he was Duke of Aquitaine in southern France, territory he had inherited from his father and ultimately from his great-great-grandmother Eleanor of Aquitaine, Queen of England; he had been Prince of Wales and Earl of Chester since 1301 (he was the first heir to the English throne to receive the title of Prince of Wales); and he had been Count of Ponthieu, a small county in northern France bordering Normandy, since the death of his mother Queen Leonor in 1290. Although Spanish, Eleanor had a French mother, Joan of Ponthieu, Queen of Castile, and had inherited the county from her. It passed to Edward as Leonor's only surviving son. He was thus a peer of the realm of France as well as King of England, and owed homage for his French lands to his overlord the King of France; this was to create huge problems for Edward in 1325, and he was unfortunate that during his reign of nineteen and a half years there were no fewer than four kings in France, to all of whom he owed the ceremony of homage. Although still called Dukes of Aquitaine, the Kings of England no longer held the entire duchy but only a part of it, Gascony.

It is entirely probable that Edward II's very first act as king was to recall a man named Piers Gaveston from the exile imposed on him by Edward's father some months before. Gaveston was a nobleman of Béarn in the far south of France near Spain, part of the area ruled by the Kings of England, and had lived in England since 1297. Edward I placed Gaveston in his son's household in or before 1300, and he was, almost beyond a shadow of a doubt, the great love of Edward II's life. Concerned about the two men's relationship, and unable to send his own son and heir out of the kingdom to separate them, in April 1307 Edward I exiled Gaveston from England instead. As soon as he could when his father died only a few weeks later, Edward II brought Gaveston back, gave him the Earldom of Cornwall, and made him a member of the royal family by marriage to his niece Margaret de Clare, second daughter of his second-eldest sister Joan of Acre and the oldest unmarried female member of the English royal family in 1307.

Not long after Gaveston's wedding, Edward II himself married. His bride was Isabella of France, only surviving daughter of the powerful French king Philip IV and Joan I, who was Queen of Navarre – another of the Spanish kingdoms – in her own right. Edward and Isabella's marriage had been arranged by the pope as far back as 1298 as a means of making peace between the warring kingdoms of England and France, and neither of them had the slightest choice in the matter. They married in Boulogne, northern France on 25 January 1308 – Edward also performed homage to his new father-in-law at this time as Duke of Aquitaine and Count of Ponthieu – and were crowned as King and Queen of England at Westminster Abbey exactly a month later. Isabella was probably born in late 1295, and was at least eleven and a half years Edward's junior and only 12 when they married. Her mother Queen Joan I of Navarre died in 1305 and was succeeded by Isabella's then 15-year-old brother Louis, who also acceded to the French throne as Louis X on the death of Philip IV in November 1314. Isabella's other brothers were Philip V and Charles IV, the last kings of the Capetian dynasty which had ruled France since 987; as the three brothers all left daughters but no sons, they were succeeded by their cousin Philip VI, son of Philip IV's brother Charles of Valois, and the first Valois King of France. Although it is often assumed that Edward II and Isabella of France's marriage was an unhappy, unloving tragedy from start to finish, this is not the case: there is much evidence that for many years they showed each other considerable affection, support and loyalty, and it was not until the 1320s that Edward's behaviour began to drive his wife and queen into opposition.

Within months of his accession to the throne, Edward II brought his kingdom to the brink of civil war by his passion for and favouritism towards Piers Gaveston. In 1308, a large group of English barons demanded that Gaveston be exiled. Edward refused for months, and both he and his opponents prepared for war; military confrontation seemed almost inevitable. Edward finally averted the threat when he agreed to send Gaveston out of England and appointed him lord lieutenant of Ireland, but then spent the next few months manipulating his barons and bribing Pope Clement V until Clement lifted the ban of excommunication on Gaveston if he returned to England, and the English barons consented to his return in June 1309.

Edward failed to learn his lesson; he continued to shower Gaveston with lands, gifts, appointments and favours, while Gaveston gave his baronial opponents insulting nicknames and acted with a haughtiness and superiority which they found unbearable. He was exiled from England for a third time in late 1311, this time leaving his royal wife Margaret de Clare behind in England, pregnant. Yet again early in 1312, Edward II brought Gaveston back to England, unable and unwilling to live without him, and restored him to the Earldom of Cornwall. A group of exasperated barons captured Gaveston in June 1312, just five months after the birth of his and Margaret de Clare's only child Joan, and had him run through with a sword and beheaded at Blacklow Hill in Warwickshire. Their leader was the richest and most powerful earl in England, a man of high royal birth: Thomas of Lancaster, Earl of Lancaster, Leicester, Derby, Lincoln and Salisbury, who was Edward II's first cousin (he was the elder son of Edward I's younger brother Edmund of Lancaster) and Queen Isabella's uncle (he was the younger half-brother of her mother Queen Joan I of Navarre). King Edward would never forgive Lancaster for this act of murder, and the hostile relations between the two cousins dominated English politics for the next decade.

Queen Isabella, now 16 or 17, was four months pregnant at the time of Piers Gaveston's murder, and on Monday 13 November 1312 at Windsor Castle she gave birth to her and Edward II's first child, the future King Edward III. Despite some modern speculation, there is no doubt whatsoever that Edward II was his son's real father. The assumption that he was not is solely a modern idea first mooted in the 1980s, and is based entirely on the presumption that because Edward II was a lover of men, he was necessarily incapable of intercourse with women. This theory is disproved by the existence of Edward's illegitimate son Adam, who was born sometime between 1305 and 1310 either before Edward's marriage to Isabella or when she was still too young to be his wife in more than name only, and by the behaviour of contemporaries: there was clearly not the slightest doubt in anyone's mind that Edward III was the true son of Edward II. Three more royal children were to follow: John of Eltham, Earl of Cornwall, in August 1316; Eleanor of Woodstock, Duchess of Guelders, in June 1318; and Joan of the Tower, Queen of Scots, born in the Tower of London in July 1321. The royal couple made a long and successful visit to Isabella's homeland in the summer of 1313 to attend the simultaneous knighting of Isabella's three brothers and her cousin Philip de Valois, an eventful stay during which Edward passed the first anniversary of Piers Gaveston's murder by watching more than fifty entertainers dance for him naked and a little later saved Isabella's life when a fire broke out in their pavilion one night. She may have suffered a miscarriage later that year.

Edward II had led an unsuccessful military campaign in Scotland in 1310–11 when he failed to engage Robert Bruce in battle or to weaken his position at all. Still confident that he was the rightful overlord of Bruce's kingdom, however, he waged a much more successful campaign against Bruce in the papal court: the popes Clement V (died 1314) and his successor John XXII (died 1334) were both firmly on Edward's side in the matter, and frequently republished the sentence of excommunication on Bruce for the murder of his rival John Comyn, Lord of Badenoch, in 1306. In the summer of 1314, Edward finally led a great army north and faced Bruce at the Battle of Bannockburn on 24 June. Only three of Edward's earls accompanied him: his nephew Gilbert de Clare, Earl of Gloucester, his brother-in-law Humphrey de Bohun, Earl of Hereford, and his cousin Aymer de Valence, Earl of Pembroke. Edward had already alienated many of his powerful earls and barons to the extent that they were unwilling to fight for him. Young Gloucester, the greatest nobleman in England after Edward's powerful and detested cousin Thomas of Lancaster, was killed during the rout, as was John Comyn of Badenoch's son John Comyn the younger, and Edward himself had to be dragged protesting from the field by the Earl of Pembroke when Pembroke realised the battle was lost. Although the king had fought bravely in the middle of the field and acquitted himself well (one chronicler says he fought 'like a lioness deprived of her cubs'), the loss at Bannockburn was a crushing humiliation which weakened his position even further. And over the next few years, things went from bad to worse.

2

THE KING AND THE
CONTRARIANTS, 1314–1324

A natural disaster occurred in England and elsewhere in northern
Europe in the years 1315 to 1317: it hardly stopped raining from
1314 to 1316, and crops rotted in the fields. Prices for such food-
stuffs as were available increased dramatically, beyond the reach of
most people. Five or perhaps as much as 10 per cent of the population starved to death, or perished as diseases swept the country, and
one chronicler even claims that some desperate people resorted to
cannibalism. Edward II finally had Piers Gaveston buried at Langley
Priory in Hertfordshire, which the king himself had founded in 1308,
at the beginning of 1315, two and a half years after Gaveston's murder.
That same year, a new man rose in Edward's affections: a knight of
Oxfordshire called Roger Damory, who had fought in the retinue of
Edward's nephew the Earl of Gloucester at the Battle of Bannockburn.
In the spring of 1317, Edward arranged Damory's marriage to his
twice-widowed niece Elizabeth de Clare, and another court favourite,
Sir Hugh Audley, married Elizabeth's sister Margaret de Clare, Piers
Gaveston's widow, at the same time. Elizabeth, Margaret and their
eldest sister Eleanor were co-heirs to the vast fortune of their late
brother the Earl of Gloucester (killed at Bannockburn in 1314), and
in 1317 Gloucester's lands in England, Wales and Ireland were divided
among the three sisters and their husbands. Eleanor had been married
to Hugh Despenser the Younger since 1306: he was the nephew of

Guy Beauchamp, Earl of Warwick, who had abducted Piers Gaveston in 1312 and imprisoned him before his assassination, and who died in 1315. Despenser's father Hugh Despenser the Elder was, however, an ardent royalist who staunchly supported Edward II for his entire reign. Edward had apparently long disliked and distrusted Hugh Despenser the Younger, but after the barons appointed Despenser as his chamberlain in 1318 against his wishes, his feelings underwent a sea change. In about 1319/20, Despenser became the king's great 'favourite', perhaps his lover, or perhaps a close friend and useful political ally. At any rate, Edward became so closely involved with Despenser that the latter was called 'the king's right eye', and in 1326 one annalist even referred to them as 'the king and his husband'.[1] All three of the king's de Clare nieces were married to men who were in some way involved in intense relationships with their uncle, though the nature of these relationships – sexual, romantic or only friendly – cannot be established for certain.

Throughout these close associations with Piers Gaveston, Roger Damory and Hugh Audley, Edward II remained on excellent terms with his queen, Isabella of France. If she was hostile to Gaveston, Damory and Audley, there is no sign of it, and indeed she is known to have given Roger Damory splendid gifts for his chapel and to have aided Piers Gaveston in some way during his third and final exile in late 1311.[2] The king's response to hearing the news of her first pregnancy in 1312 was to give her a generous gift of pearls, and he certainly did not abandon her weeping and pregnant at Tynemouth that year to save Gaveston instead, as one rather later chronicler of St Albans claimed: the chronicler confused events of 1312 with another occasion ten years later when Isabella truly was in danger of capture by Robert Bruce's forces at Tynemouth.[3] Edward paid for all of Isabella's household expenses, and the royal couple spent almost all of their time together; on the rare occasions they were apart, they sent each other frequent letters (Isabella wrote to Edward no fewer than three times in four days in February 1312).[4] Edward had publicly caused Isabella humiliation during their coronation banquet in February 1308 by ignoring her to talk to Gaveston and by hanging the latter's coat of arms on the walls of Westminster Hall instead of Isabella's, but when they married Isabella was barely even 12, and Edward came to show much more interest, respect and affection towards her as she grew older. An eyewitness who observed the couple at close quarters during their trip to France in 1313 stated that Edward loved Isabella; the two were very close on their visit and probably during the rest of their marriage, though unfortunately English observers did not bother to record the state of their king and queen's personal relationship. Edward, as well as paying all of Isabella's expenses, often gave her lands and she frequently interceded with him on behalf of others, and although most of their letters to each other sadly no longer survive, those which do reveal that Edward called Isabella his 'dear heart' while she called him 'my very sweet heart'.

Edward II failed yet again against Robert Bruce, King of Scots, when in 1318 Bruce captured the vital northern port of Berwick-upon-Tweed and Edward's siege and attempted recapture of the town in September 1319 proved entirely ineffective. The siege worsened the king's already dire relations with his powerful cousin Thomas, Earl of Lancaster, still further, and Edward publicly declared that one day soon he would take revenge for the 'wrong' done to Piers Gaveston: a threat aimed at the earl, whom Edward held responsible for Gaveston's death and whom he detested. In the summer of 1320, Edward, Isabella and a large number of the English nobility sailed to France, where Edward had to pay homage to his brother-in-law Philip V for the Duchy of Aquitaine and County of Ponthieu. His eldest brother-in-law Louis X had died in June 1316 at the age of only 26, having reigned for a mere nineteen months, and Edward had thus avoided the ceremony of homage, which he found intolerably demeaning. He had managed to put off paying homage to Philip V for three and a half years, and having finally done so in the summer of 1320, must have been annoyed when Philip died only eighteen months later, barely 30 years old. Charles IV, the last of Isabella's three older brothers, succeeded as King of France at the beginning of 1322.

Before that, Edward's favouritism towards his nephew-in-law, chamberlain and 'favourite' Hugh Despenser the Younger had once again pushed his kingdom towards civil war. In the autumn of 1320, an alliance of barons whom the king later took to calling the 'Contrariants' formed a powerful opposition to Despenser, and in May 1321 this broke out into mass civil unrest when the Contrariants attacked the lands of Despenser and his father throughout England and Wales and forced the two into exile in August 1321. Edward led a successful military campaign against the rebellious barons in the winter of 1321–22, and after the royal army under the command of the sheriff of Cumberland Sir Andrew Harclay defeated the Contrariant army at the Battle of Boroughbridge in Yorkshire on 16 March 1322, executed about twenty of them, including his own first cousin Thomas, Earl of Lancaster. Lancaster was beheaded for treason outside his own Yorkshire castle of Pontefract, though contemporaries were in no doubt that his real crime was the execution or murder of Piers Gaveston ten years before. Numerous other Contrariants were imprisoned, including Roger Mortimer, lord of Wigmore in Herefordshire, who was 35 in 1322 and a former ally of the king, and his uncle Roger Mortimer of Chirk. Both men were imprisoned in the Tower of London with a small number of attendants and a pittance to live on. The Mortimers were originally sentenced to death; Edward II commuted this to life imprisonment, a decision he surely came to regret bitterly. Mortimer of Chirk died in the Tower in 1326, aged about 70, while Mortimer of Wigmore's wife Joan Geneville was kept under house arrest with eight servants for the rest of Edward II's reign; three of his four sons were imprisoned and three of his eight daughters were incarcerated in nunneries (though not veiled as nuns). The king's former favourite and nephew-in-law Roger Damory was another of the men who died fighting against Edward during the Contrariant rebellion.

After the victory over the Contrariants, Edward II, Hugh Despenser the Younger and his father Hugh Despenser the Elder, now 61 and made Earl of Winchester in 1322, made themselves even more unpopular than they had been previously with their greed and tendency to despotism. And although Queen Isabella had always supported her husband loyally, in and after 1322 the royal marriage began to deteriorate. Edward II went to war with her brother Charles IV of France in the summer of 1324 over his failure to travel to France to swear the homage he owed to Charles for his lands in Gascony and Ponthieu: a little-known conflict between the two countries called the War of Saint-Sardos. Edward – most unfairly – treated his queen as an enemy alien. He confiscated all her lands in September 1324 and gave her instead a much smaller income from the Exchequer, and in and after 1322 Isabella rarely appears on record. She had previously wielded considerable political influence over her husband and often interceded with him, but it seems that Edward now decided that he no longer trusted her and acted as though Hugh Despenser the Younger, a man Isabella feared and detested, was his true consort. Edward did not, however, remove Isabella's children from her as is often claimed nowadays, which is a modern invention based on no contemporary sources whatsoever, and there is no real reason either to think that Isabella was in secret contact with her husband's most dangerous enemy, Roger Mortimer of Wigmore, at this time. Mortimer made a daring escape from the Tower of London on 1 August 1323, and made his way to the Continent, where he joined other English rebels and malcontents who had fled from England in 1322 such as Sir John Maltravers. It is beyond doubt, however, that Edward's confiscation of Isabella's lands and income angered her and was to push her into opposition to him and Hugh Despenser.

By alienating his queen, Edward II made a bad enemy who would ultimately bring about his and his beloved Hugh Despenser's downfall. He was beset by crises: he and Hugh Despenser, and Despenser's father the Earl of Winchester, made themselves extremely unpopular by their greed and despotism, and by 1325 they had few important allies left. One of them was Edmund Fitzalan, Earl of Arundel, formerly an enemy of the king who had attended Piers Gaveston's execution or murder but who came over to Edward's side; he was a rival and enemy of Roger Mortimer, his close kinsman. Other allies of the king included William Melton, Archbishop of York, and several other bishops including Walter Stapeldon of Exeter and Hamo Hethe of Rochester. The country generally, however, seethed with discontent. Edward II turned his back on it all and instead took part in his unconventional and highly criticised activities such as digging ditches, fishing and spending time with his lowborn subjects; carpenters, fishermen, ditchers and blacksmiths. In 1325, the final crisis of the era, the one which would end his reign and perhaps his life as well, began.

3

INVASION AND DEPOSITION, 1325–1326

Edward II, at war with France, decided to send his wife Isabella, sister of Charles IV, to her homeland to negotiate a peace settlement with her brother. Isabella left her husband's kingdom on 9 March 1325, sailing from Dover with a large retinue of attendants and thousands of pounds for her expenses from her husband. The later chronicler Jean Froissart of Hainault (born *c.* 1337) made up a very silly story that Isabella pretended to go on pilgrimage to Canterbury and, persecuted by her cruel husband, secretly fled the country from the port of Winchelsea with her son the heir to the throne; a story which was taken rather too seriously by some later writers. The author of the *Vita Edwardi Secundi* or 'Life of Edward II', a well-informed royal clerk, said more soberly that Isabella was keen to leave the company of some whom she did not like, meaning her husband's powerful chamberlain and 'favourite' Hugh Despenser the Younger and his father Hugh the Elder, Earl of Winchester. It is likely that Isabella went at the suggestion of Pope John XXII, who was keen for England and France to end their conflict and who called Isabella an 'angel of peace'. Isabella travelled around France for some months, meeting and dining with numerous relatives and visiting religious shrines, and negotiated a peace settlement between her brother and her husband after months of difficult negotiations. There is no hint that she met or communicated with her husband's enemies on the Continent, Roger Mortimer, John Maltravers and others.

In September 1325, Edward II made what with hindsight was probably the most terrible mistake of his life when he sent his son to France in his place to pay homage to Charles IV for Gascony and Ponthieu. Edward of Windsor, born in November 1312 and the eldest of Edward II and Isabella's four children, was not quite 13 at this time, and was made Duke of Aquitaine and Count of Ponthieu so that he could travel to France in his father's stead. It is often thought that Edward II fell into his wife's trap, and that Isabella had been planning and plotting to get her son to France and out of his father's control so that she could use him as a weapon against Edward. In fact Edward II agonised for weeks over sending his son to France or going himself. He had painted himself into a corner where all the options open to him were fraught with risk and would involve danger to himself, his son or Hugh Despenser, or all of them.[1]

Whether Isabella had connived to have her son join her or not, the king's heir was now under her control, and, safe at her brother's court and away from her husband, she decided to use this fact to her advantage. She loathed and feared Hugh Despenser the Younger, and imposed an ultimatum on Edward: either he must send Despenser away from him, or Isabella would remain in France and would not return to him, nor permit his son to return. To emphasise that she was entirely serious, Isabella took to wearing the clothes of a widow, and thus publicly portrayed herself as a woman in mourning for the loss of her husband and the death of her marriage. Edward II, unfortunately, failed to take his wife seriously, and refused to expel Hugh Despenser – on whom he was in some way dependent – away from his court and his side. This left Isabella with no choice but to remain in France with her elder son.

At some point in late 1325 or early 1326, Isabella began some kind of association with the escaped English rebel Roger Mortimer, who had arrived at the French court. Although often presented in much modern writing as a great and passionate love affair, there is no evidence that Isabella and Mortimer's association was anything of the sort, and it is far more likely to have been a pragmatic alliance between two people who wanted nothing more than to return to England and to be restored to their lands, income and families, at least in the beginning (it may have developed into something more later on).[2] They both loathed Hugh Despenser, and realised they could use each other to oust him from power. Despenser was so entrenched in Edward II's favour that only military action or at least the threat of it could remove him; Isabella as a woman had no capacity to lead an army, and thus needed the capable war leader Mortimer. For his part, Mortimer had no pretext for invading Edward II's kingdom or expectation of much support from its people without the queen-consort of England and her son the future king as figureheads; had he been able to do so, he would have acted against Edward II long before 1326.

Isabella arranged a future marriage between her son Edward of Windsor and a daughter of Willem, Count of Hainault and Holland, whose wife Jeanne de Valois was her first cousin. The daughter was Philippa of Hainault, who wed Edward III in early 1328 and who was married to him for over forty years until her death in August 1369. The alliance with the wealthy counties of Hainault and Holland gave Isabella and Roger Mortimer access to ships and mercenaries to invade England and the chance to bring about the downfall of the hated Hugh Despenser. Ultimately, whether Isabella had intended this or not, it also brought about the downfall of her husband Edward II. She appears, however, to have been trying to reconcile with him in 1326: she sent a letter to the Archbishop of Canterbury in February explaining that she was unable to return to him because of her great fear of Hugh Despenser, that being apart from Edward caused her much distress, and that above all else she wished to remain in her husband's company and to die there. Most unconventionally, she referred to Edward as her 'very dear and very sweet lord and friend'. She also told Roger Mortimer at some point in 1326 that she was intending to return to Edward; furious, Mortimer told her that if she did so, she would be stabbed either by Mortimer himself or by Edward II (the identification of the 'he' who would do this is not clear).

Isabella's invasion force left the port of Dordrecht in Holland on 21 or 22 September 1326. With her were her son and the heir to the English throne Edward of Windsor, almost 14 years old; Edmund of Woodstock, Earl of Kent, the younger of Edward II's half-brothers (as well as being the youngest son of Edward I, Kent was Isabella's first cousin via his mother Marguerite of France); and Roger Mortimer and other English exiles who had fled the country after the Contrariant defeat in March 1322. They landed on 24 September in Suffolk, on the lands of Edward II's other half-brother Thomas of Brotherton, Earl of Norfolk, who immediately joined them. Another powerful English nobleman who came over to the rebels' cause was Henry of Lancaster, whose brother Thomas, Earl of Lancaster, had been beheaded by Edward in 1322. Henry was Edward II's first cousin, Queen Isabella's uncle and his brother Thomas's heir, and had been deprived of much of his inheritance by his cousin the king; he joined Isabella in the hope of gaining it, and, as with the king's half-brothers who had been edged out of power by Hugh Despenser, the hope of gaining his rightful position at court. With Edward II's half-brothers and cousin on their side, as well as the queen and the heir to the throne, the remnant of the Contrariant faction of 1322, most of the northern lords (who followed Henry of Lancaster) and many bishops, the rebels' advance was inevitable, and their position swiftly became unassailable.

When the invasion force arrived, Edward II was in the Tower of London with the Despensers and his eldest and favourite niece Eleanor Despenser née de Clare, wife of Hugh the Younger, with whom Edward, bizarrely, was said by one Flemish chronicle to be having an incestuous affair.[3] Edward soon realised that he could not hold his hostile capital, and travelled towards South Wales where he hoped to find support and soldiers. With him went the Despensers and his other important noble ally the Earl of Arundel, leaving Eleanor Despenser and the king's 10-year-old second son John of Eltham in charge of London and the Tower. Isabella and her allies also moved towards the west, joined by ever more people, pillaging the lands of the Despensers and others as they went. Edward put a bounty of £1,000 on the head of Roger Mortimer; Isabella responded with one of £2,000 for Hugh Despenser the Younger. She, her son and her brother-in-law the Earl of Kent issued a proclamation, holding Despenser responsible for the ills which had befallen the kingdom; Edward II himself was not blamed, though the Bishop of Hereford, Adam Orleton, a man Edward had persecuted because he believed Orleton had supported Mortimer against himself in 1322, preached a sermon in Oxford accusing Edward of being a sodomite. Orleton later claimed that he had been talking about Despenser the Younger.

The king tried desperately to raise troops, but his support was already badly failing, and several of his allies went over to the queen. Edward, Hugh Despenser the Younger and (probably) the Earl of Arundel reached Chepstow in South Wales on 16 October, and on the 20th tried to sail from there, most likely intending to reach Ireland and attempt to launch a counter-invasion. Even the winds were against the King of England, however, and after five fruitless days bobbing about on the sea, they were forced to put in at Cardiff. On 27 October, the great port of Bristol (then England's second-largest city) fell to Queen Isabella, and on the same day she had Hugh Despenser the Elder, the 65-year-old Earl of Winchester, executed there. Winchester was hanged in his armour, his head sent on a spear to the town of Winchester in Hampshire to be publicly displayed there, and his body fed to dogs. One of Edward II's closest friends and allies fled from Bristol and back to his homeland of Scotland: Donald, Earl of Mar, nephew of King Robert Bruce. Mar had been captured and imprisoned by Edward I as a child in 1306 and seen many of his uncles executed and his aunts imprisoned, yet he later joined Edward II's household and refused to return to Scotland after Edward's defeat at Bannockburn, preferring to stay at Edward's court. Mar's long association with Edward was far from over.

Edward and the younger Hugh Despenser left Despenser's great castle of Caerphilly in Glamorgan at the beginning of November 1326, leaving Edward's money and treasure inside under the control of Despenser's eldest son Hugh or Huchon (his nickname), then aged 17 or 18 and the king's eldest great-nephew. They also left a few dozen members of Edward's household behind, and the account of the king's chamber, one of the departments of his household, was kept for the last time at Caerphilly on 31 October. Edward seems by now to have had no idea what to do, and was simply wandering around South Wales helplessly. On 10 November he appointed several men to send as envoys to Isabella, including his teenage nephew Edward de Bohun, the loyal Welsh knight Sir Rhys ap Gruffudd, and his squires John Harsik and Oliver of Bordeaux, though events overtook the king and the men were never sent. Edward was captured near Neath, South Wales on 16 November 1326 with Hugh Despenser the Younger, the chancellor of England Robert Baldock, and a few others; his disastrous reign unofficially ended at that moment. Despenser was slowly and horribly executed in Hereford on 24 November 1326 in the presence of Queen Isabella; the king's other main noble ally, Edmund Fitzalan, Earl of Arundel, had been beheaded also in Hereford a week earlier on the orders of his cousin Roger Mortimer, without a trial and with an inexperienced and inept executioner wielding an apparently blunt axe. Despenser's widow Eleanor, the king's eldest niece who had been left in charge of the Tower of London, was imprisoned there on 17 November, and three of her five daughters were forcibly veiled as nuns on 1 January 1327, even though they were still children (the eldest daughter, Isabel, was married to the executed Earl of Arundel's son Richard, and thus escaped, as did the youngest, Elizabeth, who was still a baby or not yet born).

Even at this late stage, it appears that Isabella wished to reconcile with her husband and to seek his forgiveness, at least according to one anonymous chronicle from Flanders which gives an extremely detailed and mostly accurate account of the events of 1326. It states that after Edward was captured, she went to his chamber and knelt in front of him, begging him for God's sake to 'cool his anger' with her, but he refused to talk to her or even to look at her.[4] This statement, not confirmed by any other source, is the only information we have that Isabella and Edward II came face to face in 1326–27; otherwise there is nothing to show that the royal couple ever met again after Isabella left for France on 9 March 1325. It is possible that they did, however. Edward's cousin and Isabella's uncle Henry of Lancaster was one of the men who sat in judgement on Hugh Despenser the Younger, tried and executed in Hereford on 24 November 1326, and it is certain that Edward was in Lancaster's custody after his capture on 16 November. The king therefore may well have been in Hereford at this time – though one hopes that Edward was not forced to watch the grotesque execution of a man he loved – and perhaps did meet his wife. The matter remains unclear. It is highly likely that Isabella found her opposition to Edward painful and difficult, and that she had desired

the removal of her husband's loathed favourite from his side, not necessarily the downfall of Edward himself. Isabella's kneeling before her
husband hardly indicates that she was treating him with disrespect,
even eight weeks or so after her invasion force arrived in England.
After Isabella had Hugh Despenser executed, however, there could
have been no reconciliation between the couple; this was something
Edward would never have been able to forgive.

The queen and her allies met at Wallingford near Oxford over
Christmas 1326 to discuss what should be done with the king, and it
was finally decided that he must be made to abdicate in favour of his
14-year-old son Edward of Windsor and that he would spend the rest
of his life in comfortable captivity. Parliament opened in London on
12 January 1327; the location was chosen deliberately as the city had
long been hostile to Edward II and his royal ancestors, and Edward's
ally Walter Stapeldon, Bishop of Exeter, had been murdered there in
October 1326. In a carefully stage-managed event, almost certainly
planned and carried out by John Stratford, Bishop of Winchester
and Adam Orleton, Bishop of Hereford, with Roger Mortimer's first
cousin Thomas Wake and his men planted in the crowd to shout support for the king's deposition, Edward II was deprived of his throne.
Four men, the Archbishop of York and the Bishops of Rochester,
London and Carlisle, bravely spoke out for the king, but otherwise
Edward II's downfall was rapid and, as far as we know, almost unop-
posed. Only the garrison of Hugh Despenser the Younger's castle of
Caerphilly held out against Isabella, with Despenser's son Huchon and
many former members of Edward II's household inside. Isabella was
determined to have the teenaged Huchon executed, but the garrison
refused, despite a long siege of the castle, to give him up, and finally in
March 1327 he and they were pardoned.

Edward II's deposition was a revolutionary act in England.
Although several of Edward's predecessors had stood in danger of
losing their throne, most notably his great-grandfather King John
who died suddenly in 1216 with much of his kingdom under the
control of the invader Louis of France (the future King Louis VIII
and Queen Isabella's great-great-grandfather), it had never quite
come to that critical moment. Although with hindsight Edward's

downfall, deposition and even his death have come to be seen as inevitable, they were not.

For almost four years, Isabella of France and Roger Mortimer ruled England during Edward III's minority, or at least, it can be assumed that they did despite a lack of real records proving that they were in charge of the government. They proved every bit as incompetent and greedy as Edward II and Hugh Despenser had, until Edward III overthrew them on 19 October 1330: he and twenty or so young knights launched a surprise attack at Nottingham Castle and arrested Mortimer. The young king was not quite 18, but already father to a son since June 1330, and with the succession to his throne assured, struck with speed and ruthlessness at his mother's detested favourite. He had Mortimer executed on 29 November 1330, and his mother forcibly retired. Thereafter, Edward III ruled his own kingdom, fathered a dozen children with his queen Philippa of Hainault, began the Hundred Years War against France, survived several outbreaks of the Black Death, and died in his bed on 21 June 1377 at the age of 64, following a reign of half a century.

For the first few months of Edward III's reign, his father was still alive; a curious and unprecedented situation in England, one which forced people to confront the awkward situation of what exactly was meant to be done with a former king during the reign of his successor. Although the possibility of Edward II's execution had been discussed at the Wallingford council of December 1326, this was firmly rejected, not least by Queen Isabella, and it was unclear on which grounds he might have been executed anyway. It was therefore decided that Edward would be held in comfortable captivity for the rest of his life and well looked after as befitted a man of high royal birth who had been an anointed king, was the father of the king, a son of a king, and the grandson of two more kings. And yet, the imprisonment of a former king, as was perhaps inevitable, continued to cause problems for the regime which had succeeded him. Edward of Caernarfon still had supporters, and in 1327 they acted to rescue him.

4

IMPRISONMENT OF A KING, 1327

In the early months of 1327, Sir Edward of Caernarfon lived in comfortable captivity at Kenilworth Castle, in the custody of his cousin Henry, Earl of Lancaster. Lancaster was a very different kind of man to his prickly older brother Thomas, whom Edward II had beheaded in 1322, and treated his cousin with respect. Henry of Lancaster supported his niece Isabella in 1326 and early 1327 so that he could be restored to the vast inheritance which was rightly his and which Edward II had mostly appropriated for himself, but Isabella kept him out of power and he had little if any access to the young Edward III, whose legal guardian Lancaster was. Isabella and Roger Mortimer feared Lancaster's influence and wealth, and his custody of the former king gave him a hold over them. Therefore they determined to remove Isabella's husband from Kenilworth and give Edward instead into the custody of men they could trust: Thomas, Lord Berkeley, and Sir John Maltravers. Berkeley, the powerful lord of Berkeley Castle, Gloucestershire and owner of many lands in Gloucestershire and Somerset in the south-west of England, was born in about 1295 and was imprisoned by Edward II after the Contrariant rebellion in 1322. He was freed after the invasion of 1326, but his father Maurice had died while still in prison that year. Thomas Berkeley married Roger Mortimer's eldest daughter Margaret in 1319 – Edward II had her temporarily incarcerated in a nunnery in 1324 – and because of this connection and his own recent family history, had no reason to love Edward of Caernarfon. John Maltravers, a knight of Dorset, was Thomas Berkeley's brother-in-law. Knighted with Edward, Roger Mortimer, Hugh Despenser and many others at Westminster on 22 May 1306, he also joined the Contrariants in 1321 and fled the country after their loss at Boroughbridge in March 1322, though his father John Maltravers the elder remained in England and loyal to Edward II. Maltravers spent years in exile on the Continent and was reunited with Roger Mortimer after the latter's escape in 1323, and took part in the 1326 invasion.

Almost nothing is known about it, but in about March 1327, Kenilworth Castle was attacked by a force of men determined to free Edward of Caernarfon. The attack, which failed, was led by two brothers called Thomas and Stephen Dunheved. Thomas was a Dominican friar whom Edward had sent to Pope John XXII in 1325 to complain about the Archbishop of Dublin (two fourteenth-century chroniclers heard and reported false rumours that he had been sent to procure an annulment of Edward's marriage to Isabella, which is not true for all that it has often been repeated as 'fact' ever since).[1] John XXII thought highly enough of Thomas to make him a papal chaplain when he was at his court in Avignon in September 1325, but also warned the prior provincial of all the Dominicans in England to 'keep [him] under obedience' and correct his behaviour, as being made a papal chaplain had gone to Thomas's head and led him to act as though he were free from the Dominican order.[2] Thomas was back in England by 9 November 1325, when he was paid 10s for carrying Edward II's letters to Hugh Despenser the Younger in Wales.[3] The Dominicans, also known as the Blackfriars or Friars Preacher, were Edward II's favourite order; all his confessors were Dominican, and in 1308 he had founded a Dominican priory at his favourite residence of Langley in Hertfordshire, where he buried his beloved Piers Gaveston at the beginning of 1315. In return the friars were staunch supporters of his, and the London chapter had been forced to flee from the city after Isabella's invasion of 1326, so close was the Dominicans' association with Edward.

Thomas's brother Stephen Dunheved was formerly lord of the village of Dunchurch, just outside Rugby on Dunsmore Heath in

Warwickshire. In or before 1321, he committed an unspecified serious crime for which he abjured the realm (a legal procedure whereby someone expecting execution could instead voluntarily banish themselves from England). Edward II pardoned him and allowed him to return to England, and in February 1322, during the Contrariant rebellion, Stephen Dunheved joined the king's household as a valet and was made temporary keeper of Lyonshall Castle in Herefordshire. At the same time, Dunheved was appointed to seize all the lands and goods of Roger Mortimer, who had just been arrested and sent to the Tower of London; one of the men appointed with him was John Daniel, whom Mortimer later beheaded without a trial with the Earl of Arundel on 17 November 1326.[4] Stephen Dunheved's manor of Dunchurch passed to his brother John Dunheved, who did not join his brothers in attempting to free Edward of Caernarfon in 1327 but who was pardoned for a serious felony on 5 May 1327, the day after Stephen was ordered to be arrested and taken to Queen Isabella because of his attempts to liberate the former king.[5] Both Thomas and Stephen Dunheved were fanatical supporters of Edward of Caernarfon, and the activities of Thomas in particular came to the attention of several chroniclers. The Lanercost chronicler wrote that he 'travelled through England, not only secretly but even openly, stirring up the people of the south and north to rise for the deposed and imprisoned king and restore the kingdom to him'.[6] It is more likely that in fact the Dunheved brothers and their associates had little clear idea of what they wanted to do with Edward after his release, or precisely how they might be able to restore him to his lost throne. The *Annales Paulini* also noted Thomas Dunheved's activities, and claimed that 'some magnates' (*quibusdam magnatibus*) supported him in his attempts to free Edward, though they are not named, and this statement may or may not be true.[7] The attempt by the Dunheveds and their supporters to free Edward from Kenilworth was probably another reason why he was moved to Berkeley Castle, as the *Anonimalle Chronicle* says.[8] The chronicler Adam Murimuth claimed that Edward was removed from Kenilworth because he was being 'treated too delicately' there, though this may have been written with hindsight after his supposed murder a few months later.[9]

Thomas Berkeley and John Maltravers were given legal responsibility for the custody of Edward of Caernarfon, and on 24 April 1327 were granted the massive sum of £5 per day to feed and clothe him and his household (at a time when most people in England did not even earn £5 a year). On 15 May they were given £500 for Edward's expenses from the money Edward had taken to Caerphilly Castle and left there in November 1326.[10] According to later evidence, Thomas Berkeley appointed another man to share the custody of Edward of Caernarfon with himself and John Maltravers: he was Sir Thomas Gurney, a knight of Somerset, where his family gave its name to the villages of Gurney Slade, Barrow Gurney and Farrington Gurney. The date of his appointment as one of Edward of Caernarfon's custodians is not clear. Gurney was not a lowborn killer, as he has sometimes been depicted, but a rather wealthy knight from a distinguished family that came to England with William the Conqueror in 1066. Gurney's eldest son Thomas the younger was born in February 1319, and Matthew, one of his other three sons, lived into the early 1400s and was a great warrior much admired by the chronicler Jean Froissart. Thomas Gurney, as an adherent of the Berkeleys and a long-term associate of the family and of John Maltravers, joined the Contrariant rebellion against Edward II in 1321–22, and was imprisoned in the Tower of London; he was released on 1 July 1324 and pardoned soon afterwards for a fine of £100 to be paid in ten annual instalments. Edward II trusted him enough in early 1325 to summon him to Gascony to fight for him during the War of Saint-Sardos.[11]

On Friday 3 April 1327, Thomas Berkeley took Edward of Caernarfon from Kenilworth Castle to his own castle at Berkeley in Gloucestershire, about 70 miles away to the south-west. They spent the night of 5 April, which was Palm Sunday, at Llanthony Secunda Priory in Gloucester during the journey, or perhaps at Gloucester Castle nearby, and reached the castle of Berkeley either later on 5 or 6 April.[12] Lord Berkeley presumably took as small a force with them as possible; Edward's whereabouts were not to be widely broadcast, in an attempt to keep his location secret and thus safeguard against more plots to free him. The *Annales Paulini* thought, however, that Edward was taken from Kenilworth to Berkeley 'with many armed men' (*cum multis armatis*).[13] Adam Murimuth, who correctly notes that Edward was removed from Kenilworth around Palm Sunday, comments that he 'was secretly brought to Berkeley'.[14] Berkeley Castle records show a payment of 48s for conducting the former king from Bristol.[15] Bristol in northern Somerset is considerably out of the way when travelling from Kenilworth in Warwickshire to Berkeley in Gloucestershire, being 20 miles south-west of Berkeley, so this may represent a deliberate journey in the opposite direction in order to confuse Edward's allies as to his real location. One man, though, a supporter of Edward, apparently saw them: Brother Michael atte Hulle, a canon of Llanthony Secunda Priory in Gloucester. Michael and his nephew William later joined the Dunheved brothers in their continued attempts to free Edward, and may have alerted them to Edward's whereabouts.

Contrary to popular modern belief, Edward of Caernarfon was almost certainly treated well at Berkeley Castle. Contemporary records show that he was given wine, good food and wax for his candles, that he had servants and a small kitchen staff, and that he had access to a chapel. The notion that he was mistreated at Berkeley comes solely from stories by the later chronicler Geoffrey le Baker, writing about twenty-five years later. Baker was not writing factual history: he was pushing for Edward of Caernarfon to be canonised as a saint, and was writing a hagiography of how the noble former king forgave the torments and abuse heaped on him by lesser men, whom Baker called the 'satraps of Satan'. Baker claimed that on the way to Berkeley, Edward was forced to wash himself and shave with dirty ditchwater, told his tormentors that he would indeed have hot water for shaving and immediately began crying, and was treated as though he were mad. Nor did his treatment improve after arrival: his captors tortured him by housing him in a charnel house, hoping that the stench of dead and rotting animals would suffocate him to death.

These vivid tales, like the story of the red-hot poker murder which Geoffrey le Baker also narrates, have far too often been repeated as though they are certain fact. They are not. Only le Baker and one other claim that Edward of Caernarfon was mistreated at Berkeley Castle, and the stories are disproved by castle records and by various entries in the chancery rolls. The only other chronicle which speaks of Edward's ill-treatment is a version of the French *Brut*, which claims that Edward was left alone without food and drink for two days while his jailers John Maltravers and Thomas Gurney went hunting in Selwood Forest in the West Country, and that when Gurney returned he contemptuously shaved Edward's beard with his knife. A similar detail is also in Baker, and the French *Brut* chronicle was perhaps Baker's inspiration, or a now lost account inspired them both.[16] This version of the *Brut* also has Edward giving a dignified but pointed speech in French to Thomas Gurney after the latter has shaved him with a knife: 'Thomas, you do this dishonour to me against your faith, and vengeance will come to you because of it, as it is forbidden by holy writ for a king or a chapel to be touched through malice, because they are anointed.' The author of this version, however, was also pressing for Edward to be canonised as a saint and claimed that the former king performed miracles at Gloucester after he was buried there, and therefore his tales cannot be taken too seriously for the same reason that Baker's cannot. It is a pity that Baker's lurid tales have often been taken as factual, perhaps because they are so detailed, and it is sometimes wrongly assumed that so much detail must mean a plausible tale and a reliable source, when in fact his aim was to portray Edward as a Christ-like figure, not to write an accurate account of his captivity. Queen Isabella sent Edward gifts of clothes and delicacies when he was at Berkeley, and affectionate letters, though claimed that 'the community of the realm' would not allow her to visit him.[17] There is no record of any of his family visiting him, though his son the young king had sent him two barrels of wine as a gift while he was at Kenilworth.[18] Edward's younger children John, Eleanor and Joan were only 10, 8 and 5 in early 1327, and the downfall and imprisonment of their father must have been distressing and bewildering for them; perhaps they would have been allowed to visit him somewhat later when they had had more time to come to terms with the situation.

There is no reason to think that the good food, wine and wax purchased for Edward were not in fact given to him but made their way to others, as one modern writer has suggested.[19] The records for the purchase of these items are found in Lord Berkeley's own household accounts and were not intended to be handed over to the government as proof that Berkeley was looking after the former king properly. Berkeley had no reason to falsify his own accounts and pretend to purchase items for the former king if he did not. Edward III never accused Lord Berkeley and his brother-in-law Sir John Maltravers of mistreating and abusing his father, as he would surely have done if Baker's allegation had any basis in fact. Parliament declared that Edward of Caernarfon should be treated as befitted a man of royal birth who was the king's father, which did not mean that he should be mistreated and abused, but treated with the full dignity of his royal status. The clerk and chronicler Adam Murimuth does say that although Lord Berkeley treated Edward of Caernarfon well, Maltravers behaved harshly towards him; however, as Murimuth wrongly believed that Maltravers was one of Edward's murderers, his testimony on this point is rather suspect, and this claim is not supported by any other evidence. The Fieschi Letter, written ten or so years later by a man who was a lawyer of the pope and later Bishop of Vercelli in Italy, says that one of Edward's servants at Berkeley told him that he must escape as two men were on their way to kill him. The servant offered to swap clothes with Edward so that the former king might escape more easily, which implies that Edward still wore fine and expensive clothes while at Berkeley, which would immediately make him recognisable as a man of high rank.

Edward may have been held in the keep inside the inner courtyard of Berkeley Castle, where a small but perfectly comfortable room is still shown to visitors as his. There is doubt, however, that this room really was the place where Edward lived; Berkeley Castle has been much altered internally over the last 700 years, and it is likely that Edward had larger accommodation for himself and his servants. Berkeley is a fairly small castle, and the room in which Edward was supposedly kept is located in the keep, the strongest and most defended part of any castle. An internal stairway now leads to a platform where visitors can peer through a window cut into the thickness of the keep wall into Edward's alleged chamber. In the 'king's gallery' outside this room is a long shaft, which is sometimes claimed to be the charnel house or pit where, according to Geoffrey le Baker, rotting animal corpses were kept in an attempt to kill Edward by asphyxiation. Given that Edward had servants, the stench would have killed them too, and the castle has been so much altered that it is impossible to state with any certainty that this is the pit of which le Baker speaks (which was seemingly entirely his own invention anyway). Berkeley Castle records do show payments to a smith for providing bolts, bars and other ironwork for Edward's chamber, presumably in a belated attempt to increase security after an attack on the castle, though as the payments are undated this is only speculation. Four keys were made, one for Edward's chamber, one for the chapel in the keep dedicated to St John which Edward was most likely allowed to use, one for an outer door and one for the postern gate.[20]

The Dominican friar Thomas Dunheved and his brother Stephen were still determined to free Edward from captivity, and there were some interesting characters among the men who joined them. Peter de la Rokele, who came from Wootton, Oxfordshire, was a former under-sheriff of Buckinghamshire and an adherent of the Despensers, and was also the grandfather of William Langland, author of *The Vision of Piers Plowman* and one of the great poets of medieval England.[21] The highest ranking member who joined the Dunheved gang was a knight of Wiltshire called Edmund Gascelyn, who had previously witnessed charters of the Despensers and who in a petition of early 1327 was named as a Despenser adherent.[22] There were two men called William Aylmer, both parsons, one of whom had been Hugh Despenser the Elder's steward in Soham, Cambridgeshire in 1315 and who was assaulted as a Despenser adherent during the rebellion against the Despensers in 1321. Three were formerly sergeants-at-arms in Edward II's household, Roger atte Watre, John le Botiler and Thomas de la Haye, and there was also Richard de Bircheston, lord of the manor of Barcheston in Warwickshire. Others who joined were Dominican friars called Henry de Rihale and John de Stoke of the Warwick chapter; John, a monk of Newminster Priory in Northumberland, 300 miles from Berkeley Castle; and William Russell (or Roscele as it was spelled then) parson of the church of Huntley on the edge of the Forest of Dean in Gloucestershire about 25 miles from Berkeley.[23] Russell's church perhaps provided a convenient and remote location for the gang to stay not too far from Berkeley. At the beginning of May 1327, Stephen Dunheved and the Dominican friar John de Stoke were ordered to be arrested and taken before the king.[24] The Patent Roll from March to June 1327 is full of entries accusing members of the Dunheved gang of all kinds of crimes, such as assault, theft, extortion and breaking and entering; these crimes may have been genuine, or perhaps they were fake accusations so that sheriffs and justices of the peace would arrest them and keep them safely in prison where they would be unable to attempt to free Edward of Caernarfon.[25] In early June 1327, the Dunheveds and some of their associates turned up in Chester, where the local justice (Richard Damory, older brother of Edward II's late nephew-in-law and favourite of the mid-1310s, Roger Damory) was ordered to arrest them as 'malefactors' and to 'keep them in prison until further orders'.[26]

The orders to arrest the Dominican friar John de Stoke on 1 May 1327 and Stephen Dunheved three days later came in response to a letter written by Henry, Earl of Lancaster, to the chancellor of England John Hothum on 28 April. Lancaster asked for powers to arrest Stoke on the grounds that he and unnamed others had been plotting to 'betray' Warwick Castle.[27] This probably indicates that at this point the Dunheveds and their associates still did not know, several weeks after the move to Berkeley Castle had been made in early April, where Edward of Caernarfon now was, and erroneously believed that he had been taken to Warwick Castle, only 5 miles from Kenilworth. Their presence in Chester in early June may indicate that they thought he was then somewhere nearby. This may have been a wild goose chase based on false information, or perhaps Edward of Caernarfon really was in or near Chester at some point, or we could even speculate that decoys were sent to different places accompanied by armed forces in order to conceal Edward's true whereabouts. Adam Murimuth, a well-informed royal clerk and chronicler, says that in 1327 Edward was taken to Corfe Castle in Dorset and other secret locations so that it could not be determined where he was, and that he was taken to Berkeley Castle secretly.[28] As noted, Berkeley Castle records state that Edward was brought to Berkeley from Bristol, located south-west of Berkeley, which may represent another false journey intended to conceal the former king's true whereabouts. The chronicler who wrote the English *Brut* thought that Edward was murdered at Corfe Castle; the author of one version of the French *Brut* also said Edward was taken from Kenilworth to Corfe by night, and the author of an anonymous chronicle in Flanders wrote that he was sent there in November 1326 by Queen Isabella after refusing to 'cool his anger' with her at her request.[29] This detail is of course wrong, but it seems virtually certain that Edward was indeed at Corfe Castle at some point in 1327. By mid- or late June, the Dunheved gang had finally learned that Edward was at Berkeley Castle, perhaps because Michael atte Hulle, canon of Llanthony Secunda in Gloucester, and his nephew William had by then made contact with them and informed them of his real location. Although after Edward's alleged death in September 1327 it became widely known that he had been in captivity at Berkeley Castle, few people in England between April and September 1327 were aware of that fact.

Edward of Caernarfon's close friend Donald, Earl of Mar, was also making efforts to help him in the summer of 1327. Mar returned to his native Scotland after the fall of Bristol and the execution of Hugh Despenser the Elder, Earl of Winchester, in October 1326. His uncle Robert Bruce, who evidently bore no grudge for Mar's many years of service and devotion to Edward, gave him his earldom. In June 1327 Mar led one of the three columns of his uncle's army into the north of England; the campaign was a disaster for the new English regime, as disastrous as any of Edward II's had been, and the young Edward III came close to being captured and burst into tears of rage and frustration. Although the Earl of Mar was in the north of England in the summer of 1327, he was directing his followers to help Edward of Caernarfon and perhaps attempt to free him from captivity. The Lanercost chronicle, a reliable and useful source for events in Scotland and the north of England, says that Mar 'returned to Scotland after the capture of the king, hoping to rescue him from captivity and restore him to his kingdom, as formerly, by the help of the Scots and of certain adherents whom the deposed king still had in England'.[30] Mar's followers gathered in the south-west of England in the summer of 1327 'to do and procure what evils they can against the king [Edward III] and his subjects'.[31] Queen Isabella and Roger Mortimer considered Mar such a threat they ordered two of his supporters in Staffordshire to be arrested in August 1327 merely for sending letters to him; on 14 July that year, they ordered the justice of Chester to imprison the former mayor of the town for adherence to Mar; and on 22 July they ordered the arrest of four more of Mar's supporters, and others unnamed also of his allegiance, who had returned to England from Scotland 'to do what mischief they can to the king and his realm'. Mar, one of Edward II's staunchest supporters for many years, was now called 'the enemy and rebel' of Edward's son.[32] It is perhaps not a coincidence that the Dunheved brothers were causing havoc in Chester in early June, and the town was a centre of disaffection in 1327: leading merchants were fined, and eighteen children or 'boy-hostages' imprisoned in the castle to ensure the citizens' good behaviour, at their own cost, as they had been 'disobedient and ill-behaved' towards Edward III.[33]

Probably around late June or early July 1327, with the king and his court including the powerful Roger Mortimer and Edward III's great-uncle and legal guardian Henry of Lancaster safely out of the way hundreds of miles to the north dealing with the Scottish invasion, the Dunheved brothers and their many allies attacked Berkeley Castle. Astonishingly, they achieved their objective and, temporarily at least, seized Edward of Caernarfon from custody. Little is known about the attack, and we only know that it took place because of a letter Thomas, Lord Berkeley wrote (in French) on 27 July 1327 to the chancellor of England and Bishop of Ely, John Hothum. Lord Berkeley explained that the Dunheved gang had 'marched to Berkeley Castle with an armed force, seized the father of our lord the king from our custody and feloniously robbed the said castle against the peace'.[34] This was his second letter on the subject; unfortunately the first, which informed Hothum that the men had already been indicted before him in Gloucestershire, has not survived. Berkeley named nineteen members of the group who had been indicted and asked for extra powers to arrest them, declaring that he would make an effort to do so (*jeo mettrai peine a les prendre*).

Despite the emergency, Lord Berkeley was oddly keen to stick to the rules, and carefully differentiated between the men who resided in Gloucestershire – who included a Walter Saunford, William Russell the parson of Huntley church, a monk of Hailes Abbey called Robert

Shulton and a Richard le Flesshewere, which means 'butcher' – and those who did not. He pointed out that the 1285 Statute of Winchester did not give him the authority to arrest anyone 'for the cause stated above' and that therefore he needed to be granted special powers to do so, as quickly as possible. An order to arrest the men was duly issued five days later on 1 August, naming them in the same order as in Lord Berkeley's letter and with four other names (Edmund Gascelyn, John de Hill, Roger atte Watre and William le Parker of Alcester, Warwickshire) added from Berkeley's first letter, and was entered on the Patent Roll.[35] Any mention of Edward of Caernarfon was carefully omitted in this writ and the men deemed guilty of marching towards Berkeley Castle with an armed force to plunder it, and of 'refusing to join the king in his expedition against the Scots' (a false accusation to ensure that sheriffs and justices would search for the men and arrest them). The named men were the recognised leaders of the gang who attacked Berkeley Castle, not the entire group; the number of participants in the attack is not known, but as it was so successful, they may well have numbered in the hundreds. Not all the men who took part may have had an interest in Edward II's release, though the named men surely did, but perhaps were more interested in the thought of attacking and plundering a rich castle. It is not clear from Lord Berkeley's letter whether Edward was ever taken outside the castle, only that he was snatched from Berkeley's custody. If the Dunheved gang did succeed in removing him from Berkeley Castle, from later events we can assume that he was swiftly recaptured, and Lord Berkeley's letter betrays no anxiety that the former King of England had escaped and was still free when he wrote the letter perhaps a month or so after the attack. There were times when neither Thomas Berkeley nor John Maltravers was present at Berkeley Castle – for example when they and Berkeley's younger brother Maurice Berkeley were sent to Bristol Castle, 20 miles away, on 30 April 1327 to collect armour for the impending royal campaign in Scotland – and perhaps the attack on the castle took place on one of these occasions.[36]

Lord Berkeley's letter of 27 July 1327 further informed John Hothum that another plot to free Edward of Caernarfon existed in the south-east of England: 'I have heard from certain members of my household, who have seen and heard of it, that a great number of people are assembling in Buckinghamshire and adjoining counties for the same cause', i.e. attempting to free Edward of Caernarfon. Berkeley described two men called John Redmere and John Norton as 'great leaders of this company', and went on to say that they had been captured and imprisoned on this account in Dunstable, Bedfordshire, which adjoins Buckinghamshire. Redmere and Norton were both Dominican friars, as many of Edward of Caernarfon's supporters were; Redmere was the former keeper of Edward's stud-farm, Norton his clerk and occasional attorney, and also surveyor of the king's works at Westminster and in the Tower of London. Both men thus knew Edward personally, and Norton had served him since 1312 or earlier and Redmere since 1317 or earlier.[37]

Traces of this Buckinghamshire/Bedfordshire plot can still be found in the records, and confirm Lord Berkeley's story. On 11 August 1327, the bailiffs of Dunstable were ordered to send John Redmere and John Norton 'in prison in their custody' to captivity at Wallingford Castle, which belonged to Queen Isabella, instead. The order of 4 May 1327 to arrest Stephen Dunheved also stated that he should be taken to Wallingford.[38] Evidently this order was not carried out, as another was issued on 21 October to take Redmere and Norton from Dunstable to Newgate prison in London. Two other men were then named with them, presumably other members of their plot to free Edward who had been found and arrested in the meantime: Robert of Ely and Nigel Mereman of Cornbury, Oxfordshire.[39] What seems to have prompted this move to Newgate appears in another entry on the Close Roll three days earlier: four men called Thomas atte Halle, John Salbot, Philip de Wibbesnade (i.e. Whipsnade, near Dunstable) and Robert Duraunt, and 'other malefactors' not named, were said to be 'riding about armed in diverse parts of the county [Bedfordshire], lying in wait day and night for the prior of Dunstable and his men, and committing other evils there'. The sheriff was ordered to arrest them.[40]

Given the timing and the men's attempts to 'lay in wait' for those who were holding Redmere and the others prisoner, it seems likely that these were further members of the plot to free Edward of Caernarfon, and were now occupied with trying to release their associates from captivity. Philip de Wibbesnade, Thomas atte Halle and Robert Duraunt joined a rebellion led by Henry, Earl of Lancaster against Lancaster's niece Queen Isabella and Roger Mortimer a little over a year later.[41] An undated petition of John Redmere and John Norton, which must belong to the period August to October 1327, still exists in The National Archives. In it, the two friars complained to the king and his council that they had merely been hearing Mass in the local Dominican house when the bailiffs of Dunstable burst in and arrested them for conspiring to free Edward of Caernarfon from Berkeley Castle. They claimed that their imprisonment was so harsh that they were 'at point of death' as a result.[42] Although John Redmere vanishes from history after the order to send him to Newgate, John Norton was apparently alive and at liberty in October 1333 (assuming this is not another man with the same rather common name).[43]

As for the Dunheved gang, they scattered, and most disappear from the records in and after 1327: either they fled abroad or went into hiding in England, or perhaps some of them were killed. A 1328 document of King's Bench records the trial of several men 'for trying to seize the [former] king', but sadly there are few details of the men or their fate.[44] At least two appear on record again only after Edward III overthrew his mother and Roger Mortimer and took over control of the kingdom in October 1330. Peter de la Rokele, former under-sheriff of Buckinghamshire, appears again on 21 January 1331, just three months after the young king's coup d'état, when his son Eustace, father of the great poet William Langland who may have been born around this time, acknowledged that he owed him £100.[45] The knight Edmund Gascelyn remains very obscure after 1327, and is mentioned briefly in October 1336 when he was ordered to appear before King Edward III, only some months before he died in September 1337.[46]

Thomas Dunheved, the Dominican friar and leader of the gang, was captured in the village of Budbrooke, 18 miles from his family's home in Dunchurch, Warwickshire, according to the *Annales Paulini* (though the *Annales* give the date of 11 June for his capture, which is too early and surely pre-dates the attack on Berkeley Castle). The *Annales* also say that Dunheved was taken to Queen Isabella then imprisoned at Pontefract Castle in Yorkshire, where he died in misery after trying to escape.[47] The Lanercost chronicler also noticed Thomas Dunheved's fate, but says merely that 'the foolish friar' was arrested and imprisoned, and died in captivity. The *Anonimalle*, meanwhile, says that Dunheved and unnamed others were imprisoned in York because of their plots to free Edward.[48] Precisely when Thomas Dunheved died is not clear, and it is just possible that he was still alive and active in 1329–30, and played some kind of role in the Earl of Kent's plot to free Edward of Caernarfon that year. His brother Stephen Dunheved fled to London, and on 1 July 1327 an order was issued to the mayor and sheriffs to arrest and imprison him.[49] They did so, but Dunheved escaped from the notorious Newgate prison shortly before 7 June 1329 and 'wanders at large against the king's will'; he certainly made more efforts to aid the release of Edward of Caernarfon in 1329–30.[50] One of the two parsons called William Aylmer was arrested in Oxford sometime before 20 August 1327. The order to the sheriff of Oxfordshire to release him from prison if he found mainpernors (guarantors) to ensure that he appeared before King's Bench surprisingly states openly that Aylmer was arrested 'for consenting to and abetting the robbery of Berkeley Castle, and the taking of Edward de Carnarvan, the late king'.[51] Most of the members of the gang who attacked Berkeley Castle, however, never appear on record again.

In September 1327, yet another plot was hatched to rescue Edward of Caernarfon from Berkeley Castle. This latest attempt consisted of Welsh supporters of the former king; Edward, born in Wales, had long been popular there, far more so than in England. The leader of the plot was Sir Rhys ap Gruffudd of South Wales, who had fought for Edward during the Contrariant rebellion of 1321–22. Edward had arranged his marriage to an heiress named Joan Somerville some years later, and Gruffudd remained loyal to the king until the very end: on 10 November 1326, just six days before the king's capture, he was one of the men Edward appointed to send as an envoy to Queen Isabella.[52] Another of those appointed as envoy with Gruffudd was Edward's squire John Harsik, who years later would also join a plot to free Edward, after his supposed death. Other members of the September 1327 plot included Sir Gruffudd Llwyd of North Wales, also a long-term and loyal supporter of the king, and (in the idiosyncratic spelling of Welsh names used by English scribes at the time), Ath' ap Eignon, Hywel ap Luspa, Madoc Loithe, David Vagh and Llywelyn ap Ken'. The plot was betrayed to the deputy justice of Wales, William Shalford. By 26 October 1327, he and his superior Roger Mortimer had imprisoned thirteen of the men in Caernarfon Castle, ironically enough Edward II's birthplace.[53] Rhys ap Gruffudd managed to escape with seven other Welshmen and they fled to Scotland, where they may have sought shelter with Donald, Earl of Mar. Gruffudd was granted several pardons throughout 1328 for fleeing from the realm and for 'all other offences committed in England and Wales', but ignored them and stayed in Scotland.[54] In 1329–30 he and Mar would again become involved in Edward of Caernarfon's affairs.

This latest plot appears to have convinced some people that Edward of Caernarfon was too dangerous to be allowed to live any longer. According to a court case brought by Hywel ap Gruffudd in 1331, William Shalford wrote to Roger Mortimer from the island of Anglesey in North Wales on 14 September 1327 informing him of the plot, and added that if Edward were released from prison, Mortimer and all his allies would be destroyed. Shalford also wrote that Mortimer should 'ordain such a remedy regarding the above-mentioned matters that neither the said Sir Rhys [ap Gruffudd] nor anyone else in England or Wales should have cause to think of his [Edward's] deliverance'. It was claimed in 1331, whether correctly or not, that the Welsh plot to free Edward was carried out with the 'assent of some of the great lords of England' (*par assent dascuns des grantz de la terre Dengleterre*), and that those involved were raising men in both North and South Wales. Hywel ap Gruffudd also claimed in 1331 that William Shalford was guilty of advising and encompassing the death of Edward II, who was 'feloniously and treacherously killed and murdered' (*felonousement et traiterousement occis et murdretz*).[55] In mid-September 1327, Roger Mortimer, according to the 1331 court case, was away from the king and the dowager queen in Lincoln and was in Abergavenny, South Wales, from where he sent a messenger named William Ockley or Ogle to Berkeley Castle with a message after he received Shalford's letter. Ockley was a man-at-arms, apparently Irish or of Irish origin: in March 1326, he was appointed as the attorney of a 'Stephen Ocle', presumably a relative, in Ireland.[56] Ockley was probably the 'William de Okleye' who accompanied Roger Mortimer's wife Joan Geneville during her imprisonment after the Contrariant rebellion in 1322 (she was held under house arrest with eight attendants), and thus was a long-term Mortimer adherent.[57] The stage was set for the murder of a king.

PART II

THE KING IS DEAD

5

THE MURDER OF A KING

On Monday 21 September 1327, or perhaps during the night of 21–22 September, Sir Edward of Caernarfon died at Berkeley Castle. 21 September is the feast day of St Matthew the Evangelist, and in 1327 it was also the first anniversary of Queen Isabella's invasion force leaving Dordrecht for England. Both Edward II and Roger Mortimer were born on the feast day of St Mark the Evangelist, 25 April – Edward in 1284, Mortimer in 1287 – so perhaps 21 September was deemed a satisfactory day for the former king to die for this reason.[1] Sir Thomas Gurney set off to inform Edward's son the young king, who was holding Parliament 160 miles away at Lincoln, either on 21 September or early in the morning of the 22nd. Berkeley Castle records say that Gurney was sent to Nottingham. Either this was an error by the clerk who wrote it, or it was genuinely believed at the castle that Edward III was indeed at Nottingham, and perhaps Gurney rode there first; it would not have been too far out of his way. Edward III, who was still only 14 years old – he would turn 15 on 13 November 1327 – sent a letter on Thursday 24 September to his first cousin John de Bohun, Earl of Hereford, whose mother Elizabeth (d. 1316) had been Edward II's sister. The letter, in French, began, 'Very dear cousin, news came to us this Wednesday the 23rd day of September during the night that our very dear lord and father has been commanded to God' (*Trescher cosin novelles nous vyndront y ce meskerdy le xxiii iour de septembre de deinz la nuyt qe nostre trescher seignur et piere est a dieu comaundez*).[2] This may be one of several letters which the young king sent and the only one which fortuitously survives, or it may be unique. It demonstrates that Edward III immediately began disseminating news of his father's death, taking the news brought to him by Thomas Gurney at face value. Lord Berkeley's letter does not survive, only the reference to Gurney being sent with it to the king, so we have no way of knowing what Berkeley told Edward III about his father's death in the letter or what Gurney may have told the king in person. The Rochester chronicler says that Gurney informed Queen Isabella of the news of her husband's death at Lincoln on 22 September, which must be an error; this is impossibly fast for Gurney to have travelled the 160 miles from Berkeley in Gloucestershire, unless the chronicler was implying that Gurney was sent to tell Isabella about Edward's death before it had even happened.[3]

Parliament broke up on 23 September, and although it was probably too late to make an official announcement of Edward II's death to the attendees, some of them still in Lincoln may have been informed before they left the city. At any rate, the news soon spread throughout the country. Thomas Gurney must have galloped hard to reach Lincoln during the night of 23–24 September, and presumably set off from Berkeley either on 21 September or as early as possible on the morning of the 22nd, depending on what time Edward died. At this time of year, there are approximately twelve hours of daylight every day in England, the hours during which Gurney could have travelled. Edward II himself had received the news of his father's death near Carlisle on 7 July 1307 four days later and about 310 miles away in London. This represents a journey of just under 80 miles a day by the royal messengers coming to inform him, but they had relays of horses, and the hours of daylight in early July and thus the part of the day when they could ride are much longer than in the third week of September. Not only must Sir Thomas Gurney have ridden extremely hard to cover the 160 miles from Berkeley Castle in Gloucestershire in barely two days (and if the Berkeley Castle account is correct and he went to Nottingham first, this would have delayed him by some hours), William Shalford's letter also reached Roger Mortimer and then Berkeley Castle remarkably quickly. According to the 1331 court case, although we have no other confirmation of this, Shalford was at 'Rosfeyre', i.e. Rhosyr or Newborough as it is now called, on the island of Anglesey in North Wales, when he wrote to Roger Mortimer on 14 September 1327.[4] Mortimer himself was supposedly at 'Bergeuenay', i.e. Abergavenny in South Wales, though we have no independent confirmation of this either. Newborough to Abergavenny is a good 150 miles and the Menai Strait from Anglesey to the mainland must be crossed first, and in fourteenth-century Wales, with its mountains, rough terrain, few roads and sparse population, 150 miles was far from an easy journey. Having received the letter, Mortimer then had to respond to it more or less immediately and send William Ockley to Berkeley Castle. This would be almost 60 miles from Abergavenny given that the journey required crossing the River Severn, probably at Gloucester where there was a bridge; this would take a messenger rather out of the way and make the journey longer than it would be nowadays, when there are two suspension bridges over the Severn.

The timing of the whole venture, from Anglesey on 14 September to Abergavenny some days later to Berkeley Castle on the 21st and finally to Lincoln on the night of the 23rd, when Gurney informed Edward III of his father's death – a total journey of at least 350 miles in just nine days – is just about possible but extremely tight, especially as it was autumn and the days were not nearly as long as they had been in summer, and the weather may have been wet. It also seems to leave no time at all for the protagonists to reflect and think before they made a major and life-altering decision relating to the murder of a king, the father of their present king. Although the later medieval Kings of England who were deposed were murdered in captivity (Richard II, Henry VI and probably Edward V), no English king had been forced off his throne before Edward II and there was as yet no concept that a deposed king must be murdered to ensure the safety of his successor. The decision to kill Edward of Caernarfon in September 1327 cannot have been one that was made lightly with little thought, especially as his son was bound to punish anyone responsible for killing and hurting him when he came of age.

For over three years, until the downfall of Queen Isabella and Roger Mortimer, the fiction was maintained by the English court that Edward of Caernarfon had died a natural death, though surely many people must have suspected foul play given that Edward was only 43 (his father Edward I lived until he was 68 and his paternal grandfather Henry III died at 65) and had always been healthy, strong and fit. Numerous fourteenth-century chroniclers comment on Edward II's enormous physical strength. The *Scalacronica*, for example, says 'physically he was one of the strongest men in his realm'; the *Polychronicon* says he was 'fair of body and great of strength'; and the *Vita Edwardi Secundi* says he was 'tall and strong, a fine figure of a handsome man'. Edward was also known for enjoying 'rustic' pursuits such as digging ditches, thatching roofs and swimming, which surely kept him in good shape.

In November 1330 after Edward III overthrew his mother Isabella and her favourite Roger Mortimer, it was stated by Parliament for the first time that Edward II had been murdered, and three men (and indirectly a fourth) were accused of his murder. The means of murder, however, was never stated officially, and contemporary chroniclers filled the gap with their own speculation or rumours they had heard. It is important to bear in mind that no official cause of murder was ever given out by Edward III or his government and that no-one involved in the death of Edward II ever spoke publicly about it, and that fourteenth-century chroniclers give a wide variety of causes of death. There is therefore no way to know for sure what happened to Edward of Caernarfon at Berkeley Castle on 21 September 1327. Most chroniclers do give this date correctly, though some state 20 or 22 September. Edward III and his sons, and his mother Queen Isabella, kept the anniversary as the 21st; they heard Mass and gave out alms to the poor to mark the day, as was customary in the fourteenth century. Thomas Berkeley and John Maltravers also claimed expenses for looking after Edward until 21 September, the date of his death – the record simply says that 'King E. the father died at Berkeley' – then for keeping the corpse until 21 October when it was moved to Gloucester. They claimed £1,005 in total, for 201 days at £5 per day, and had already received £700.[5]

One of the earliest surviving references to Edward's death comes on 23 October 1327, when his close friend and ally William Melton, Archbishop of York, offered an indulgence to all in his diocese who prayed for the soul of the late king. Melton mentioned Edward's *fatalis casus*.[6] This seems to mean 'a fatal accident', though *casus* can also mean 'fall', perhaps meant more in the metaphorical sense of a downfall than a literal fall; only one other source, a Flanders chronicle, states that Edward died of a fall. The *Annales Paulini*, the annals of St Paul's Cathedral in London, were written very soon after 1327 and say only that on 20 September [*sic*], 'King Edward, who was called of Caernarfon because he was born there, died (*obiit*) in Berkeley Castle, where he was held in custody.'[7] Adam Murimuth, the royal clerk who was the only chronicler in the south-west of England in 1327, gives 22 September as the date, and says at first merely that Edward 'was dead' (*fuit mortuus*) while in captivity at Berkeley Castle, then adds rather mysteriously that it was common knowledge that he was 'killed by a trick' or 'craftily killed', *per cautelam occisus*, on the orders of Sir John Maltravers and Sir Thomas Gurney. He also states later, when discussing the Parliament of November 1330 and Roger Mortimer's execution, that Edward was suffocated or smothered, *fuerat suffocatus*.[8] His comment about the murderers is partially incorrect. Although John Maltravers was sentenced to death in absentia at the Westminster Parliament three years later, this was for his entrapment of Edward of Caernarfon's half-brother the Earl of Kent earlier in 1330, and he was never officially accused of any complicity in Edward's death, either in 1330 or at any other time in his very long life; Maltravers lived for many years on the Continent, returned to England in the late 1340s and died in 1364, well into his 70s and thirty-four years after his death sentence.

The Lichfield chronicler in the early 1330s thought that Edward had been strangled (*iugulatus*).[9] The *Anonimalle*, also in the 1330s, said that Edward died of an illness:

The king fell ill there [at Berkeley Castle] and died on the day of St Matthew the Apostle [21 September] before St Michael [29 September], and was buried in Gloucester on the eve of St Thomas [20 December], when he had reigned nineteen years, three months and two weeks, on whose soul may God have mercy, amen.

The chronicler is specific but not quite correct about the length of Edward II's reign: he became king on 8 July 1307 and the final day of his reign was 20 January 1327, or nineteen years, six months and two weeks. The dates in this account are otherwise correct.[10] Some continuations of the French *Brut* chronicle say that Edward became grievously ill and died *de grant dolour*, which means 'of great grief' or 'sorrow' but might also be taken to imply 'of great pain'.[11] The Peterborough chronicle says that Edward was 'healthy in the evening but was found dead in the morning' (*Edwardus vespere sanus in crastino mortuus est inventus*), which implies death by natural causes, and the Woburn chronicle, the chronicle of Robert de Avesbury, and the annals of Newenham Priory in Devon written in the early 1330s, say only that Edward died at Berkeley Castle without further information.[12] An anonymous chronicle written in the county of Flanders in northern France gives the bizarre and unique story that one day Edward was placed in some kind of box and raised up high, that 'those who had him in their keeping' pushed his head forward outside the box, and that the box was suddenly hurled down to the ground so that he died. The chronicler comments that he has no idea on whose orders this was done, but that Edward died without acknowledging his own culpability, always blaspheming, and full of anger.[13] This story sounds rather like something his father Edward I had done to two Scottish noblewomen, Mary Bruce and Isabella MacDuff, in 1306, as punishment for their support of the new King Robert Bruce: the women were placed in cages which were winched up a castle wall, though they were not killed. It is the only chronicle which gives any support to the idea of William Melton, Archbishop of York, that Edward had died literally of a *fatalis casus*, a 'fatal fall', if that was the sense in which Melton meant the word.

The chronicler of Lanercost Priory in the far north-west of England, writing in the 1340s, stated rather unhelpfully that Edward 'died soon after [the Dunheved plot], either by a natural death or by the violence of others'.[14] The author of another northern chronicle, Bridlington in Yorkshire, stated also in the 1340s:

With regard to the king's decease various opinions were commonly expressed. I prefer myself to say no more about the matter, for sometimes, as the poet says, lies are for the advantage of many and to tell the whole truth does harm.[15]

This passage has sometimes been understood to mean that the chronicler had heard of the notorious red-hot poker story and did not believe it, or wish to perpetuate it. The *Scalacronica* was written around 1360 by a knight named Sir Thomas Gray. Gray's father of the same name had fought for Edward II at Bannockburn in 1314 and been captured by the Scots, and (although his son does not mention this rather inconvenient fact) served in the retinue of and was very close to Hugh Despenser the Younger in the 1320s. Although Gray was writing decades later, his own father had been a close eyewitness to events of Edward II's reign, and had personally known Edward and Despenser very well. Gray wrote in the *Scalacronica*, rather movingly, that Edward 'was taken from Kenilworth to Berkeley, where he died, by what manner is not known, but God knows it'.[16] Apparently he had not heard the red-hot poker story, or if he had, gave it no credence. The author of the *French Chronicle of London* wrote that Edward had been 'vilely murdered' without saying how, while the chronicler of Wigmore in Herefordshire, the seat of Roger Mortimer and his family, was insistent that Edward died a natural death at Berkeley Castle, whatever anyone else might say (though given the close association of Roger Mortimer with Wigmore, the chronicler might not be unbiased).[17] The Rochester chronicle, written by an associate of the Bishop of Rochester, Hamo Hethe, who was an ally of Edward II and spoke out for him at the Parliament of January 1327, says that Edward died while in the hands of enemies who had long planned to harm him and who wished to put him to a most shameful death.[18] The 1331 court case against Roger Mortimer's deputy justice of Wales, William Shalford, said that Edward had been 'feloniously and treacherously killed and murdered' without stating how the murder had taken place, an echo of what Edward's own son Edward III stated at the Parliament of November 1330: Edward was 'traitorously, feloniously and falsely murdered and killed'.

Jean Froissart, a chronicler from Valenciennes in the county of Hainault in modern-day Belgium and northern France, the home of Edward III's queen Philippa, spent three days at Berkeley Castle in September 1366 in the company of Hugh Despenser the Younger's 30-year-old grandson Edward, Lord Despenser (a great knight whom Froissart much admired and praised). The lord of the castle then, thirty-nine years after Edward of Caernarfon's murder, was Maurice Berkeley, who was the son of Edward's 1327 custodian Thomas and was also the grandson of Roger Mortimer via his mother Margaret, Mortimer's eldest daughter. Maurice Berkeley's wife was Edward Despenser's aunt, Hugh Despenser the Younger's youngest daughter Elizabeth, who had escaped Queen Isabella's orders to force her older sisters into a lifetime as nuns as she was only a baby at the time of her father's execution in November 1326. Despite the family connections, Froissart learned nothing about Edward of Caernarfon's death at Berkeley Castle except that a very old squire told him that 'they shortened his life for him' in the same year as he was taken to the castle, which Froissart must have known anyway. That was all Froissart had to say on the matter. Either the inhabitants of Berkeley Castle genuinely did not know what had happened to the former king almost four decades previously or did not wish to talk about it. Maurice Berkeley was probably only born in 1330, years after Edward II was imprisoned and murdered in his father's castle and the year his grandfather Mortimer was executed. He may never have been told what happened to Edward, or if he was, he kept quiet about it.[19]

Chroniclers who give the famous or rather infamous 'red-hot poker' story of Edward II's murder include the *Polychronicon* of *c*. 1350, written by a monk of Chester called Ranulph Higden, and the English *Brut* of the 1330s. This is the earliest chronicle to mention the story, and has Thomas Gurney, which it spells Toiourneye, and (wrongly) John Maltravers coming into Edward's chamber as he slept. It says that they turned him onto his stomach and laid a table on him, holding it and him down, and took:

> A horn, and put it into his fundament as deep as they might, and took a spit of copper burning, and put it through the horn into his body, and oftentimes rolled therewith his bowels, and so they killed their lord, that nothing was perceived.

This, the chronicler claims, was done on Roger Mortimer's orders sent to Thomas Berkeley, whom the chronicler calls Maurice, actually the name both of his father who had died in 1321 and of his son. The writer of the *Brut* wrongly believed that Edward was killed at Corfe Castle in Dorset, which is strongly associated with Edward of Caernarfon in 1327 and which will be discussed again later.[20] Geoffrey le Baker in the early 1350s also repeated the red-hot poker story:

These cruel bullies, seeing that death by foetid odour would not overcome so vigorous a man, during the night of 22 [*sic*] September, suddenly seized hold of him as he lay on his bed. With the aid of enormous pillows and a weight heavier than that of fifteen substantial men they pressed down upon him until he was suffocated. With a plumber's red-hot iron, inserted through a horn leading to the inmost parts of the bowel, they burned out the respiratory organs beyond the intestines, taking care that no wound should be discernible on the royal body where such might be looked for by some friend of justice.[21]

A manuscript of the French *Brut* now held at Corpus Christi College, Oxford, gives a different version of the red-hot poker story. It says that Lord Berkeley and his wife Margaret Mortimer deceitfully welcomed the former king to their castle with 'great honour', having 'plotted his death before his arrival' (*la compassement de sa mort avaunt sa venue*). While Edward was being 'royally assisted at table', they gave him poison (*venyme*) in his potage, i.e. soup or stew. The poison began to work immediately, and Edward hastily left the table unable to keep his food down, and retired to his chamber to get undressed, presumably because he had vomited over himself. Sitting on his bed naked, Edward 'heard the false plotting of his enemies', Thomas Gurney, John Maltravers and unnamed others, which aroused terrible suspicion in him. He resolutely took hold of an iron bar to defend himself, crying out loudly 'Hail Mary, I beg for your mercy', which somehow was heard by all the inhabitants of nearby Berkeley village. 'The traitors', as the chronicler calls them, seized him by his private parts and by a cloth around his neck, battled him to the ground and, to make sure that he died, pushed a horn inside his anus and then a 'burning iron' (*un fer ardaunt*) inside that so that his entire body was burned from the inside out. This version of the *Brut* is, like Geoffrey le Baker, most sympathetic to Edward, calling him a martyr and 'the gentle king' who 'for the love of God' performed miracles at his burial place in Gloucester.[22] It is, to my knowledge, the only chronicle which accuses Thomas, Lord Berkeley and his wife Margaret Mortimer of complicity in Edward's murder: although they do not kill him directly, they plot his death before his arrival at their castle and give him poison in his food while pretending to treat him with honour and respect, and thus weaken him and force him to retreat to his chamber where he is murdered. No other chronicle so much as hints that Thomas Berkeley was involved in Edward II's murder, even though it took place in his castle.

The *Polychronicon*, Geoffrey le Baker and the *Brut* were all very popular texts which strongly influenced chroniclers of the late fourteenth century such as John of Reading, Henry Knighton, Thomas Walsingham and the Meaux chronicle, who also all give the red-hot poker as the cause of Edward of Caernarfon's death, often in combination with suffocation. The *Polychronicon* alone survives in more than 160 manuscripts.[23] The story of the red-hot poker by the end of the fourteenth century and beyond was often repeated as though it was certain fact, and the dramatist Christopher Marlowe, writing his play about Edward II and his downfall and death in the early 1590s, probably never read any other tale, despite the great variation of fourteenth-century chroniclers' accounts. It is interesting to note that Ranulph Higden of Chester, one of the most influential of all fourteenth-century chroniclers, was summoned to Edward III on 21 August 1352, probably not long after he had written his story of the murder by red-hot poker of Edward III's father, 'with all your chronicles and those in your charge to speak and treat with the [royal] council concerning matters to be explained to you on our [the king's] behalf'.[24]

A man named John Trevisa translated Higden's *Polychronicon* from Latin into English in about 1388, and left the red-hot poker story intact. Trevisa was a chaplain of Lord Berkeley at Berkeley Castle, and it has often been assumed that because he translated that part without comment or correction, the poker story must be correct. However, Trevisa was born in about the early 1340s, fifteen or so years after

Edward of Caernarfon's murder, and in Cornwall; he had no connection to the village of Berkeley or Gloucestershire until much later in life. He studied at Oxford in the 1360s, and arrived at Berkeley probably in 1387, sixty years after Edward had died there. The lord of Berkeley in the 1380s and until his death in 1417 was Thomas, the namesake grandson of Lord Thomas who had been Edward's custodian in 1327. Thomas the elder died in 1361, and his son and heir Maurice, who was probably only born in 1330, died in 1368, two years after the visit of his nephew-in-law Edward Despenser and Jean Froissart, and long before John Trevisa's arrival. Thomas Berkeley the grandson, born in 1353, may have had no better idea than anyone else about Edward of Caernarfon's fate at his castle many decades previously, and thus there is no reason to think that his chaplain Trevisa did either, or that Trevisa's failure to correct the red-hot poker story points to its truth. The tale of the poker was widespread by the late fourteenth century, and probably neither Lord Berkeley nor Trevisa had ever heard anything else. There is no reason to suppose that the fourteenth-century chroniclers who relate the red-hot poker story were any better informed than the ones who did not, and none of them was close to Berkeley Castle in place or time or to anyone involved in Edward of Caernarfon's death. Geoffrey le Baker also wrote a very silly story about Edward's death which is still sometimes repeated today: he claimed that Queen Isabella sent a letter to Berkeley Castle which said, in Latin, *Edwardum occidere nolite timere bonum est*. This could either mean 'Do not kill Edward, to fear is good' or 'Kill Edward, not to fear is good', depending on where the comma was placed. This is a complete fabrication and should not be taken seriously.

No fourteenth-century chronicler doubted that Edward of Caernarfon died at Berkeley Castle on or around 21 September 1327, and for a time, neither did anyone else. The first funeral of a King of England since Edward I's twenty years before, and the last until July 1377, was about to take place.

6

THE FUNERAL OF A KING

Edward II's body was probably embalmed shortly after death: his son Edward III's body was embalmed 'immediately' after he died in 1377, and it is reasonable to assume that Edward II's was too. Royal burials of the fourteenth century involved covering the face and body entirely with cerecloth, or wax-impregnated cloth, and a payment for 100lb of wax, and for palls and other cloth, dyes and spices, appear in Lord Berkeley's accounts ending on 29 September 1327. Edward I's remains, when examined in 1774, still bore traces of this cloth over his face, and after the murder of Edward II's great-grandson Richard II in 1400, cerecloth was removed from his face so that he could be identified.[1] The procedure of embalming Edward II was carried out by a woman whose name and position are lost to history, probably a local wise woman. Although it has been postulated that Edward of Caernarfon's body was embalmed by this obscure woman and not a royal physician in order to cover up the crime of Edward's murder, and that it was done 'secretly', there is no real reason to suppose that this is the case. Perhaps Lord Berkeley and others at the castle thought it was necessary to have the body embalmed soon after death to prevent too much unpleasant physical decomposing, and were unwilling to wait for the few days it would take a royal physician to arrive at Berkeley Castle.[2]

Thomas, Lord Berkeley paid 37s 8d for a silver vessel in which to place Edward's heart; it was sent to his widow Isabella.[3] This may seem macabre by modern standards, but separate heart burial was entirely usual, albeit not universal, in royal English burials of the thirteenth and fourteenth centuries. Edward II's paternal grandmother Eleanor of Provence was buried at Amesbury Priory in Wiltshire in 1291, and her heart was given to the Greyfriars (Franciscans') church in London. Edward's mother Leonor of Castile was buried at Westminster Abbey in late 1290, and her heart and the heart of her third son Alfonso of Bayonne were given to the Blackfriars (Dominicans') church in London; Leonor must have kept Alfonso's heart for six years after his death in August 1284. A later tradition has it that Isabella of France was buried at the Greyfriars church in London on 27 November 1358 with her husband's heart on her chest, though the truth of this story cannot be verified. It is sure, however, that Isabella was buried with the clothes she had worn at her wedding to Edward fifty years previously.[4]

For a month, from 21 or 22 September (depending on when exactly during that day or night Edward's murder is meant to have taken place) until 21 October, Edward of Caernarfon's body was guarded at Berkeley Castle by one man: William Beaukaire. He and he alone received 12d per day from the Exchequer in London for staying *juxta corpus regis*, 'next to the king's body'.[5] Beaukaire was a royal sergeant-at-arms who in June 1328 was named, as 'Willelmus Beauquer', as a member of Edward III's household and who thereafter disappears from the records of English history.[6] Presumably he was a Frenchman, as Beaucaire is a town in the Languedoc-Roussillon region of southern France about 15 miles south-west of Avignon where the popes resided in the fourteenth century, and on the opposite side of the River Rhône from the town of Tarascon. William Beaukaire, rather curiously, was one of the men who held out against Queen Isabella for a few months in 1326–27 at Caerphilly Castle, the great South Wales stronghold of Hugh Despenser the Younger. Also in the castle when it was besieged for several months on Isabella's orders, after Edward II and Hugh Despenser the Younger abandoned it at the beginning of November 1326, were Despenser's teenage eldest son Hugh (Huchon) and many members of Edward II's household, such as Walter Cowherd, Peter Plummer, John Edrich and Henry Hustret. The Caerphilly garrison finally surrendered in March 1327 when Isabella agreed not to execute the young Huchon Despenser, and he was imprisoned instead for the rest of her period in power while the rest of the garrison was allowed to go free. William Beaukaire's name, now spelled 'Gills Beaucair' ('Gills' presumably being a nickname for Guilhem or Gulielmus, the southern French or Latin form of his name), appears seventh on the list of men pardoned on 20 March 1327 for holding out against the queen at Caerphilly. The name after his is Giles of Spain, a squire of Edward II's chamber in the 1320s who in 1330 was to join Edward's half-brother the Earl of Kent in his plot to free Edward and who in 1331 was sent to his homeland of Spain by Edward III to pursue Thomas Gurney, supposedly one of Edward II's murderers. Also among the Caerphilly garrison with Beaukaire were Roger atte Watre, another royal sergeant-at-arms who took part in the Dunheved attack on Berkeley Castle in the summer of 1327, and Benet or Benedict Braham, a Despenser adherent who was also to join the Earl of Kent's plot of 1330. The name 'Stephen Dun', another man in Caerphilly Castle, may mean Stephen Dunheved.[7]

The choice of William Beaukaire – seemingly either a former member of Edward II's household or an adherent of Hugh Despenser, or both, who just six months before Edward's murder was associated with a number of men who would later attempt to free Edward from captivity and who were fiercely resisting Queen Isabella and protecting Despenser's son – as the sole guardian over Edward's body is rather curious. The date of Beaukaire's arrival at Berkeley is unknown, though seemingly he was already there at the time of the former king's supposed murder, as he immediately began keeping watch over the body. An undated expense roll of Berkeley Castle records a payment of 20s to William 'Beuquere'.[8] As Beaukaire was apparently already at Berkeley Castle, and as he was given sole responsibility of guarding the late king's body, Thomas Berkeley evidently felt he was to be trusted, despite his allegiance of some months earlier.

Presumably William Beaukaire was present at the viewing, or viewings, of Edward II's body by knights, abbots, priors and burgesses of Bristol and Gloucester which chronicler Adam Murimuth talks about: Murimuth says that a number of these men were allowed to see Edward's body *superficialiter*, 'superficially', presumably while it still lay at Berkeley Castle.[9] Other than stating that the knights, abbots, priors and burgesses saw the body 'whole' (*integrum*), Murimuth does not give any more details: whether they came in groups or separately, how they were invited and to what purpose. In short, his statement is frustratingly unclear, and no information on this matter is available from any other chronicler, the chancery rolls or Berkeley Castle records. Murimuth was the only chronicler anywhere in the vicinity of Berkeley Castle in 1327, albeit a hundred miles away in Exeter, and although he is usually reliable, he did make errors, such as stating that Edward of Caernarfon was murdered on 22 September and that John Maltravers was one of the murderers. It is not clear whether the visitors from Bristol and Gloucester were invited to make sure that Edward of Caernarfon was dead, to identify the body, or simply as a mark of respect to the dead king and his son. There were certainly many knights, abbots and other men in the south-west of England who would have met Edward II or seen him during his reign, and would be able to recognise him. Neither is it clear what Murimuth meant by the statement that the men only saw Edward's body 'superficially'. Edward III himself did not send anyone to Berkeley Castle to view his father's body, or at least there is no record that he did or that any other member of the former king's family saw his body at any point, either at Berkeley Castle or later at Gloucester. One modern historian has claimed that the visitors were only allowed to view the body 'superficially' because 'what was feared was discovery of the manner of death'.[10] Murimuth's statement might indeed mean that the visitors were not allowed to inspect the body of the former king closely in order to avoid anyone spotting that he had been murdered, or even perhaps (given later events) that it was not Edward II's body at all. Another historian makes the point that the apparent efforts to prevent anyone inspecting Edward's body too closely, perhaps because he had been murdered or mistreated at Berkeley Castle, may have backfired, and led to the later rumours that Edward was still alive on the grounds that no-one had really had the chance to see him dead.[11]

On 21 October, Edward's body was given into the custody of John Thoky, abbot of St Peter's Abbey in Gloucester, and taken the 20 miles to that town, where the former king would be buried.[12] A story told by one of Thoky's successors later in the fourteenth century had it that only the monks of Gloucester dared to brave the wrath and displeasure of Queen Isabella and courageously bury the body, and that other abbeys refused to accept it, but there is no reason to think that this was the case.[13] St Peter's was not an unsuitable location for a royal burial: Edward II's grandfather Henry III had hastily been crowned there as a 9-year-old in 1216 (he was re-crowned in Westminster Abbey some years later), and William the Conqueror's eldest son Robert, brother of William II and Henry I, was buried there. Edward himself may have preferred to rest at Westminster Abbey with his parents Edward I and Leonor of Castile and his grandfather Henry III, but as he died intestate and never stated his burial wishes, this is not certain; it is also possible that he would have liked to be buried at his own foundation of Langley Priory in Hertfordshire, near Piers Gaveston. As early as 6 October 1327, the abbot and convent of Croxden Abbey in Staffordshire were granted permission to hold 'an anniversary on St Matthew's day [21 September] for the soul of the late king, and for the souls of his progenitors forever'.[14] On 23 October 1327, as noted above, William Melton, Archbishop of York, offered an indulgence to all in his diocese who prayed for the soul of the former king.

On 20 October, the day before Edward of Caernarfon's body was taken from Berkeley Castle to Gloucester, several other men joined the sergeant-at-arms William Beaukaire in keeping watch over the body. They were knights called Robert Hastang or Hastings and Edmund Wasteneys, who received 6s 8d and 5s per day respectively for remaining with the body until 20 December, the day of Edward's funeral; two royal chaplains called Bernard Burgh and Richard Potesgrave, at 3s each per day; two sergeants-at-arms called Bertrand de la More and John Enfield at 12d per day; and Andrew, a royal *candelarius* or candlemaker.[15] On the day Edward's body arrived at Gloucester, 21 October, the Bishop of Llandaff, a Dominican friar named John Eaglescliff, also joined the watchers.[16] As Edward II had been a strong supporter of the Dominicans, which support they returned in equal measure, this was a thoughtful gesture. A gatehouse in Gloucester just outside the abbey of St Peter's, which became Gloucester Cathedral after the Dissolution in the sixteenth century, carries a plaque to this day about Edward's body passing through there, and is still called King Edward's Gatehouse. Meanwhile in London, royal clerks began to arrange Edward's funeral; he was referred to respectfully as 'the king' rather than as 'the father of our lord the king' as had been customary throughout 1327. On 22 October, a royal clerk named Hugh Glanville or Glaunvyl was appointed to pay the wages to the men watching over Edward's body and any other expenses relating to the former king's death. He paid out a total of £77 12s, which included William Beaukaire's wages for watching over the body for three months.[17] Edward II's funeral cost over £350 in total.[18]

From 21 October to 20 December 1327, Edward's body lay in state at St Peter's Abbey in Gloucester. He had been most unpopular in life, but the sudden death of a deposed king was bound to arouse considerable public curiosity: Glanville's account refers to four great pieces of oak sawn into bars or barriers by carpenters, designed to resist the pressure of crowding people pushing for a glimpse. Edward had visited Gloucester and the vicinity several times during his reign, and certainly many people there would have known what he looked like, but neither the body nor the face of the dead king was visible. He lay under a cover which was decorated with 800 gold leaves, with a wooden effigy of himself on top of it. This is the first time any such wooden effigy is known to have been used for a royal burial in England.[19] The effigy, for which 40s was paid, was carved in the likeness of Edward, and was crowned with a copper gilt crown which cost 7s 3d. Edward's coronation robes from 1308 were sent from London, and used to dress the effigy. The whole lay on a hearse which was decorated at the four corners with great lions, made by a court painter called John de Eastwick; the lions wore mantles with the royal arms of England embroidered on them. Also on the hearse stood four images of the Evangelists, Saints Matthew, Mark, Luke and John, presumably in a nod to Edward II's birth on the feast of St Mark and perhaps, rather less than tactfully, to his death on the feast of St Matthew. Outside the hearse stood images of eight angels carrying censers (containers for incense) and two more great lions. A first hearse was hired from Andrew the candle-maker, but another was made between 24 November and 11 December.[20]

Edward II's funeral took place at St Peter's on Sunday 20 December 1327; not much is known about it. His son Edward III, who had turned 15 a month earlier, was certainly present – this was long before English royal etiquette began to demand that kings should not attend funerals – and so was his widow Isabella. Roger Mortimer had himself a new black tunic made for the occasion, a piece of hypocrisy which the young king remembered three years later when he had Mortimer dragged to his execution wearing it. Edward II's niece Elizabeth de Burgh née de Clare was there, having left her two young daughters in the care of Hugh Despenser the Younger's sister Isabel Hastings, and so was Edmund of Woodstock, Earl of Kent, the younger of Edward II's two half-brothers.[21] Most probably, other relatives of the late king also attended, including Edward's other half-brother Thomas of Brotherton, Earl of Norfolk, Edward's three younger children John of Eltham, Eleanor of Woodstock and Joan of the Tower (now 11, 9 and 6), his cousin Henry, Earl of Lancaster, his nephew-in-law John de Warenne, Earl of Surrey, and as many of the English bishops and lords as were able to travel to rather remote Gloucester in winter. Several days after the funeral, the woman who embalmed Edward II was brought to his widow Isabella in Worcester: the clerk Hugh Glanville recorded this as 'bringing a certain woman who disembowelled the king to the queen by the king's [Edward III's] orders'.[22] It seems that Glanville tried to hide this fact in his accounts, and that the barons of the Exchequer later queried a suspicious gap or alteration when they audited them. The order to bring the woman to her, although issued in the young king's name, is far more likely to have come from Isabella herself. The woman's name is not known, nor what she said to the dowager queen, nor what became of her afterwards; yet another mystery of Edward II's death.

7

THE MURDERERS OF A KING

The royal court did not stay long in Gloucester after Edward of
Caernarfon's funeral, though they returned to the area a year later and
spent the first anniversary in the town on 20 December 1328. In early
1328 they were 170 miles away in York, where on or about 25 January
15-year-old Edward III married Philippa of Hainault, aged about 13
or 14, in a ceremony performed by the Archbishop of York, William
Melton. Whether by accident or design, the young king's wedding
took place on his parents' twentieth wedding anniversary, Edward II
and Isabella of France having married in Boulogne on 25 January 1308.
It was also the first anniversary of the first official day of the young
king's reign. For years the underage Edward III was forced to watch
the disastrous regency of his mother Isabella and Roger Mortimer
bankrupting his kingdom and tarnishing the name of the monarchy
as much as his father had. On 19 October 1330, a few weeks before
his eighteenth birthday and four months after the birth of his and
Queen Philippa's first son Edward of Woodstock, Edward III arrested
Roger Mortimer at Nottingham Castle in a sudden coup d'état, placed
his mother under house arrest and took over the rule of his kingdom. Mortimer was walled up, literally, at the Tower of London until
Parliament began at Westminster on Monday 26 November, when he
was taken before Parliament tied up and gagged. The fourteen charges
against Mortimer reflect the young king's rage that his mother's ally

and favourite had used and abused royal power to which he was not entitled, being neither of royal birth nor elected to an official position on the regency council appointed to rule during the young king's minority. Edward III also said that Mortimer had filled his household with spies who reported his every move to Mortimer, with the result that the king 'was unable to do as he wished, so that he was like a man living in custody'.[1]

One of the charges against Mortimer at this Parliament stated that:

Whereas the father of our lord the king was at Kenilworth by the ordinance and assent of the peers of the realm, to remain there at their pleasure in order to be looked after as was appropriate for such a lord, the said Roger by the royal power usurped by him, was not satisfied until he had him at his will, and ordained that he be sent to Berkeley Castle where he was traitorously, feloniously and falsely murdered and killed [*treterousement, felonessement, et falsement murdre et tue*] by him and his followers.[2]

On 29 November 1330, Roger Mortimer was dragged from the Tower of London to Tyburn, forced to wear the black tunic he had had made for Edward II's funeral three years earlier, then hanged naked. He was buried at the Greyfriars church in Coventry, though his widow Joan Geneville petitioned the king a few months later to have his body moved to his family's main seat at Wigmore in Herefordshire, and it is merely a romantic myth that Queen Isabella was lain to rest next to him when she died twenty-eight years later in 1358; she was in fact buried at the Greyfriars in London. It is absurd to imagine that Edward III would have allowed his royal mother, through whom he claimed the throne of France, to lie for eternity next to a man he had executed for treason.

It was also stated at the Westminster Parliament that Sir Thomas Gurney, the knight of Somerset who brought Edward III the news of his father's death at Lincoln on 23/24 September 1327, and William Ockley, the man-at-arms sent by Roger Mortimer to Berkeley Castle shortly before 21 September 1327, 'falsely and traitorously murdered' Edward II. The means of murder was never given out officially, either now or at any other time. The king offered a reward for the capture of the two men: £100 for Gurney alive or 100 marks (£66) for his head; 100 marks for Ockley alive or £40 for his head. William Ockley presumably fled from England, and was never heard of again. Thomas Gurney fled to Spain and then to Italy, where Edward III pursued him relentlessly, either to have him punished for the murder of Edward II or to gain information from him, or probably both; letters sent by Edward III in 1331 indicate that he was extremely keen to hear Gurney's confession.

Without the fortunate survival of the court case against William Shalford by Hywel ap Gruffudd in 1331, we would have no idea why William Ockley was charged with Edward II's murder, as no chronicler mentions him at all: the case says that Roger Mortimer sent Ockley to Berkeley Castle with a message informing them of the Welsh plot to free Edward and telling them to act on the contents of the letter from Shalford 'in order to avoid great peril'.[3] A writ to arrest Thomas Gurney and William Ockley was issued to all the sheriffs of England and the bailiffs of eight ports on the south coast on 3 December 1330, on the grounds that they were 'charged with diverse offences in this realm, [and] propose leaving the realm secretly, and diverse evils may arise through their malice'.[4] This was a full week after the commencement of Parliament and four days after the execution of Roger Mortimer, and would therefore seem to have been issued a little later than one might expect for a writ demanding that the murderers of the king's father be prevented from leaving the country and arrested.

Roger Mortimer's ally Sir Simon Bereford was executed just before Christmas 1330, vaguely accused of aiding Mortimer in all his felonies, which presumably included the murder of Edward II. No chronicler mentions Bereford's involvement in the murder, though the Fieschi Letter (of which much more later) does:

Afterwards the servant who was keeping him [Edward II], after some little time, said to your father [Edward III's father, i.e. also Edward II]: Lord, Sir Thomas Gurney and Sir Simon Bereford, knights, have come with the purpose of killing you.

If the Fieschi Letter really was Edward II's account of how he had escaped from Berkeley Castle which he related to Manuele Fieschi, Edward would have heard of the knights Thomas Gurney and Simon Bereford but not of William Ockley, a man-at-arms who was of much lower birth and rank, and if he heard that Bereford was executed at the end of 1330, might have put two and two together and assumed that Bereford was one of his would-be killers. Simon Bereford is a shadowy figure whose role in the events of Roger Mortimer and Isabella of France's regime is not at all clear, though Edward III evidently thought he had enough reason to execute him. He was the only other man executed at this time.

Whether out of bravery, foolhardiness or a clear conscience, Thomas, Lord Berkeley himself did not flee from the country but turned up at the November 1330 Parliament, in time to witness his father-in-law Roger Mortimer condemned to death and executed. When asked how he wished to acquit himself of involvement in the death of the king's father, Lord Berkeley made a most curious statement, recorded by a clerk in Latin (though he surely said it in French): *nunquam fuit consentiens, auxilians, seu procurans, ad mortem suam, nec unquam scivit de morte sua usque in presenti Parliamento isto.* This translates as 'He never consented to nor aided nor procured his death, nor did he know about his death until this present Parliament.'[5] As it was Lord Berkeley's letter to Edward III in September 1327 taken to the young king by Thomas Gurney which informed him of his father's death, which news the king had immediately begun disseminating, Berkeley's statement that in fact he had not known that Edward II was dead until he arrived at the Parliament of November 1330 is surprising and peculiar. His words have often been over-elaborately translated by modern historians to say that Berkeley was claiming he knew nothing of the circumstances of Edward II's death (although it had taken place in his own castle) or that he did not know Edward had been murdered, but that is not what his testimony says. It says, simply, that he 'did not know about (or of) his death until this present Parliament'.[6]

This answer was not accepted and it was demanded that Berkeley give another account, whereupon he claimed that he was away from Berkeley Castle on the night of Edward's death, at his manor of Bradley about 7 miles away, and was suffering from 'so great an illness' that he 'remembers nothing' of the events of 21 September 1327. A dozen knights turned up at Parliament on 20 January 1331 and perjured themselves by stating that Berkeley's claims of absence from his castle that day and convenient amnesia were indeed true, though Berkeley's lies were exposed 300 years later in John Smyth's *Lives of the Berkeleys*. Smyth found documents demonstrating that Lord Berkeley was indeed at Berkeley Castle on 21 September 1327, and did not leave for Bradley until the 28th.[7] Thomas Berkeley was not punished in any way, though was held responsible for appointing Thomas Gurney and William Ockley 'to carry out the keeping of the lord king', and was officially committed to the custody of the king's household steward, Sir Ralph Neville. On 16 March 1337, over six years later, Berkeley was finally deemed 'guiltless' of all charges relating to the death of Edward II and pardoned.[8] This was a few weeks before the death of his wife Margaret Mortimer, Roger's eldest daughter, on 5 May 1337. Whether coincidentally or not, six months after this pardon Edward III made his first personal visit since the downfall of his mother and Roger Mortimer to his father's tomb in Gloucester.[9]

As early as 20 May 1331, Edward III learned of Thomas Gurney's whereabouts: he had fled to Spain, and on that day, the king wrote to Alfonso XI of Castile remarking that Gurney had been 'charged with sedition against the person of the late king and with conspiracy of his death'. Gurney had been arrested and imprisoned in the town of Burgos in the north of Castile (where, incidentally, Edward III's grandparents Edward I and Leonor of Castile had married in 1254) by Alfonso's chamberlain. Edward thanked Alfonso and his chamberlain for this, 'and offers himself prepared for those things that shall please Alfonsus upon all occasions'. He also asked Alfonso and the mayor and community of Burgos to have Gurney delivered to Sir John Hausted, steward of Gascony (the territory ruled by the Kings of England in the south-west of France, which bordered Castile) on the grounds that it was 'unfit that such iniquity should be left unpunished'.[10] According to a version of the French *Brut* chronicle, Gurney and Sir John Maltravers (who had fled from England with Gurney after also being sentenced to death at Parliament) were spotted in Burgos by an

English pilgrim called Isolda Belhouse, who notified the authorities. Maltravers escaped before he could be captured, at which juncture he presumably went to Flanders where he lived for many years. Thomas Gurney, meanwhile, was placed in irons by the highway.[11] On 30 May 1331, ten days after writing to Alfonso, Edward III sent Giles of Spain, who in 1329–30 had been involved in a plot to free the supposedly dead Edward II, 'to bring to the king Thomas de Gurney, knight, arrested beyond seas for compassing the death of the late king'. This order was repeated on 25 June, though in fact Giles had left England on 11 June.[12] Edward explained to Alfonso XI, his chamberlain and various others that he wished Gurney to be questioned by the citizens of Bayonne in Edward's duchy of Gascony:

> Concerning the sedition and conspiracy [to kill Edward II] aforesaid and the assent, instigation and procuration made concerning it, and by whom and in what manner they were made, and to cause his confession to be put into writing by a notary public.

This order was repeated to the men of Bayonne, and the king told them to give Gurney's confession to Giles of Spain, who would bring it to Edward III in person.[13] Evidently the king was very keen to learn exactly who was responsible for his father's death and how it happened, and Gurney's confession, if he ever made one, would be a wonderfully informative document for historians. It is apparent from Edward III's own letters that he was pursuing Gurney for information, which he wanted to be written down, notarised and brought to him in person. Unfortunately, the plan went awry when Thomas Gurney managed to escape from a Burgos prison (leaving behind his valet John Tilly, whom Giles of Spain seized and imprisoned in Gascony), and made his way to Naples in Italy, which was then ruled by Edward II's second cousin King Robert 'the Wise'. Gurney was finally captured in Naples in 1333 by the Yorkshire knight Sir William Thweng. To cut a very long story short, he died in Bayonne, Gascony in about June 1333 before he could be returned to England, almost certainly of ill health or stress and exhaustion. His body, however, was delivered to Edward III in the north-east of England, and Gurney may have been beheaded after death, or at least had his body displayed in public. The chronicler Geoffrey le Baker thought that he was executed by being beheaded on board ship, which may be a garbled version of what really happened.[14] The valet John Tilly and another associate of Gurney named Robert Lynel were arrested and ordered to be brought to England because of 'certain things committed against the king in this realm [England]'.[15] It is notable that none of Edward III's letters and orders referring to Thomas Gurney in the early 1330s state directly that Gurney had murdered Edward II, only that he had conspired to do so, and had thus committed sedition against the person of the former king.

However Edward II died on 21 September 1327, for a full five and a half centuries hardly anyone ever doubted that he did indeed die. There was seemingly little or no question about this. Then in the 1870s, a letter was discovered which cast doubt on the whole story of the king's murder and whether he had even died at all, and some years later, another letter appeared which cast further doubt on the whole issue. Most curiously, it turned out that in the 1330s an English archbishop and an Italian lawyer, later a bishop, committed their belief that Edward was alive past 1327 to parchment. And they were far from being the only ones. The peculiar story of Edward II was far from over.

PART III

LONG LIVE THE KING

8

THE RESCUERS OF THE KING

For more than a year after Edward II's supposed death on 21 September 1327, there is no evidence that anyone in England doubted that he really was dead. A Parliament took place at Salisbury in the second half of October 1328 during a particularly fraught period of Queen Isabella and Roger Mortimer's regime. Mortimer used the opportunity to bestow the unprecedented Earldom of March on himself, meaning earl of all the English–Welsh borderlands, to the disgruntlement of many, especially Queen Isabella's uncle and Edward II's first cousin Henry, Earl of Lancaster. Being deprived of the custody of Edward of Caernarfon in April 1327 had angered the earl. In 1328, Isabella and Mortimer freed Sir Robert Holland from prison. He had been a close ally of Lancaster's brother Thomas but had betrayed him in 1322, not long before Thomas was execued. Holland's release added fuel to the fire, and some Lancastrian knights decapitated him in an Essex wood in October 1328 and sent his head to Henry, who shielded them from justice.

Mortimer's grandiose earldom and his and Isabella's continued control of the government, when they had not even been appointed to an official position on the regency council which was meant to rule in the underage king's name, was the last straw. In late 1328, Henry of Lancaster raised an army against the pair, and attempted to seize the young king. Edward III's uncles the Earls of Norfolk and Kent joined the rebellion temporarily, which fizzled out in early 1329 when Roger Mortimer marched to the Earl of Lancaster's main power base of Leicester and sacked it. Just after the Salisbury Parliament ended, on 5 November 1328, Henry of Lancaster sent an interesting letter to the mayor and aldermen of London, telling them that 'the earl of Kent had made certain communications to him, which he could not put into writing, but which the bearer would report by word of mouth'.[1] The Earl of Kent was Edmund of Woodstock, younger of Edward II's two half-brothers, and then 27 years old. The possible significance of this communication from Lancaster only became apparent later (and it is only a possible significance; we cannot know for sure what Lancaster meant with this communication).

On 8 March 1329, eight men were ordered to come to Edward III immediately, 'laying aside all excuse, as the king wishes to have colloquy with [them] upon certain affairs'.[2] The men were William Culpho, John Molyns, Thomas Staunton, Roger Waltham, John Wymondeswold, John Flete, John Harsik and William Dunstable (on the same day, Dunstable was also ordered to be arrested 'wherever found' and brought to the king).[3] As with the Earl of Lancaster's letter, the significance of this only became apparent a year later, when several of the men were named as conspirators who had taken part in a certain plot of the Earl of Kent and their arrest ordered. John Molyns had formerly been a valet of Hugh Despenser the Younger and was pardoned by Edward III for adherence to the Despensers; John Harsik was a former squire of Edward II's household whom the king had appointed as one of his envoys to Queen Isabella in his last days of freedom (with Rhys ap Gruffudd, who had tried to free Edward from Berkeley Castle in September 1327).

On 24 March 1329, the Earl of Kent began making plans to leave England: he and members of his household received a series of safe-conducts permitting them to travel, and appear to have left the country on or shortly after 11 June 1329.[4] Edward III himself, now 16 years old, left England on Friday 26 May 1329 in order to pay homage to his mother's cousin Philip VI of France for his French lands, and returned to Dover on 10 June.[5] Possibly uncle and nephew met at this point. Kent travelled to Avignon to meet and talk to Pope John XXII, and also spent time in Paris, where he met the English lords Henry, Lord Beaumont and Sir Thomas Roscelyn in the chamber of his nephew Duke John III of Brabant (only child of Edward II's sister Margaret, who was also Kent's half-sister). The earl was in Gascony at the end of September and back in England by early December 1329 or sooner.[6] Rather intriguingly, John XXII commuted the vow of Kent and his wife Margaret Wake to go on pilgrimage to Santiago de Compostela on 30 September 1329 on the grounds that Kent 'has learned that plots are laid against him in Spain [so] he is unable to go there'.[7]

None of this seemed particularly important or unusual until rather later: on 13 March 1330, the Earl of Kent was dramatically arrested while attending a Parliament in Winchester which had begun two days before, and was charged with treason against his nephew the young king. Kent admitted that he believed Edward II was still alive and had been trying to free him from captivity, and that he went to see the pope to 'see what thing might best be done touching his [Edward's] deliverance'.[8] And he was far from alone in this belief. Edward II's friend William Melton, Archbishop of York, had certainly believed that he was dead, and offered an indulgence on 23 October 1327 to anyone in his diocese who said prayers for Edward's soul.[9] On 10 October 1329, however, Melton received news that Edward of Caernarfon was still alive, brought to him by a man called William of Kingsclere:

> Announcing to him and emphatically asserting that Edward, the late King of England, the father of the present king, was alive and in good health in the prison of Corfe Castle [in Dorset] and asking him if he would furnish any advice or help in releasing him.

Melton replied that he would sell everything he had excepting one vestment and one chalice, 'and would spend freely to obtain his release'.[10] Melton found the news convincing enough to send Kingsclere, with 20s for his expenses, to Edward II's old friend Donald, Earl of Mar in Scotland. Mar and his followers had made attempts to help Edward while at Berkeley Castle in 1327. Back in Scotland now, married, and close to the throne – he was the son of Robert Bruce's eldest sister and the first cousin of the 5-year-old new king David II, and later was briefly regent of Scotland – Mar was still intensely interested in the fate of the man he had served loyally for many years. He informed Melton via Kingsclere that he would come to England with an army of 40,000 men in order to bring about Edward of Caernarfon's release.[11] It is impossible that Mar would have been able to raise such a vast number of fighting men, which was three times the size of Edward II's unprecedentedly large army at Bannockburn in 1314, but the exaggerated number emphasises his desire to help the former King of England, his close friend.

This news slipped out and came to the ears of Queen Isabella and Roger Mortimer: on 7 December 1329, they or whoever was controlling chancery at the time warned many sheriffs and justices of the kingdom to arrest anyone spreading 'false rumours inventing the arrival of foreigners', *falsos rumores confingunt de adventu alienigenarum*, in England.[12] When the Archbishop of York appeared before King's Bench on 23 April 1330 to answer a charge of treason, on the grounds that he had invited a Scottish army into England, it was said that:

> If so great a host of foreigners, powerfully armed, were to come into England to the terror of the people of the realm, it would greatly yield and contribute to the shame of the king [Edward III] and his crown and to the destruction and impoverishment of his people.[13]

The Earl of Kent had returned to England some days or weeks before the proclamation about false rumours of foreigners, and rejoined the court on or before 3 December 1329, when he witnessed a royal charter issued at Kenilworth.[14] The 17-year-old Edward III and his family and household spent a prolonged period at Kenilworth Castle in late 1329; Queen Philippa was pregnant with the royal couple's first child Edward of Woodstock, who was born on 15 June 1330.

On 14 January – almost certainly in 1330, though the year is not given – at his manor of Cawood in Yorkshire, the Archbishop of York sent a letter to his kinsman the mayor of London, Simon Swanland.[15] Having begged Swanland to keep what he was about to tell him strictly secret, Melton went on to say that he had 'certain news of our liege lord Edward of Caernarfon, that he is alive and in good physical health in a safe place by his own wish [or command]' (*certeins noueles de nostre seignur lige Edward de Karnarvan qil est en vie et en bone sancte de corps en enseur leu a sa volonte demeign*).[16] The wording 'Edward is alive and in good physical health' echoes what Melton had been told by William of Kingsclere on 10 October 1329, three months before he wrote to Swanland. Melton went on to express his joy at Edward's survival, and asked Swanland to procure a loan of £200 in gold, 'if you can have it brought secretly to the said lord [Edward] from us for his comfort'.

Two points are important here. Firstly, Melton must have known, or at least believed, that he knew where Edward was, but did not commit this to the letter. Presumably, as the letter asks Swanland to have the £200 taken directly to Edward, Melton's messenger must have informed Swanland orally where Edward was. Secondly, gold was rarely used in England in 1330, the only coin in general circulation being the silver penny. Gold was used far more regularly on the Continent, however, so Melton appears to have assumed that Edward would go abroad. Whether this meant to find permanent and secret shelter, or to attempt to raise an army and regain his throne, is not clear.

Simon Swanland was a draper by profession and had previously supplied cloth to Edward II's household; he was named as a squire of Edward III's household in June 1328 and in 1330.[17] Edward II knew and trusted him: when he fled from London in early October 1326, he left some personal possessions in Swanland's safekeeping, including two 'good and beautiful' Bibles, one with a red leather cover, a cloth-of-gold cloak edged with pearls and silver, three velvet garments with green stripes and a matching hat, a cushion cover of vermilion sendal (a fine, light silk), and a green coverlet with three matching hangings.[18] In January 1330, Melton asked Swanland, in his capacity as a draper, to obtain numerous items for the supposedly dead Edward of Caernarfon:

Two half cloths of different colours, a good cloth and intimate clothing and good fur of miniver [expensive fur from ermine or squirrel] for six garments, and three hoods, with miniver for finishing the hoods, and two coverlets of different colours of the largest size, with the hangings, and two belts and two bags, the best you can find for sale, and twenty ells of linen cloth dyed red, and ask for his cordovan [or 'cordwain', expensive Spanish leather] so that we will have six pairs of shoes and two pairs of boots, and have all the above-mentioned things packaged up in a bundle as mercers [cloth merchants] carry their goods.

It is possible that Melton wrote to other men he trusted at this time as well, asking them to procure other items, and that the letter to Swanland is the only one which fortuitously happens to survive (it is now in the Warwickshire County Record Office).

It is remarkable that Melton was ordering clothes, shoes and other provisions for Edward of Caernarfon over two years after Edward's funeral. The archbishop asked Swanland to deliver the bundle of items to Brother William Cliff, whose identity is not entirely clear but who was either a clerk of Melton or (less probably) a man of this name who had been a clerk of both Edward II and the Despensers and whom Hugh Despenser the Younger appointed as his attorney in July 1322. This William Cliff was pardoned for adherence to the Despensers in March 1327.[19] Melton also sent a horse to Swanland to carry the items, and asked him to come to Melton in person as soon as he could and as soon as the items were delivered, 'to advise us how we will borrow a great sum of money for the said lord, as we wish that he may be helped as far as we and you are able to arrange'.

Extracts from the Melton Letter were first published in the journal *Notes and Queries* in 1911 by J. Harvey Bloom, though Bloom did not appear to recognise the significance of what he had found and describes the letter merely as a request to Swanland 'to obtain certain articles for the king's wardrobe', despite citing the part which states (in French) that 'our liege lord Edward of Caernarfon is alive'.[20] For almost a century the Melton Letter was ignored, until its existence was communicated to Ian Mortimer and he briefly referred to it in his 2006 biography of Edward III, *The Perfect King*.[21] In 2009, Professor Roy Martin Haines edited the letter for the *English Historical Review*, but most curiously failed to deal with it as possible evidence of Edward II's survival past 1327 and merely assumed that Archbishop Melton must have been 'misled' and 'so easily convinced' and 'deceived' into believing that Edward was still alive when the letter was written.[22] Simply assuming that Melton was 'deceived' and 'misled' without even speculating as to who did this and why, and how they so easily deceived a highly intelligent, capable and astute archbishop and politician, is not a satisfactory way of dealing with a letter which is a strong piece of evidence that Edward II really was alive in 1330. Also rather curiously, Professor Seymour Phillips barely even mentions Melton's letter in his magisterial 2010 biography of Edward II for Yale University Press, even in his sections entitled 'Deposition and Death' and 'Afterlives' in which he discusses the possibility of Edward living past 1327 (and dismisses it).[23]

Melton and his letter are also not mentioned in J. S. Hamilton's 2008 article 'The Uncertain Death of Edward II?', though in fairness this was published the year before Haines edited the letter in the *English Historical Review*; it is also barely mentioned in Andy King's 2016 article in *Fourteenth Century England IX*, 'The Death of Edward II Revisited'. A full English translation of Melton's letter appears in Ian Mortimer's 2010 book *Medieval Intrigue*; it is also cited in full in French and English in Appendix 2 in the present book and is briefly discussed in my previous books *The Unconventional King* and *The Rebel Queen*. The Melton Letter has been rather ignored and dismissed by historians who are committed to the narrative that Edward died in 1327, perhaps because it cannot easily be discarded as evidence that Edward was indeed alive in 1330.

It is important to note that William Melton was not trying to incite a rebellion against Queen Isabella and Roger Mortimer, at least not at the time of writing the letter, but begged Simon Swanland 'not to tell any man or woman of the world' about Edward's survival. The argument of dissatisfaction with the regime is often used against Melton's ally the Earl of Kent, who also strongly believed that Edward II was still alive in 1330: that Kent and his allies did not truly believe in Edward's survival but were merely using his name in order to foment and spread discord against the regime of the unpopular pair ruling England in the underage Edward III's name. On the contrary, William Melton was extremely keen to keep the news of Edward II's survival secret, and also took the precaution of not committing certain important details to his letter, such as Edward's whereabouts. Swanland did keep the letter secret; it, and his involvement in the plots of 1330, were never discovered. Melton and his messenger William Cliff, who were both arrested, kept quiet about Swanland, and in July 1330 Swanland led a deputation of twenty-four men to Edward III at Woodstock. The king had summoned them to him to question them about the city of London's loyalty to him.[24]

It is likely that William Melton had attended Edward II's funeral, assuming he had been able to make the long journey from Yorkshire to Gloucester in the dead of winter, and he certainly believed in October 1327 that the deposed king was dead. Melton had joined the future king's household in early 1297 when Edward was only 12, or perhaps even earlier, and had thus known Edward for most of the king's life. Melton showed Edward considerable loyalty and affection for many years, but was not simply a yes-man, and was not afraid to stand up to Edward when he felt it necessary.[25] He had bravely spoken out for Edward at the January 1327 Parliament, and refused to attend the coronation of Edward III soon afterwards out of loyalty to the young king's father, though he was soon reconciled to him and married him to Philippa of Hainault a year later. Edward III thought highly of Melton and trusted him, appointing him treasurer of England soon after taking over governance of his kingdom in October 1330, and Melton's contemporaries also praised him. The Lanercost chronicler wrote that he 'led a religious and honourable life', and the *Vita Edwardi Secundi* said that although he lived long at court he was untainted by its corruption, and 'by the grace of God remained always unpolluted'.[26] The pious Melton often forgave debts owed to him by the poor, and when he died in April 1340 there was widespread grief in his archdiocese.[27] Probably in his 50s in 1330, a highly experienced politician, churchman and administrator, a past and future treasurer of England, a man of humble birth who had reached his high position entirely on merit, Melton was not an ignorant, credulous and uneducated person who could easily be deceived. His belief that Edward II was still alive in 1330, a belief so strong that he was willing to take the risk of committing it to parchment and being accused of treason (as in fact happened), therefore carries weight.

According to the *Brut* chronicle, written some years later, and the contemporary *Annales Paulini* (the annals of St Paul's cathedral), it was widely believed in England in the late 1320s that Edward II was still alive.[28] The *Brut* says 'common fame is throughout all England that he was alive, and whole and safe' and that people were afraid whether it were true or not; the *Annales* say that men in the entire realm of England asserted that Edward II was still alive in parts beyond sea, and that his brother the Earl of Kent was shortly going to attempt to restore him to the throne. It is often claimed that Queen Isabella and Roger Mortimer had begun these rumours of Edward's survival themselves in order to lure the Earl of Kent into treason, but in fact they ordered all the sheriffs of England and the justice of Wales (Roger Mortimer, who appointed himself to the position for life) to arrest and imprison anyone who said that Edward II was still alive.[29]

It is beyond doubt that Edmund of Woodstock, Earl of Kent, believed that his half-brother was still alive. On 13 March 1330, he was arrested and charged with treason against his nephew Edward III. He made a confession before the coroner of the royal household, which was later repeated in front of Parliament and in the nineteenth century was published as an appendix to the chronicle of Adam Murimuth. Kent named a handful of some of his most important adherents, the men who took part in his plot to free his supposedly dead half-brother; there were many more.[30] Orders began to be issued for the arrest of his adherents, some of them as early as 10 March, before Kent had even officially named them and three days before his own arrest. The *Brut* chronicle says that when Kent returned to England in the autumn or early winter of 1329 after visiting the pope to seek his advice regarding Edward and travelling to Gascony, he was informed by 'some of the Friars Preacher' (i.e. the Dominicans), that Edward was alive at Corfe Castle in the keeping of Sir Thomas Gurney.[31] The Lanercost chronicle comments that Kent acted to free his brother at the instigation of many of the bishops and lords of England, and 'especially at the instigation of a certain preaching friar of the convent of London, to wit, Friar Thomas Dunheved', and three other Dominicans called Edmund, John and Richard.[32] Lanercost also says that Thomas Dunheved told the earl that he had raised up the devil, who told him that Edward II was still alive. This statement, minus the information that the friar was Thomas Dunheved, is found in the Earl of Kent's confession: Kent claimed that a Dominican of London raised the devil and that two other Dominicans called Edmund Savage and John were among the 'chief dealers' of the whole matter. The bizarre tale of a devil-raising friar may be either a detail inserted into the confession to discredit Kent, or his own invention to conceal his real source.[33] It is basically impossible that men such as the Archbishop of York and the Bishop of London, not to mention all the secular lords who joined him, would have followed Kent on the strength of a devil-raising friar. As with the Melton Letter of two months previously, Kent's confession does not state where he believed Edward of Caernarfon to be hiding or imprisoned; neither man gave the location as Corfe Castle.

A story told by the unreliable chronicler Geoffrey le Baker in the early 1350s – the writer who claimed that Edward of Caernarfon was mistreated at Berkeley Castle and killed by red-hot poker – has another version of how the Earl of Kent came to hear of his half-brother's survival.[34] Baker says that some people pretended that Edward II was still alive at Corfe, and laid on festivals with lights and feasts to give the local inhabitants the impression that some important person was living there. Rumours spread that this important person was none other than Edward of Caernarfon, and reached the ears of Edmund, Earl of Kent, who sent a Dominican friar to Corfe to see what was happening. Seated at yet another great feast, the friar (dressed in secular clothes) saw a man he believed to be the former king, and informed Kent. The earl was subsequently beheaded after trying to free this fake 'Edward' from the castle. Chronicler and well-informed royal clerk Adam Murimuth says that the story of Edward II being alive was 'completely false' and, sarcastically, that it 'would have been a ghost'.[35]

Archbishop William Melton, nearly 300 miles away in Sherburn, Yorkshire, was told on 10 October 1329 (almost certainly while the Earl of Kent was still overseas) that Edward II was at Corfe Castle, and the Fieschi Letter of a few years later also states that he was there for some time after his supposed death. The association of Corfe Castle with Edward in 1327 is strong. Corfe is an ancient fortification on the Isle of Purbeck in Dorset, 85 miles more or less directly south from Berkeley Castle. The present castle was built in the eleventh century by William the Conqueror and mostly demolished after the civil war in the seventeenth, but Corfe's history goes back even further: in 978 it was the site of the murder of the King of England, Edward the Martyr, perhaps by his stepmother so that her son Ethelred would become king instead. In the fourteenth century it was a royal castle, sometimes used as a prison: Edward II imprisoned some of the Contrariants there in and after 1322, and one, Sir Robert Walkfare, was pardoned in 1327 for escaping from Corfe.[36] Adam Murimuth says that Edward was imprisoned at Corfe Castle at some point in 1327 and two other chroniclers mention his presence there that year; in the 1330s the *Brut*, though it gives the almost certainly mythical red-hot poker as the cause of his death, thought that he was actually killed at Corfe.[37] Edward's joint custodian in 1327, Sir John Maltravers, came from the area and was the constable of Corfe Castle for four years from November 1326. Two villages still called Worth Matravers and Langton Matravers, named after his family, lie 4 or 5 miles from Corfe, and a third village, Lytchett Matravers, is 10 miles away. Thomas, Lord Berkeley sent letters to John Maltravers at Corfe shortly before 29 September 1327, around the time that Edward was supposedly killed at Berkeley Castle, and at the same time Maltravers was said to be 'on the service of the king's father in Dorset', for which he received the large sum of £258 8s 2d.[38] Corfe had several advantages as a location to hide the former king: it was remote, Edward had few friends in the area, Maltravers was influential there, it was on a hill and easily defensible, and it was near the sea. It seems extremely likely that Edward of Caernarfon was indeed at Corfe Castle at some point in 1327, though exactly when is not known.

Two men evidently at Corfe in late 1329 or early 1330 were John Deveril, who was probably a man-at-arms, and Sir Bogo Bayouse (or Bayeux or Bayonne), a knight of Yorkshire who had been captured fighting against Edward II's army at the Battle of Boroughbridge in March 1322. His name is spelled in a variety of creative ways in extant contemporary documents, including Begyn de Baeus and Bugues de Baiocis. The Earl of Kent made a fatal error. Desperate to reassure Edward of Caernarfon that he was doing his best to liberate him, he asked his wife Margaret Wake to write a letter for him (a fact which raises some interesting points about literacy and education among the English nobility and especially among women of the early fourteenth century). The letter, recorded in the *Brut* chronicle in Middle English though surely in French in the original, stated:

> Worships and reverence, with a brother's liegeance and subjection. Sir knight, worshipful and dear brother! If it please you, I pray heartily that you be of good comfort, for I shall so ordain for you that soon you shall come out of prison, and be delivered of that disease that you be in. And understand of your great lordship that I have unto me assenting almost all the great lords of England, with all their apparel, that is to say, with armour, with treasure without number, for to maintain and help your quarrel so that you shall be king again as you were before; and that they all have sworn to me upon a book, and as well prelates as earls and barons.[39]

If this letter is correctly recorded by the author of the *Brut*, and if the Earl of Kent was not lying or exaggerating, he had considerable support among the earls, lords and bishops of the realm. Unfortunately, his letter was delivered into the hands of Roger Mortimer's adherents Sir Bogo Bayouse and John Deveril at Corfe, who revealed it to Mortimer. The merciless speed and ruthlessness with which Kent was subsequently arrested, convicted and executed might suggest that his and his allies' plot to free Edward was a genuine one. His fate was a foregone conclusion: only two days after his arrest and the day before he even made his confession, on 15 March, he was already being referred to as 'the late earl of Kent' and one of the 'late enemies of the king and his realm'.[40]

The usual explanations for Kent's plot are inadequate, and the whole situation makes little sense unless Edward of Caernarfon either genuinely was still alive, or that there was truly compelling evidence which led a large number of men to behave as though he was.[41] According to the *Brut* chronicle, the queen mother Isabella, 'through counsel of the [Roger] Mortimer, and without any other counsel, sent in haste to the bailiffs of Winchester that they should smite off the head of Sir Edmund of Woodstock, Earl of Kent', and the young King Edward was deprived of any opportunity to intervene and was 'wonder sorry' when he heard of his uncle's death. The *Brut* wrongly gives the date of Kent's execution as 10 October in the third year of Edward III's reign, i.e. 1329, which curiously enough was the date on which the Archbishop of York was told that Edward II was alive.[42] On 19 March 1330, the 28-year-old Earl of Kent, a son, brother, uncle and (although he couldn't have known it) grandfather of kings, was taken out on to a scaffold in Winchester. Terrified, he had promised to walk barefoot from there to London with a rope around his neck in order to save himself, but to no avail. The executioner fled, unwilling to take part in the judicial murder of such a highly born man, and Kent was forced to wait around all day in his shirt until a latrine cleaner, under sentence of death himself, was persuaded to wield the axe in exchange for a pardon. An order to send the earl's heavily pregnant wife Margaret Wake, Roger Mortimer's first cousin, with their young children (who included the toddler Joan of Kent, Richard II's mother) with only two attendants to Salisbury Castle in Wiltshire had been issued five days previously on 14 March. Countess Margaret was in fact allowed to remain at her home of Arundel Castle in Sussex, at least temporarily, presumably because it was discovered that she was eight and a half months pregnant and unable to travel. She gave birth to the Earl of Kent's posthumous son John there on 7 April. The rapid downfall and execution of his uncle at the hands of his mother and her favourite was surely a major factor in Edward III's determination to overthrow Isabella and Roger Mortimer and take over his own kingdom. The sudden coup d'état which removed them from power took place on 19 October 1330, seven months to the day after Kent's death.

9

THE RESCUERS OF THE KING
PART 2

On 21 March 1330, two days after the Earl of Kent's execution, several men including John Maltravers were ordered 'to make inquisition' to 'discover his adherents' in Hampshire, Dorset, Norfolk and Suffolk.[1] Kent admitted at his trial that he 'had made in parts beyond the sea and on this side of the sea, confederacies and alliances of men-at-arms and others'.[2] His followers were thought to be particularly numerous in Norfolk and Suffolk, and on 4 May the sheriff was ordered to find and identify them.[3] On 3 April 1330 there was still chaos throughout the country: the sheriffs of seventeen counties in the south of England and the Midlands were warned that many men were going about armed, and told to imprison them and confiscate their horses and armour.[4] All the sheriffs of England and the justice of Wales were informed on 13 April that the Earl of Kent had gathered a large number of armed men on both sides of the English Channel, and were ordered to arrest everyone who said that Edward II was still alive.[5] One of the earl's co-conspirators was Sir Rhys ap Gruffudd, who had fled to Scotland in September 1327 after attempting to free Edward II from Berkeley Castle and whose arrest as a Kent adherent was ordered on 31 March 1330. On 8 August that year, Roger Mortimer as justice of Wales gave himself an order to arrest and imprison Gruffudd's adherents in Wales; many people in that country were said to be 'of his confederacy and alliance'.[6] William Melton, Archbishop of York, appeared in person before King's Bench on Monday 23 April 1330 charged with inviting Donald of Mar and a large Scottish army to England in order to secure Edward II's release. In the end the case was never heard, and on 11 December 1330 Edward III, finally in full control of his own kingdom, declared Melton (now his treasurer of England) 'completely guiltless'.[7]

For decades, historians have tried to explain the plot of 1329–30 in terms of the Earl of Kent only, and have condemned him as stupid, gullible and unstable, either ignoring his many adherents or dismissing them as a mere handful of disaffected clerics. A few friars and clerics did join Kent (one of them was no less a person than the Bishop of London), but the vast majority of his followers were secular, and included four sheriffs, several dozen lords and knights, squires, sergeants-at-arms, merchants, and men so obscure they cannot be traced. Looking at the many records relating to the Earl of Kent's plot created by the English government in 1330, which make it perfectly clear that many dozens and probably many hundreds of men were supporting the earl in 1329–30 across England and Wales, the insistence that Kent was acting more or less alone and that he only believed his brother was still alive because he was stupid and gullible is peculiar. Kent's allies continued to be sought and charged for months after his execution, until as late as August 1330. Many were still in prison or exile when Edward III overthrew his mother and Roger Mortimer on 19 October.

When the Earl of Kent confessed to the crime of trying to release his supposedly dead brother from captivity – one wonders where the act of freeing a dead man from unlawful imprisonment was recorded as a felony – he named one man in particular who played a vital role in liaising between himself and several of his fellow plotters. Sir Ingelram Berenger, a knight of Wiltshire, was born in 1271 or earlier and had served in the retinue of Hugh Despenser the Elder, Earl of Winchester, for more than a quarter of a century; his name is frequently found accompanying Despenser abroad or on military campaigns for the last few years of Edward I's reign and all of Edward II's.[8] At the Lincoln Parliament of early 1316, Hugh Despenser the Younger attacked and assaulted a baron named John Ros who had tried to arrest Berenger for an unspecified reason.[9] Berenger was lucky to

survive the Despensers' downfall in 1326 unscathed, and was pardoned for allegiance to Hugh the Elder on 24 February 1327; he had
already been restored to his lands on 28 December 1326.[10] Berenger
was a landowner in Wiltshire, Hampshire, Dorset and Somerset, and
was twice appointed sheriff of Buckinghamshire and Bedfordshire by
Edward II in the 1320s.[11]

Aged around 60 in 1330, Berenger was a highly experienced politician, administrator, landowner and knight, and his belief in Edward II's
survival cannot lightly be dismissed. Berenger was not a natural ally
of Edmund of Woodstock, Earl of Kent: Kent had been one of the
judges who condemned both Hugh Despensers to death in 1326,
and thus was partly responsible for destroying Berenger's livelihood.
Berenger met the earl in London and brought a message from William
la Zouche, lord of Ashby de la Zouch in Leicestershire, who told
Kent via Berenger that he would 'give as much as he could for the
deliverance of his brother [i.e. Edward of Caernarfon]'. Berenger also
brought news that Sir John Pecche, lord of Hampton-in-Arden in
Warwickshire and a former constable of Corfe Castle, wished to help
the plot; Pecche's son Nicholas also joined.[12] On 15 March 1329,
Ingelram Berenger and William la Zouche jointly acknowledged a
debt of £300 to John Pulteney, rich merchant and future mayor of
London, which may give us some idea of the date when they met and
discussed the issue of Edward's survival (though this may also simply
be a coincidence). This was a week after eight men, some of them later
arrested as adherents of the Earl of Kent, were ordered to go to the
king immediately, and nine days before Kent began making plans to
leave England and visit the pope to ask his advice about Edward. On
3 July 1329, Berenger and la Zouche again acknowledged a joint debt,
to a London merchant named Peter Araz.[13]

William la Zouche of Ashby was an interesting man to become
involved in a plot to free Edward of Caernarfon. In November
1326 he had been one of the men who captured Edward and Hugh
Despenser the Younger in South Wales, and thus was, like the Earl of
Kent himself, not a natural ally of the long-term Despenser adherent
Ingelram Berenger. In early 1329, la Zouche abducted and married
the younger Despenser's widow, Edward of Caernarfon's niece and

Edward III's first cousin Eleanor de Clare, which seemingly prompted him to change sides (he and Eleanor were busily besieging Caerphilly Castle, her birthplace and part of her inheritance, in February and early March 1329).[14] La Zouche visited his stepson Hugh 'Huchon' Despenser, eldest son and heir of Hugh the Younger and in prison at Bristol Castle for the whole of Queen Isabella and Roger Mortimer's regency, and Huchon offered his support to his great-uncle the Earl of Kent.[15] La Zouche also spoke to his stepdaughter Isabel Despenser's teenage husband Richard Fitzalan, son of the Earl of Arundel executed without a trial by Roger Mortimer and Queen Isabella in 1326. Apparently Richard agreed to join the alliance, or at least was independently plotting against Mortimer and Isabella: a commission was ordered on 4 June 1330 to discover his adherents in Shropshire and Staffordshire, and Fitzalan, called 'the king's enemy and rebel', fled abroad.[16] William la Zouche met the Earl of Kent in person after two men had assured the earl that he could be trusted, and they rode together between Woking and Guildford in Surrey as they discussed the issue. The two men were Ingelram Berenger and William Cliff, who was the Archbishop of York's messenger to the mayor of London Simon Swanland in January 1330 regarding Edward II's survival.[17] Ingelram Berenger also acted as the liaison between Kent and the Bishop of London, Stephen Gravesend.

Kent claimed that two other men 'did travail and take pains' to help him free Edward II in the company of Ingelram Berenger: John Gymmynges and Sir Malcolm Musard. Musard was a notorious gang leader in Worcestershire and also a former adherent of Hugh Despenser the Elder, whom he had served from 1296 onwards. He had thus known Berenger for decades, and accompanied him abroad in Despenser the Elder's retinue in 1305 and again on later occasions.[18] Musard had nevertheless switched sides on occasion during Edward II's turbulent reign, and although he served the king in early 1322 during the Contrariant rebellion, he was arrested and imprisoned in the Tower of London in 1324 for adhering to the Contrariants.[19] He was pardoned for this in 1326 and supported Edward II during Queen Isabella's invasion; Isabella confiscated his lands in May 1327 on the grounds that he had aided the Despensers against herself and her son.[20]

The same year, Musard was accused of theft in Gloucestershire with Richard de Bircheston of Warwickshire, one of the men named as an associate of the Dunheved brothers in 1327 and who attacked Berkeley Castle with them that summer.[21] John Gymmynges, who was intended to play a vital role in the Earl of Kent's release of Edward II from captivity, was also a former adherent of the Despensers and Edward II: in May 1321 he was appointed as keeper of the great stronghold of Caerphilly Castle, which Hugh the Younger had surrendered into the king's hands during the rebellion against him, and then and in September 1322 was named as a valet of Edward II.[22]

Several other men not named in the Earl of Kent's confession of 16 March 1330, but who were ordered to be arrested between March and May 1330 for aiding him, were also former Despenser adherents: Sir Nicholas Dauney of the West Country, Sir William Cleydon, Sir William Spersholt, Thomas Staunton, Brother Richard Bliton, formerly Hugh the Younger's confessor who had been with Despenser and Edward II when they attempted to sail from Chepstow in October 1326, and Benet Braham, yet another of the men who held out at Caerphilly Castle in 1326–27 with Despenser's son.[23] Former adherents of the Despensers had good reason to dislike the Earl of Kent, who had taken part in the trial of both Despensers and condemned them to death, and had sent his household to plunder their lands far and wide in the aftermath of the 1326 invasion. That such men were prepared to follow Kent in 1330 indicates that they thought his plot to free Edward was a genuine one. The idea that Ingelram Berenger joined the Earl of Kent's plot to free Edward II not out of belief in the former king's survival, but out of revenge for Queen Isabella and Roger Mortimer's destruction of the Despensers or dissatisfaction with their regime, seems untenable. They had shown him mercy, restored him to his lands as early as December 1326 even before Edward II's official deposition, and did not imprison him for his long adherence to their enemies. Berenger had sworn homage and fealty to Edward III sometime before 12 January 1328, and seems to have been reconciled to the new regime.[24] Berenger's arrest for 'sedition' was ordered on 10 March 1330 and again on the 22nd three days after Kent's execution, and he was to be taken immediately to the king when found.

His lands in Wiltshire and Hampshire were still in the king's hands on 15 August 1330, when they were granted to Sir Bogo Bayouse and John Deveril of Corfe Castle.[25]

Other important English secular lords who joined the Earl of Kent's conspiracy to free Edward II were Sir Fulk Fitzwarin, lord of Whittington in Shropshire, who met Kent in person at Westminster to discuss the matter and who fled the country after the discovery of the plot; Sir John Say, lord of Martock in Somerset; Henry, Lord Beaumont, titular Earl of Buchan in Scotland, a relative of both Edward II and Queen Isabella; Sir Thomas Roscelyn, who had been with Roger Mortimer for years on the Continent and who took part in the 1326 invasion; Sir Nicholas de Sandwich; and Sir Thomas Wake, lord of Liddell in Cumberland. Wake, whose sister Margaret was married to the Earl of Kent, was said to have 'secretly withdrawn from the realm' on 4 April 1330, before he could be arrested.[26] He was Roger Mortimer's first cousin, had been one of the men who led Hugh Despenser the Younger from South Wales to his execution in Hereford in November 1326, and played a vital role in the Parliamentary proceedings which deposed Edward II.

Another Kent adherent in 1330 was Sir Roger Reyham, whom Edward III appointed as sheriff of the county of Kent a few months later; another was Adam Wetinhale, whom Edward II had made chamberlain of North Wales in 1320; and yet another was Sir William Aune, who had been constable of Tickhill Castle in Staffordshire for most of Edward II's reign and been high in his favour. Besides Ingelram Berenger and Roger Reyham, two other former or future sheriffs joined the earl: John Hauteyn and William Orlaston. Kent's fellow conspirators also included former members of Edward II's household and Edward's close associates: his tailor Henry de Cantebregge, merchant of London; his usher Peter Bernard; his squires Giles of Spain, who was at Caerphilly Castle in 1326–27, and John Harsik, who was with Edward until his capture in South Wales and whom he appointed as an envoy to Isabella on 10 November 1326; his valets John de Toucestre, William Daumarle and William Marenny; his chaplain John Coupland; and his close friend William, abbot of Langdon. Duke John III of Brabant allowed Kent to meet several of his fellow plotters in the duke's chamber in Paris, which at least implies sympathy with Kent's aims and perhaps even that the duke shared his belief in Edward II's survival.[27] John III was the son of Edward II's third sister Margaret, whom Edward had last met (as far as we know) when she and her husband Duke John II attended his coronation at Westminster in February 1308. It is unclear when Margaret died, but she was certainly alive in late September 1326 when Edward II wrote to her and her son, and she may still have been alive in the early 1330s.[28] Kent's confession states that he 'opened his heart' to two men in particular about his plan to free Edward. The first was Edward Monthermer, who was his half-nephew, youngest of the eight children of Edward II's second sister Joan of Acre, who had played little if any role in his uncle's reign. Monthermer was imprisoned in Winchester (where Kent was arrested and executed) on or before 24 March 1330 and given 12*d* per day for his sustenance.[29] The second man was George Percy, not a knight and apparently a squire or man-at-arms; he and his son John had been members of Kent's retinue since at least February 1320, when Kent was only 18 and not yet an earl.[30] John Percy, the son, was old enough to be married by July 1318, so George must have been considerably older than the Earl of Kent.[31] In 1309 and 1311 George had been a valet in the household of Edward II.[32] The arrest of George Percy, Ingelram Berenger, Fulk Fitzwarin and William la Zouche was ordered on 10 March, three days before the Earl of Kent himself was even arrested.[33] Fulk Fitzwarin immediately fled the country, and his sons Fulk and Ivo were captured and imprisoned 'safely and honourably without duress' in Shrewsbury in his place. His wife Eleanor was given an allowance of 40 marks a year on 31 May to sustain herself and her other children, and Fitzwarin's lands were seized on 27 April.[34]

It is unclear if the Lanercost chronicler's statement that the Dominican friar Thomas Dunheved was involved is true or not; he is usually thought to have died in prison after temporarily freeing Edward in 1327, but it is not impossible that he escaped and took part in the 1330 plot. His brother Stephen certainly escaped from Newgate prison in London in 1329 and was named as an adherent of the Earl of Kent twelve days after Kent's execution. The Welsh plan to free Edward from Berkeley Castle in September 1327 had prompted Roger Mortimer to deal with the entire situation of Edward's continued imprisonment, and in early 1330, Welshmen were also involved in Kent's plot. They were Sir Rhys ap Gruffudd, leader of the 1327 plot, and Ieuan Llwyd, son of Sir Gruffudd Llwyd who was one of the men imprisoned in Caernarfon Castle after it failed (Gruffudd Llwyd died in 1335 so may have been too elderly or infirm to take part himself in 1330).

Sir William Aune, formerly a close ally of Edward II and his constable of Tickhill Castle in the Midlands for many years, was constable of Caerphilly Castle, South Wales between 12 March 1329 and 5 February 1330, and again from 4 March to 5 April that year. On 10 August 1330, William Aune was 'indicted for adhesion' to the Earl of Kent, having apparently escaped notice for several months.[35] One of his mainpernors (guarantors) was Sir John Pecche, lord of Hampton-in-Arden and former constable of Corfe Castle, who had joined Kent's plot with his son Nicholas but was pardoned and restored to his lands and goods the day before acting as Aune's mainpernor.[36] The lands of Sir Ingelram Berenger and others remained confiscated until restored to them a few months later when Edward III, finally acting under his own agency after he overthrew his mother and Mortimer, deemed the men 'guiltless'. John Maltravers and two other men were given a commission of *oyer et terminer*, 'to hear and to determine', regarding the adherence to the Earl of Kent of Berenger and unnamed others, on 3 August 1330.[37]

At the November 1330 Parliament which condemned Roger Mortimer to death, William Melton, Archbishop of York, William, Abbot of Langdon, and many others petitioned Edward III to pardon them for adherence to the Earl of Kent (the king did so). Melton had been summoned by a writ of privy seal to appear before King's Bench on 23 April 1330, his accuser one John of Lincoln, but the case was never heard. According to John of Lincoln, William of Kingsclere informed Melton at Sherburn in Yorkshire on 10 October 1329 that Edward II was then still alive and in good health at Corfe Castle. William of Kingsclere is obscure and almost impossible to trace on record, and must have been the messenger of someone far more important; the fact that he was called 'of Kingsclere', the place where he came from, also implies that he was of low birth and importance, and he may simply have been a boy or young man from the village of Kingsclere used as a messenger. Historian Andy King has suggested that he was working for Roger Mortimer, and gave Melton a false account of Edward II's survival in order to lure Melton into treason so that Mortimer had an excuse to act against him. The *Annales Paulini* say that 'some of the worst spies' were spreading rumours that Edward was still alive, and King suggests that William of Kingsclere was one of them.[38] This seems unlikely, however; King thinks that Roger Mortimer would have wanted to act against William Melton and lure him into treason because of Melton's former support of Edward II (Melton was one of the four men who spoke out against Edward's deposition in the Parliament of January 1327 and had long been loyal to him) and because Melton therefore might be an opponent of Mortimer. It is unclear why Mortimer would have waited until October 1329, almost three years after Edward II's downfall, to act against Melton if he believed the archbishop to be a danger to himself and his political position. That Melton was supporting Edward III in 1329–30 might in fact be a more plausible rationale for Mortimer wishing to act against him than because of the archbishop's previous support of Edward II, as the young king asserting himself against his mother and her favourite with the support of an archbishop was indeed a threat to Mortimer's continued political survival.

Mortimer had no need to invent a conspiracy involving the fake survival of Edward II in order to lure William Melton into trouble; Melton already was. The archbishop had an ongoing quarrel with Louis Beaumont, Bishop of Durham, which by 25 October 1329 had become so potentially violent that the sheriff of Yorkshire was ordered to take the *posse comitatus* or county militia to deal with the situation as Melton and Beaumont were both raising forces of armed men. Melton and Beaumont were ordered to appear before the king's council on 7 December 1329. This was the same day as sheriffs and justices across the country were warned about the 'false rumours' of foreigners, meaning the Scottish army of Donald of Mar invited by Melton, arriving in England. Bishop Beaumont claimed on this day that he 'fears harm from armed men assembled by the said archbishop'.[39] On 19 October 1329, nine days after he supposedly heard of Edward II's survival from William of Kingsclere, Melton cited Louis Beaumont to appear before him in York Minster on 21 November, and on 24 April 1330 (the day after his appearance for treason before King's Bench) gave '10,500 small florins of Florence' to Simon Swanland, recipient of his letter regarding Edward II's survival three months earlier, to 'prosecute our [Melton's] cause in the papal court against the Bishop of Durham'.[40]

Andy King points out correctly that no action was taken against William of Kingsclere in 1330, which is true; he was not named as one of the Earl of Kent's many supporters whose arrest was ordered between March and August 1330, and therefore King supposes that he may have been working for the government. However, some of the men named in Kent's confession of 16 March were not ordered to be arrested either, such as Aleyn or Alan, a messenger of the Archbishop of York to the Earl of Kent; no effort at all seems to have been devoted to discovering this man's identity or arresting him.[41] If William of Kingsclere were simply the humble messenger of a much more important person, as seems to be the case given that he is almost impossible to find on record, there would be no particular need for the government to pursue him, as they did not pursue the messenger Aleyn. The Earl of Kent's confession names a clerk of his household called William of Durham and another man called Brother Thomas Bromfield, whom Kent named as 'they who most abetted him and enticed him to do these things aforesaid', i.e. the attempts to free his half-brother Edward.[42] No arrest warrant was issued for Durham or Bromfield either, despite their enthusiasm for stirring up the earl to aid his supposedly dead brother. Queen Isabella and Roger Mortimer did not arrest everyone named in connection with the Earl of Kent's plot, which does not necessarily mean that those not arrested were their own agents. Sending a messenger to tell an archbishop that the former king was still alive because the archbishop had supported the king years previously and consequently might be an opponent of the current regime seems a rather odd and unaccountable thing for Mortimer to have done.

Kingsclere is a village in Hampshire between Newbury and Basingstoke, and in 1329 the manor of Kingsclere belonged to the archbishop, dean and chapter of Rouen in Normandy, France. It had been taken temporarily into Edward II's hands in December 1324 with two other English manors belonging to the Archbishop of Rouen because Edward was then at war with his brother-in-law Charles IV of France, of whom the archbishop (a man called Guillaume Durfort) was a subject. Kingsclere was still in Edward III's hands 'for certain causes' in May 1327 but was restored to Archbishop Durfort and his chapter in December that year, with the other lands they held in England. Its keeper in the meantime had been Robert Wyvill, parson of Kingsclere church and a secretary of Queen Isabella, who was appointed Bishop of Salisbury in April 1330 and held the position until his death forty-five years later.[43] In February 1335, the Archbishop of Rouen – then Pierre Roger, elected Pope Clement VI in 1342 – granted the manor of Kingsclere to none other than William Melton, Archbishop of York, and Melton still held it at the time of his death in April 1340.[44] Wyvill was parson of Kingsclere until his appointment as Bishop of Salisbury when he was succeeded as parson by his brother Walter Wyvill.[45]

It seems most unlikely that Archbishop Guillaume Durfort of Rouen would have sent a messenger to William Melton about Edward II's survival; Durfort was elderly in 1329 and died in November 1330, and probably never even set foot in England. The village of Kingsclere lay in the diocese of Winchester, but the Bishop of Winchester also seems an unlikely person to have notified the Archbishop of York: in 1329 he was John Stratford, later Archbishop of Canterbury, who had been persecuted by Edward II in 1323 and played an important role in his deposition in early 1327. Robert Wyvill, or Walter his brother and successor as parson of Kingsclere, seem to be more plausible candidates for the person who sent William of Kingsclere as a messenger to William Melton with news of Edward II's survival. Robert Wyvill, as the secretary of Queen Isabella, may have been privy to secret information, and both he and Walter had links to Manuele Fieschi, the Italian papal notary and bishop who some years later told Edward III that his father had survived for years past 1327. Manuele Fieschi's attorney Thomas de Luco was Walter Wyvill's executor when Pope John XXII made

Walter canon of Wells in 1332. Fieschi himself, Thomas de Luco and both Wyvill brothers were all canons of Salisbury, 30 miles from the village of Kingsclere.[46] On 18 September 1330, just a month before Edward III overthrew his mother and Mortimer, a letter written in the young king's name said that Bishop Robert Wyvill was 'assisting Queen Isabella and the king in directing the affairs of the realm' but that a Nicholas of Ludlow, who was also a canon of Salisbury, was suggesting to the pope 'certain things to the injury of the bishop's person and the blackening of his fame and intends prosecuting them, whereby shame and blame may arise to Queen Isabella and the king'.[47] The nature of the rumours being spread about Robert Wyvill is unfortunately unspecified. Another canon of Salisbury at this time was Giovanni Fieschi, son of Niccolino Fieschi who was called 'the Cardinal of Genoa' and who may have been Manuele Fieschi's uncle (and was certainly a relative); Robert Wyvill's accuser Nicholas of Ludlow was Giovanni's executor when the latter was made a canon of York on 7 July 1329.[48] Yet another canon of Salisbury in 1329–30 was John Arundel, brother of the Earl of Arundel who remained with Edward II after Queen Isabella's invasion and was executed on 17 November 1326. John Arundel's teenage nephew Richard fled from England in or a little before June 1330 after joining the Earl of Kent's plot.

William Melton's clerk Robert de Taunton had accompanied the Earl of Kent abroad in 1329, and William Cliff, Melton's messenger who told the mayor of London in January 1330 that Edward II was still alive, was also in touch with the Earl of Kent and with his adherent William la Zouche, lord of Ashby. In addition, Melton sent an unidentified chaplain called Aleyn to the earl, promising Kent that he would give the huge sum of £5,000 to aid his deliverance of Edward, and also sent a Brother Richard of Pontefract to meet the Earl of Kent at Kensington near London at the coronation of Philippa of Hainault as Queen of England on 18 February 1330.[49] Richard of Pontefract was said to be the confessor of Isabella, Lady Vescy, a second cousin of Edward II, whose involvement in the plot cannot otherwise be confirmed. She was the sister of the Bishop of Durham with whom Archbishop Melton was quarrelling in 1329, and of Henry, Lord Beaumont, titular Earl of Buchan, who certainly was involved in Kent's plot. Evidently there was considerable contact between the Archbishop of York and the Earl of Kent in 1329–30 (and also between the earl and Sir Ingelram Berenger, liaising with some of his other adherents), which makes it highly likely that William Melton heard of Edward II's survival from various different sources, not only from the obscure and mysterious William of Kingsclere.

As for Kingsclere himself, there is a rather curious postscript to his story. After the Earl of Kent's adherent Giles of Spain returned to England in 1332 following his unsuccessful attempt to bring Thomas Gurney back with him, he supposedly arrested William of Kingsclere at Rochester in Kent on 25 July 1332. Giles subsequently arrested two other men named Sir Richard de Well and John le Spicer as well, and all three men were alleged to have been involved in some way in Edward of Caernarfon's death and were imprisoned in the Tower of London. Giles then returned to his native Spain and re-arrested Thomas Gurney's valet John Tilly. The statement that William of Kingsclere was arrested for complicity in the murder of Edward II, however, is only found in an article published in 1838, which does not cite its source.[50] If Giles of Spain did arrest Kingsclere, Well and Spicer, this must have been done in compliance with Edward III's order to him on 1 July 1332 to arrest anyone he found to have conspired towards the death of Edward II, though it is unclear what these men had done in connection with the death or what became of them after their alleged arrest and imprisonment. Richard de Well, although supposedly a knight, is also very difficult to find on record. Giles of Spain's arrests of John Tilly and Robert Lynel are well documented in *Foedera*, as is Edward III's order of 1 July 1332, but his supposed arrests of Kingsclere, Well and Spicer are not mentioned there.[51]

Sir John Maltravers, Sir Bogo Bayouse and John Deveril of Corfe Castle were condemned to death in the November 1330 Parliament for their role in the judicial murder of the Earl of Kent in March 1330. The charge against Maltravers confused several contemporary chroniclers, who believed wrongly that Maltravers was charged with the murder of Edward II, which he was not, neither in 1330 nor at any point in his long life. Like William Ockley, John Deveril disappeared after November 1330 and was never heard of again. Neither he nor Ockley was a knight and, being therefore much less well-known and recognisable, found it much easier to flee and simply vanish. Deveril was believed to be hiding in Wiltshire, Somerset or Dorset on 22 August 1331, when five men, including of all people John Maltravers' father John Maltravers the elder, were ordered to search for him and bring him to the king, and to arrest anyone found to have been sheltering him.[52] On 15 July 1331, two men named as Benedict Noght and John le Taverner of Mousehole in Cornwall, and unnamed others, were accused of helping John Maltravers and Thomas Gurney to 'pass beyond seas from Cornwall' after they had been sentenced to death and the ports of England closed to them. They were also accused of supplying Maltravers and Gurney with 'corn, armour and victuals' and of continuing to assist them long after their escape.[53]

The arrest of John Maltravers and John Deveril, though not Bogo Bayouse, was ordered on 3 December 1330, along with Edward II's supposed murderers Thomas Gurney and William Ockley.[54] This was a full week after Parliament had opened and four days after the execution of Roger Mortimer, which hardly gives the impression that Edward III was desperate to catch the men. Maltravers' second wife Agnes Bereford was allowed to take possession of some of their lands on 27 March 1331, at the request of Queen Philippa, and in July 1332 was allowed to travel abroad, ostensibly on pilgrimage but almost certainly to visit her husband.[55] Maltravers went to Flanders after his near-capture in Burgos in 1331 and lived there openly for many years entirely unmolested by the English government, spoke to Edward III's friend William Montacute in 1334 and briefly returned to England the next year, and was eventually allowed to come back permanently. As late as 29 October 1330, ten days after the arrest of Roger Mortimer at Nottingham Castle, Edward III had granted Maltravers custody of the royal manor of Clarendon in Wiltshire.[56] Ten days after the king had overthrown his mother and her favourite and was ruling the kingdom himself, he evidently did not think that Maltravers had done anything wrong, or suspect him of mistreating his father in 1327; if he had, he would never have given Maltravers custody of a royal manor when he was acting under his own agency. Imposing a death sentence on Maltravers for entrapping the Earl of Kent appears to have been nothing more than a gesture, and had the king really wanted to execute him, he could have had him brought back from Flanders at any time he wished.

On 23 March 1334, Edward III sent his good friend William Montacute (who had helped him arrest Roger Mortimer in October 1330 and whom he made Earl of Salisbury in 1337) abroad to talk to John Maltravers, on the grounds that Maltravers 'was desirous to reveal to him [the king] many things concerning his honour and the estate and well-being of his realm'.[57] Montacute, John Molyns (a former Despenser adherent who was now in the king's household) and Sir Nicholas de la Beche were pardoned for receiving Maltravers, who had temporarily returned to England, on 29 March 1335. On 3 June that year, Maltravers' brother-in-law Thomas, Lord Berkeley; Thomas' brother Maurice Berkeley; the Abbot of Malmesbury in Wiltshire and a knight called William Whitefield were pardoned on the same grounds.[58] In February 1342 Maltravers' wife Agnes was allowed to stay with him in Flanders as long as she wished; by early October 1343 Maltravers was working on Edward III's behalf in Flanders, and in August 1345 he submitted to the king in person when Edward visited the county and claimed that he had suffered an injustice on the rather hilarious grounds that in 1330 he had been condemned unheard by Parliament (he had not spoken in his own defence because he had chosen to flee the country rather than attend). Maltravers also claimed that he had lost all his goods in Flanders and was 'depressed in many ways'. He returned to England in early 1347, and died in February 1364, in his mid-70s or older; he had been knighted in May 1306 with Edward of Caernarfon, Roger Mortimer and Hugh Despenser the Younger, and thus cannot have been born later than about 1290.[59] His brother-in-law Thomas, Lord Berkeley also lived a long life, dying well into his 60s in October 1361. Edward III's treatment of the two men is not at all consistent with the claim by chronicler Geoffrey le Baker that they had abused and tormented his father at Berkeley Castle in 1327, or that Thomas Berkeley had been involved in Edward II's murder. In the meantime, Sir Bogo Bayouse, also sentenced to death for entrapping the Earl of Kent, and his wife Alice fled to Italy. They lived for some years in

Rome in a house rented to them by an unidentified Italian countess, and Bayouse died in poverty in the city on 26 July 1334.[60]

The November 1330 Parliament gave the Earl of Kent a posthumous pardon, and his elder son Edmund (only a young child) was recognised as heir to all his lands and his title. Edmund died in 1331, leaving Kent's posthumous younger son John to inherit; John in turn died childless in 1352 and thus the Earldom of Kent passed to Edmund of Kent's daughter Joan, later Princess of Wales and Aquitaine, who married Edward III's eldest son Edward of Woodstock and was the mother of Richard II. The record pardoning the Earl of Kent in late 1330 is excessively, amusingly concerned to state that Edward II was dead in March 1330 – really, truly dead – and that therefore it had been impossible for Kent to rescue him, because he was certainly dead; this is stated no fewer than four times. Hugh Despenser the Younger's son Hugh or Huchon, in prison at Bristol Castle where his jailer had been Thomas Gurney, was pardoned on 15 December (presumably for the crime of being Despenser's son), and on the same day Edward III also gave permission for Hugh the Younger's remains to be collected from London Bridge, Bristol, Carlisle, York and Dover four years after his execution.[61] They were buried at Tewkesbury Abbey in Gloucestershire, where his tomb still exists, just 10 miles from Edward II's in Gloucester.

The plan of Edward of Caernarfon's allies in 1329–30, as far as we can tell from the Melton Letter and the Earl of Kent's confession, went like this: the mayor of London and draper Simon Swanland would procure money, clothes and other items for Edward, and would send them to the former king in his 'safe place'; Melton's messenger William Cliff must have informed Swanland of the location orally. The order to Melton to appear before King's Bench in April 1330 names the location as Corfe Castle in Dorset, which fits well with other evidence. It seems that Melton thought Edward would freely be able to receive the goods, i.e. that he was not in prison, and he told Swanland that Edward was well and healthy in a safe place *a sa volonte demeign*, which can either mean 'by his own wish', 'at his own bidding' or even 'at his own command'. It does not seem as though Melton thought Edward was being held in captivity against his will. This perhaps fits with a statement in the Fieschi Letter that Edward escaped (or thought he escaped) from Berkeley Castle with one companion and spent a period of time at Corfe Castle voluntarily, and was not imprisoned there. Possibly Melton asked other men to procure other items for Edward, but the letters have not survived. He may have intended the clothes, cushions and tapestries he asked Swanland to procure to alleviate Edward's rather less than comfortable living conditions, or perhaps they were meant for the journey by water from Corfe Castle to Arundel Castle, which Melton might have expected to be unpleasantly cold in the late winter of 1329–30.

The Earl of Kent was evidently planning to travel to Corfe Castle himself and leave with Edward. Either Kent also believed that Edward was at Corfe voluntarily and that there would therefore be no issue in removing him, or he expected to use his authority as the son, brother and uncle of kings to demand entry and simply leave with a prisoner (though according to the *Brut*, when the earl tried to gain access to the castle to see Edward, John Deveril would not permit it, forcing Kent to write a letter to his brother instead).[62] The former Despenser adherent John Gymmynges and his cousin, a monk of Quarr on the Isle of Wight, would provide a ship, a boat and a barge for the various stages of taking Kent and Edward along the coast of southern England to Kent's castle of Arundel in Sussex, 'and from there wherever should have been appointed'. This sounds as though Edward himself would decide where to go and what to do, in consultation with Kent and perhaps Melton and others. Where Edward would have gone, and to do what, cannot be known. Perhaps Scotland, where he had his close ally and friend Donald, Earl of Mar; Brabant in the Low Countries, where his nephew Duke John III ruled and where his sister Margaret was perhaps still alive, and from where his friends plotted an invasion of England in the summer of 1330; the Spanish kingdom of Castile, his mother's homeland; the papal court in Avignon, where the Fieschi Letter says he did go and which Edward, a pious man who kept in frequent contact with the pope during his reign, might have seen as a haven; Gascony, where he had allies such as Arnaud Caillau and Bérard Lebret; or Ireland, from where Edward may have been intending to launch a counter-invasion of his kingdom in the autumn of 1326.

The plan may even have been considerably bigger than this, and involved a concerted effort to raise armies and try to force Edward II's restoration to the throne. It is possible that Rhys ap Gruffudd and William Aune (constable of Caerphilly Castle for much of 1329–30) would attempt to raise South Wales and Ieuan Llwyd the north, while Donald of Mar would invade England from Scotland with an army, aided by Henry, Lord Beaumont (titular Earl of Buchan in Scotland) who was then on the Continent, perhaps with the aid of Edward II's nephew Duke John III of Brabant. Adherents of the Earl of Kent stretched across Wales and the south and Midlands of England and were particularly numerous in East Anglia, or at the very least were believed to be. On the other hand, William Melton showed the same loyalty to Edward III as he did to Edward II, and may not have wished to join a plot which would have harmed the young king in any way; the same applies to the Earl of Kent, Edward III's uncle. Although we cannot know what they intended to do with Edward of Caernarfon, perhaps it is more likely that their concern was more to help Edward escape captivity rather than restore him to his throne. Several prominent Londoners also took part in the Earl of Kent's plot: the bishop, Stephen Gravesend; the mayor, Simon Swanland; John Hauteyn, sheriff of the city in 1328; John de Everwyk and Henry de Cantebregge, merchants and citizens (i.e. important men) of the city, and possibly John Pulteney, a wealthy draper and moneylender, and future mayor of London four times. This London involvement is especially interesting given the previous hostility of the city to Edward II and the support many of the prominent citizens and inhabitants gave to Queen Isabella in 1326. Isabella's enemy and Edward II and the Despensers' ally Walter Stapeldon, Bishop of Exeter, had been murdered in the city not long after the queen's invasion, and the Parliament which deposed Edward II in January 1327 was held in London deliberately because the king had few friends there.

In his confession of 16 March 1330, the Earl of Kent revealed that the plan was for Henry, Lord Beaumont and Sir Thomas Roscelyn to land near Scotland and invade England with the aid of Donald of Mar, but he said that the time for this had 'passed' by then. In fact, this invasion was still feared in the summer of 1330. In mid-July, Queen Isabella and Roger Mortimer (presumably it was they) ordered all the sheriffs of England to array knights, squires and other men who bore arms:

> To set out against certain contrariants and rebels who lately withdrew
> secretly from the realm and who have assembled a multitude of armed
> men in parts beyond the sea and have prepared ships of war and other
> things and who propose entering the realm to aggrieve the king and
> his people.[63]

In late July and early August, more measures were taken: mayors, sheriffs and bailiffs in London and more than thirty other towns were ordered to array knights and men-at-arms against 'certain rebels who lately withdrew from the country by stealth [and] are said to intend to return and do what mischief they can'. Roger Mortimer and his deputies were to array fighting men in Gloucestershire, Herefordshire, Worcestershire and Shropshire.[64] Louis Beaumont, Bishop of Durham, was ordered on 10 August also to array fighting men to be ready to 'set out against the said rebels if they invade the realm'.[65] Louis Beaumont was the brother of Henry Beaumont, one of the rebels in Brabant, and evidently it was feared that Louis would aid the invasion force and allow them to land in his bishopric. Eight days before this, the keeper of the town of Kingston-upon-Hull on the north-east coast had been told to stay in the town and guard it well with two other men newly appointed, because of the 'danger and loss likely to happen at the present time, unless the town is safely and securely kept'.[66] It is unclear whether this planned invasion had anything to do with the plot of the Earl of Kent and was intended to try to free Edward of Caernarfon, or whether it was a side issue and a result of the discontent felt by some English barons towards the rule of Queen Isabella and Roger Mortimer (particularly by men like Henry Beaumont, cut off from any possibility of gaining his lands and earldom of Buchan in Scotland after Isabella and Mortimer made a permanent peace settlement with Robert Bruce in the summer of 1328). The invasion in fact never took place, perhaps because the rebels did not want to be seen acting against the young king himself, with whom they had no quarrel. Isabella and Mortimer, however, received a taste of their own medicine when they were threatened with an invasion from the Low Countries, as they themselves had done to Edward II. By 1330 they had few allies left, and few people shed a tear at their downfall that October at the hands of Isabella's son, furious at their execution of his uncle Kent and at Mortimer wielding royal power which did not belong to him.

The Earl of Kent's plot to free Edward of Caernarfon years after his official death has been described by a modern historian as 'bizarre', 'farcical' and a 'disorderly charade'.[67] A plot to free a man who had supposedly died two and a half years before might at first sight seem bizarre, but the men who took part in it did not find it so. The Earl of Kent died because of it. The Archbishop of York was indicted for treason before King's Bench. Sir William Cleydon, one of Kent's adherents, was imprisoned in Essex shortly before 4 May 1330 and died in prison sometime before 1 August.[68] Many others were arrested and their lands and goods seized, and at least eighteen important men fled the country; they obviously did not find the plot 'bizarre'. Edward III, once he overthrew his mother and Roger Mortimer, released Kent's adherents still in prison and invited the men who had hurriedly departed from England to return, and restored their lands and goods. Contrary to the often-repeated claim that most of Kent's supporters were clerical, seventeen of the eighteen men restored to their lands and goods by Edward III in late 1330 were secular lords.[69] Roger Mortimer admitted just before he was executed on 29 November 1330 that the Earl of Kent had 'died wrongfully' (*torcenousement morust*).[70] He did not, contrary to what one modern historian has claimed, admit to 'practising deceit' on the earl.[71] Sir John Maltravers, in the judgement against him at that Parliament, was said to be:

> Guilty of the death of Edmund, Earl of Kent, the uncle of our present lord the king, in that he principally, traitorously, and falsely plotted the death of the said earl, since he knew of the death of King Edward, nevertheless the said John by ingenious means and by his false and evil subtleties led the said earl to understand that the king was alive, which false plotting was the cause of the death of the said earl and of all the evil which followed.

Bogo Bayouse and John Deveril were convicted of the same offence.[72] On 24 March 1330, a letter was sent to the pope in Edward III's name, delivered via a clerk named John Walwayn, explaining why the Earl of Kent had been tried and executed. John Walwayn, like Manuele Fieschi, Fieschi's attorney Thomas de Luco, the late Earl of Arundel's brother John, and the Wyvill brothers Robert and Walter, parsons of the village of Kingsclere, was a canon of Salisbury. John XXII did not reply until 5 September, and expressed surprise that anyone had believed that:

> He, for whom solemn funerals had been made, was alive. The pope believes and holds firmly that those who were present at the funeral were not deceived, and did not attempt to deceive … Had the pope believed such a report [of Edward II's survival] he would have dealt, not with that noble, or any other, but with the queen [Isabella] and her son, touching the restoration to liberty and production in public [of the former king].[73]

And yet, according to the Earl of Kent's testimony, John XXII had indeed 'dealt' with him and even promised him his support, without breathing a word to Isabella or her son the young king. In *c.* late 1329, the pope also received a letter from Edward III sent via Edward's trusted friend William Montacute: the king, kicking against the regency of his mother and her hated favourite Roger Mortimer, asked John XXII for his support against the pair, and sent John a sample of his handwriting so that he would know in future which letters came from Edward personally and which came from his mother or others sent in his name. The pope kept faith with the young king, and did not breathe a word of that to Isabella either. Whatever John XXII said in public, in private he kept his own counsel, and also did not inform Edward III when, probably in 1331, he met a man in Avignon who claimed to be Edward's father. The tale of Edward II was about to take another strange turn.

10

THE KING IN FRANCE, GERMANY AND ITALY

One man who was a notary and associate of John XXII at the papal court in Avignon and who was probably very well aware of the Earl of Kent's plot and what was happening in England in 1330 was Manuele Fieschi, later Bishop of Vercelli in Piedmont, northern Italy. Fieschi wrote another important piece of evidence relating to the possible survival of Edward II past 1327: the Fieschi Letter. This is a text discovered in an archive in Montpellier, southern France, in the late nineteenth century, and was probably written in the late 1330s, or written in the early 1330s and updated later.[1] Fieschi's letter was addressed to Edward III, though Edward's copy of it, assuming he ever received it, has not survived. The Fieschi Letter states that Edward II escaped from Berkeley Castle to Corfe Castle and then to Ireland, and that in and after c. late 1330 he travelled through France dressed as a hermit, secretly met John XXII in Avignon, and spent fifteen days or more with him. Edward then travelled to Paris, Brabant in modern-day Belgium, Cologne in Germany, and Milan in northern Italy, and ended up in a hermitage in Italy which can be identified as Sant'Alberto di Butrio in Lombardy. The letter presents itself as Fieschi telling Edward III the story he had heard directly from Edward II (or so he claimed), whom he refers to as 'your father' throughout, not 'the man claiming to be your father'. Perhaps this meeting took place at Avignon, where Fieschi says that Edward went some months after leaving Ireland, landing briefly at the port of Sandwich in Kent, and travelling through France to the papal court in Avignon, during the fifteen days he allegedly spent there with John XXII.

The Fieschi Letter, which is in Latin in the original, begins:

> In the name of the Lord, Amen. That which I heard of the confession of your [Edward III's] father I wrote by my own hand and afterwards I took care to make it known to your highness. First he says that feeling England in subversion against him, afterwards on the admonition of your mother, he withdrew from his family in the castle of the Earl Marshal by the sea, which is called Chepstow. Afterwards, driven by fear, he took a barque with lords Hugh Despenser and the Earl of Arundel and several others and made his way by sea to Glamorgan, and there he was captured, together with the said Lord Hugh and Master Robert Baldock; and they were captured by Lord Henry of Lancaster, and they led him to the castle of Kenilworth, and others were kept elsewhere at various places; and there he lost the crown by the insistence of many. Afterwards you [Edward III] were subsequently crowned on the feast of Candlemas next following. Finally they sent him to the castle of Berkeley.[2]

It is interesting to note that 'First he says' is written in the present tense, as though Manuele Fieschi was writing the letter to Edward III while consulting a text he had written down of his conversation with his father, or even as he was talking to the former king personally. It is not absolutely clear when and where Fieschi met Edward II, or the man claiming to be Edward II; presumably when Edward arrived at the papal court in *c.* 1331 as detailed later in the letter, but this is not certain. This part of the letter is generally correct in its details and in the outline of events after Queen Isabella's invasion: in October 1326 Edward II did take refuge in the castle of Chepstow in South Wales, which belonged to his half-brother the Earl of Norfolk who was also the Earl Marshal of England, and sailed in a boat from there perhaps intending to reach Ireland or Lundy Island in the Bristol Channel. Contrary winds forced him to put in at Cardiff a few days later. This particular fact is not recorded by any English chronicler until Geoffrey le Baker about a quarter of a century later, though several fourteenth-century chroniclers outside England did know the story. The Florentine writer Giovanni Villani also talks about Edward II's sea journey, albeit with very inaccurate details: he believed that Edward put to sea at Ipswich, Suffolk, which is over 200 miles from Chepstow on the other side of the country. This may be Villani confusing Edward's journey with the arrival of Isabella's invasion force in Suffolk a month previously, and he also wrongly states that Edward fled towards Scotland, not Wales – an error probably rooted in an ignorance of British geography. Villani worked for the Bardi banking firm of Florence, who had ties to Cardinal Luca Fieschi, of whom much more below. An anonymous chronicle from Flanders states that 'Edward was on the sea and did not know what to do' while Queen Isabella was in Bristol, although the king had equipped two ships and had set sail with his household, and the much later Hainaulter chronicler Jean Froissart (who was not born until about 1337) declares that Edward and his companions spent eleven days in a boat, unable to go anywhere because the weight of their sins was dragging them down. He wrongly states, however, that this happened at Bristol and that Edward and Despenser the Younger witnessed the execution of Despenser's father the Earl of Winchester there on 27 October, on which date Edward had in fact already returned to land in South Wales.[3] Other than Baker and inaccurate accounts in chronicles written outside England, Edward II's flight from Chepstow is only known to modern historians from the fortunate survival of his last chamber account, the only chamber account of his entire reign which is still completely extant and is now in a library in London.[4]

Hugh Despenser the Younger was certainly with Edward in South Wales and specifically on the sea with him; the whereabouts of the Earl of Arundel are unclear, and Edward's biographer Seymour Phillips has stated that he was not with Edward in October 1326 and that the Fieschi Letter is therefore wrong on this detail.[5] Phillips cites no source for this statement, however, and in fact Arundel's location after the invasion is uncertain until he was executed in Hereford on 17 November 1326 on the orders of his cousin Roger Mortimer (a date noted by the writers of the *Anonimalle* and the *Annales Paulini*).

I have found no source which definitely places Arundel away from South Wales when Edward II was there, except for one anonymous chronicle from Flanders which says that he was in Bristol with Hugh Despenser the Elder. This is possible but not confirmed by any other source, and the chronicle states wrongly that Arundel was executed in Bristol with the elder Despenser on 27 October, three weeks before he was actually beheaded in Hereford.[6]

The Fieschi Letter, quite correctly, does not mention Arundel's presence when Edward was captured on 16 November with the younger Hugh Despenser and the cleric Robert Baldock. Edward was taken to Kenilworth and forced to abdicate his throne there, while Despenser, Baldock and the others with them were 'kept elsewhere at various places'. It does seem odd that an account supposedly narrated by Edward II himself does not place more emphasis on the slow and painful execution of Hugh Despenser the Younger, a man Edward had loved and been extremely close to for many years, or indeed even mention his death at all. As an account of Edward II's downfall from the perspective of Edward himself, this section of the Fieschi Letter does not entirely convince, though perhaps this is explicable by its being written down a few years later by a lawyer and couched in unemotional language, or perhaps Fieschi considerably edited Edward's original descriptions down to what he considered the salient points. An error, though perhaps not a significant one, is that Edward III's coronation in fact took place on 1 February 1327, which is the eve of Candlemas, not on the feast itself as the letter states. The phrase 'finally they sent him to the castle of Berkeley' may be a reference to Edward's being moved around different places in 1327 to conceal his real location.

The letter continues:

Afterwards the servant [or 'a servant'] who was keeping him, after some little time, said to your father: Lord, Sir Thomas Gurney and Sir Simon Bereford, knights, have come with the purpose of killing you. If it pleases, I shall give you my clothes, that you may better be able to escape. Then with the said clothes, as night was near, he went out of the prison; and when he had reached the last door without resistance, because he was not recognised, he found the porter sleeping, whom he quickly killed; and having got the keys of the door, he opened the door and went out, with his keeper who was keeping him. The said knights who had come to kill him, seeing that he had thus fled, fearing the indignation of the queen, even the danger to their persons, thought to put that aforesaid porter, his heart having been extracted, in a box, and maliciously presented to the queen the heart and body of the aforesaid porter as the body of your father, and as the body of the said king the said porter was buried in Gloucester.

As of this point in the letter we have no way of knowing whether its statements are true, with the exception of the heart presented to Queen Isabella, which fact is independently verified in Berkeley Castle records: Thomas Berkeley bought a silver vessel in which to place the heart and send it to Isabella. It is not clear, however, how a fugitive Edward II would have known that 'his' heart was sent to his wife in some kind of container.[7] Royal burials of the thirteenth and fourteenth centuries sometimes, though not invariably, involved separate heart burial. The men charged with Edward II's murder in late 1330 were Sir Thomas Gurney, knight, and William Ockley, man-at-arms, not Gurney and Sir Simon Bereford. As noted above, however, this may be explained by Edward II's having heard of the knights Gurney and Bereford and perhaps being aware of Bereford's execution on a charge of aiding Roger Mortimer in all his felonies, whereas he had probably never heard of the obscure man-at-arms and Mortimer adherent William Ockley.

The identity of 'the servant who was keeping him', or 'a servant' – Latin does not distinguish between the definite and indefinite articles – at Berkeley Castle is mysterious. The idea that the former King of England might have escaped from Berkeley by the simple expedient of killing one porter who was asleep implies a casualness and lack of security at the castle which is difficult to accept, as is the notion that he was not recognised by any of the staff while escaping. Edward of Caernarfon was a tall, well-built and physically powerful man, and even if we assume that months of incarceration had diminished his physique, that he was wearing his keeper's clothes, and that it was dark (the letter says he escaped 'as night was near'), his height would have been impossible to disguise. One would also imagine that security was tightened at the castle after the Dunheved gang attacked it and temporarily seized Edward in June or July 1327. On the other hand, the Contrariant Sir Robert Walkfare and other knights, imprisoned at Corfe by Edward II in 1322, escaped from the castle in 1325 or 1326 by killing one guard, William le Foulere.[8] This fact is either evidence that it could indeed be possible to escape from a guarded castle by killing one man, or perhaps that Walkfare and the others' flight was used as the inspiration for a fake story explaining how Edward might have escaped from Berkeley.

There is also an assumption here that Gurney and Bereford had gone to kill Edward on the orders of his wife Isabella, who was so determined that he should die that Gurney and Bereford feared her wrath if they admitted to her he had escaped before they could kill him. They were, apparently, so scared of her reaction that they even assumed a 'danger to their persons' if they admitted that they had not killed Edward, and so presented the porter's heart to her as her husband's. This hardly fits with Isabella's behaviour of 1327, when she sent loving letters and gifts to Edward at Berkeley, and even if we assume that she changed her mind and realised that she would be safer with her husband dead, she was never accused of any complicity in Edward's death, and her son Edward III's treatment of her for the rest of her life does not indicate that he held her in any way responsible. Neither was Isabella anything like as fearsome as her much later reputation as a 'she-wolf', a nickname only given to her four centuries after her death, might imply. The assumption that she would be enraged by the two men's failure to kill her husband seems more likely to be Manuele Fieschi's rather than Edward II's; Fieschi surely never met her, while Edward was married to her for almost two decades and for much of that time, the couple seem to have been happy together.

The idea that the porter's body was buried in Edward's place in Gloucester on 20 December is perhaps just about plausible, given that the body of the supposed former king was guarded by only one man for a month after death, that the knights, abbots and burgesses who (according to one chronicler) saw it only did so 'superficially', and that the face and body were not visible after the body arrived at

Gloucester either. The Earl of Kent certainly attended the funeral and was firmly convinced that Edward was still alive, and it is likely that some of the men who joined him in his later conspiracy attended it as well. If Edward II was not murdered or did not die of natural causes in September 1327, someone must have been buried in his place that December. That it was the dead Berkeley Castle porter is possible, though may be Edward II's own later assumption rather than an accurate account. Although it was not necessary for the face and body of a man buried in Edward's stead to resemble him greatly, given that few if any people saw the body closely between September and December 1327, one wonders how likely it is that a porter was tall enough to be passed off as the former king even from a distance; Edward II almost certainly stood a good 6ft. Then again, even men of humble birth in the fourteenth century could be taller than we might think. When the remains of William Melton, Archbishop of York, were examined centuries after his death, he was found to have also been about 6ft tall, and Melton came from a humble family background.[9] So perhaps it is not impossible that the porter killed at Berkeley was a tall man, and therefore could have stood in for Edward and been buried in his place. The notion, however, sits uneasily with the fact of the dead man's heart being sent to Queen Isabella, who was buried at the Greyfriars church in London in 1358 with the clothes she had worn to her wedding half a century earlier and (according to a later story) with Edward II's heart on her breast. If this is true, she would hardly have wanted to be buried for eternity with the heart of a castle porter.

The Fieschi Letter continues:

And after he had gone out of the prisons of the aforesaid castle, he was received in the castle of Corfe with his companion who was keeping him in the prisons by Sir Thomas, castellan of the said castle, the lord being ignorant, Sir John Maltravers, lord of the said Thomas, in which castle he was secretly for a year and a half. Afterwards, having heard that the Earl of Kent, because he said he was alive, had been beheaded, he took a ship with his said keeper and with the consent and counsel of the said Thomas, who had received him, crossed into Ireland, where he was for nine months. Afterwards, fearing lest he be recognised there, having taken the habit of a hermit, he came back to England and landed at the port of Sandwich, and in the same habit crossed the sea to Sluis. Afterwards he turned his steps in Normandy and from Normandy, as many, going across through Languedoc, came to Avignon, where, having given a florin to a servant of the pope, sent by the said servant a document to Pope John, which pope had him called to him, and held him secretly and honourably for a further fifteen days.

The custodian of Corfe Castle in 1327 was Sir John Maltravers, and the identity of 'Sir Thomas' is unclear. Perhaps this represents a mix-up with Thomas, Lord Berkeley, who is never named in the Fieschi Letter. Yet this mysterious 'Sir Thomas' knows who Edward is and helps him hide at Corfe Castle and later escape to Ireland. This may be a garbled account of Edward's belief that he had escaped from Berkeley Castle with the connivance of Thomas Berkeley (and perhaps he had heard of the latter's peculiar statement to Parliament in November 1330 that he had not heard of Edward's death before then), or perhaps it is just simply wrong and should not be taken too seriously. Berkeley Castle accounts state that John Maltravers was at Corfe Castle 'on the service of the king's father' in September 1327, so it is odd that the Fieschi Letter states that he was 'ignorant' of Edward's arrival and sojourn there. Maltravers was appointed custodian of Corfe on 17 November 1326, the day after Edward II's capture in South Wales; although the appointment was made in the king's name, he had nothing to do with it and was almost certainly unaware of it.[10]

When Edward supposedly arrived at Corfe after fleeing from Berkeley in September 1327, he was probably still unaware that Maltravers was the castle's constable, though he should have been able to recognise Maltravers, with whom he had been knighted at Westminster in May 1306 and whom he must have seen on plenty of other occasions afterwards (though not after March 1322, when Maltravers fled the country following the failure of the Contrariant rebellion and their army's defeat at the Battle of Boroughbridge). It is fortunate that we have confirmation of John Maltravers' presence at Corfe Castle in September 1327 from Berkeley Castle accounts, as we have confirmation of Edward II's sailing from Chepstow in

October 1326 from his own chamber account. With reference to 'the lord being ignorant', there are a couple of pieces of evidence in the chancery rolls which suggest that the constable of Corfe Castle had a deputy: in December 1330, when custody of Corfe was being given to Sir William Montacute, the entry on the Fine Roll appointing him refers to 'the keeper thereof or his lieutenant'.[11] In May 1330, John Deveril was ordered to arrest a man named Robert le Bore and imprison him at Corfe, which suggests that Deveril was then the constable's second-in-command.[12] John Deveril and Bogo Bayouse were the members of the Corfe garrison condemned to death in late 1330 for entrapping the Earl of Kent, and the *Brut* also says that Deveril was at Corfe in 1329 or 1330. The 'Sir Thomas' mentioned in the Fieschi Letter may be a reference to the deputy. If Sir John Maltravers was 'ignorant' of Edward's presence at Corfe, then Edward III sending his friend William Montacute to talk to Maltravers in Flanders in 1334 is unlikely to be related to Edward II's supposed survival. It is difficult to see how the Fieschi Letter might be correct on this point of Maltravers' ignorance, however, as we know Maltravers was at Corfe in September 1327, and even if he was an absentee constable most of the time, it is hard to imagine how the former King of England could have stayed at the castle for any length of time without its constable becoming aware of this.

The next part also appears to be an error: if Edward II escaped from Berkeley to Corfe and then left Corfe after the execution of his half-brother the Earl of Kent, this should be a period of two and a half years, September 1327 to March 1330, not a year and a half, as the letter states. This could be a simple miscalculation either by Edward or Manuele Fieschi, or a scribal error, or perhaps it is not even a mistake at all. The letter states that Edward was at Corfe for a year and a half and 'afterwards, having heard that the Earl of Kent, because he said he was alive, had been beheaded' took a ship and went to Ireland. It does not say that he went to Ireland immediately after receiving the news, and it also does not say directly that Edward was still at Corfe when he heard of his half-brother's execution or that he left there as a result of it, only that he went to Ireland with the 'consent and counsel' of the mysterious Sir Thomas, the putative castellan of Corfe. Perhaps here there is a gap of a year in the account from March 1329 to March 1330, when Edward went elsewhere and either did not inform Fieschi about it, or Fieschi did not include it in the letter.

There is no explanation as to why Edward would remain at Corfe Castle for eighteen months (or two and a half years) and not attempt to flee abroad or to Wales or Scotland, where he had friends. Berkeley Castle is not far from the Welsh border. If Edward had genuinely escaped from Berkeley, one might imagine that men were looking for him and that they would arrive at Corfe sooner or later. Edward must surely have realised this, and that he would most probably be safer in Wales, a far more sparsely populated country where he had always been reasonably popular, than in England. Nor is there any explanation why Edward went to Corfe of all places when he must have known that John Maltravers, his joint custodian, was prominent in the area and was, whether he knew it or not, the castle's constable. As we have already seen, however, there is much other evidence that Edward was at Corfe Castle at some point in 1327, albeit not of his own volition. Of all the places where Edward might have hidden, it seems a very odd choice, though he may not have known about the Welsh plot to free him in September 1327 or knew that it had taken place but that the plotters were either in prison or exile, and therefore did not see Wales as a potential safe place to hide.

Berkeley Castle is at least 270 miles from the Scottish border, and the Earldom of Mar, held by Edward's friend and ally Donald of Mar, who would certainly have given him any help he could, was more than 200 miles beyond that. It seems unlikely that Edward had the faintest idea whereabouts in Scotland the Earldom of Mar was located even if he made the long and risky journey on foot to the northern kingdom. Edward, free, may simply not have known to whom he could turn for help. His only surviving sister in England was Mary, who was a nun at Amesbury Priory in Wiltshire and not really in a position to offer him much useful support; his beloved eldest niece Eleanor Despenser was imprisoned at the Tower of London for much of Isabella and Roger Mortimer's regency, and he had alienated her sisters Margaret and Elizabeth by his shabby treatment of them; his half-brothers the Earls of Norfolk and Kent and cousin the Earl of Lancaster had supported

Isabella and Roger Mortimer; his nephew-in-law the Earl of Surrey had also gone over to Isabella in late 1326; his friends the Archbishop of York and the Abbot of Langdon were many miles distant in Yorkshire and Kent respectively; even the members of the Dunheved gang had scattered and he probably did not know where or how to find them. There were houses of Dominican friars in the towns of Gloucester, Bristol and Oxford, all of which were much closer to Berkeley than Corfe Castle, and Dominicans would always be willing to help and support Edward II, yet the Fieschi Letter does not say that he went to them or even to another religious house, where the former king would surely have felt much safer than in a castle under the command of his enemy John Maltravers. This is difficult to explain unless the mysterious servant or keeper who accompanied Edward during his escape was in some way directing his actions and that Edward, although believing himself to be at liberty, was doing what other people wanted him to: perhaps being allowed to 'escape' from Berkeley Castle but in fact still in captivity at Corfe. This, however, is speculation.

The nine months which Edward and the servant supposedly spent in Ireland would take us from sometime after 19 March 1330, when the Earl of Kent was beheaded, to c. December 1330, shortly after Roger Mortimer's execution on Edward III's orders on 29 November. The comment 'fearing lest he be recognised there' is peculiar, and it is not clear why Edward II feared that people in Ireland would recognise him. Edward, although Lord of Ireland, had never visited that country, though certainly there were members of the Anglo-Irish nobility who had spent time in England and would know him. Perhaps this implies that Edward had been inside a castle for a long time and was now out in the open for the first time in years and therefore feeling vulnerable. His close ally John de Bermingham, whom he had made Earl of Louth after Bermingham's victory over Robert Bruce's brother Edward at the Battle of Dundalk in October 1318, was murdered in the Braganstown Massacre of 9 June 1329 along with many of his family, a few months before Edward supposedly arrived in the country (Bermingham had also been a close ally of Roger Mortimer, before Mortimer joined the 1321/22 rebellion against Edward). Bermingham's father-in-law Richard de Burgh, Earl of Ulster, had been Edward's other close ally in Ireland, but he died in July 1326 leaving his 13-year-old grandson William as his heir. William de Burgh, who turned 18 in September 1330, was also Edward II's great-nephew, and had married one of the six daughters of Edward's first cousin Henry, Earl of Lancaster, in 1327. William, Earl of Ulster, divided his time between England and Ireland: he was certainly in Ireland in October 1329 and again in February 1331.[13] His grandfather Richard de Burgh's son-in-law Maurice Fitzgerald, Earl of Desmond, was alive until 1356, and another of Richard's many sons-in-law was the English baron Sir John Darcy, sometime justiciar of Ireland. Sir Anthony Lucy, appointed justiciar of Ireland by Edward III in February 1331, was also a former ally of Edward II.[14] These may have been men to whom Edward could turn for help, but again this is only speculation. Perhaps more to the point, Roger Mortimer was a major landowner in Ireland, and had spent much of the 1310s there as Edward's lieutenant and justiciar. A close ally of Mortimer was James le Botiler or Butler, who in 1327 had married Edward II's niece Eleanor de Bohun and who in 1328 received the Earldom of Ormond at the same time as Mortimer appointed himself Earl of March. If Edward II was not acting under his own agency when he travelled to Corfe and then to Ireland, then presumably Roger Mortimer, favourite of the dowager queen and the real ruler of England, was controlling his actions via trusted men in England and Ireland. The Fieschi Letter is, unfortunately, entirely silent on where Edward stayed in Ireland and whom he might have met.

At this point in the tale, the unnamed servant or keeper who had been with Edward for more than three years, since Berkeley Castle, simply disappears and is, rather unsatisfactorily, never mentioned again. Edward puts on the clothes of a hermit – presumably as a disguise, although this is not stated – travels to Sandwich in Kent, south-east England, and from there sails to Sluis on the Continent. Sandwich was one of the major English ports in the Middle Ages (nowadays it is 2 miles inland), and would have been full of people. It is odd that the Fieschi Letter says that Edward was worried about being recognised in a country he had never visited but not in his own realm where he had spent his entire life, and setting foot in England, and in such a busy port in particular, seems incredibly risky. The port of Sluis is now in the

Netherlands close to the Belgian border and not far from the towns of Bruges and Ghent, and in the fourteenth century lay in the county of Flanders. The Count of Flanders in the early 1330s was Louis, whose wife Marguerite was a niece of Edward's queen Isabella and a first cousin of his son Edward III. If Edward left Ireland at the end of 1330 or beginning of 1331, as the Fieschi Letter indicates, this would have been the middle of winter, which would surely have caused delays and difficulties in travel by water from Ireland to England and England to the Continent, and also in travel by land. In January 1308, for example, Edward had arrived several days late for his wedding to Isabella in Boulogne, almost certainly because of unfavourable weather in the Channel, and had to wait for five days in the port of Wissant on the way home in early February until it was possible to travel. In late 1330 and early 1331, the period when Manuele Fieschi says that Edward was travelling from Sandwich to Sluis and then elsewhere, it is likely to have been cold at least some of the time, and perhaps there was snow or heavy rain and floods as there often is at that time of year, which would have affected Edward's ability to travel and perhaps forced him to rest in one place on one or more occasions. The spring and early summer of 1331 were dry for the most part, however, at least in the south of England and perhaps also in France.[15]

Given that he was dressed as a hermit, Edward probably travelled on pilgrim routes and stayed in religious houses along the way or in hospices which were set up along these routes and catered to the pilgrims. Mingling with people was also potentially risky and brought with it the chance of recognition, though he had little other choice in winter and could not have slept outside, and perhaps he thought that no-one could possibly be expecting to see the supposedly dead former King of England as a hermit in France. Going on pilgrimage could be a great opportunity for meeting and socialising with all kinds of people (it is no coincidence that Chaucer wrote his *Canterbury Tales* a few decades later about a group of pilgrims on their way to Thomas Becket's shrine), the pilgrim routes of Europe were well-trodden, and it is difficult to imagine that Edward could have remained alone for very long. There was also safety in numbers on the dangerous roads of fourteenth-century Europe, an era with a rate of violent crime and murder far in excess of our own. Edward's first language was French, which would have been far more useful on the Continent than English, but as only the English elite spoke French, revealing himself as an English hermit or pilgrim who was fluent in the language might also have been hazardous. He needed money to pay for food and accommodation, which he would have had to acquire somewhere; William Melton's letter to Simon Swanland in January 1330 mentions that Melton was trying to obtain £200 in gold for Edward, and it is not impossible that Melton or Swanland succeeded in getting a sum of money to the former king. In April 1331 Edward's son Edward III's mother-in-law Jeanne de Valois, Countess of Hainault and sister of King Philip VI of France, was travelling in the opposite direction to Edward, returning from a seven-month visit to the French court in and around Paris back to her husband's county of Hainault, which lay between the northern border of France and the duchy of Brabant ruled by Edward II's nephew John III.[16] Edward II, if the Fieschi Letter is true and it really was he, would have had to exercise caution in such situations when he ran the risk of encountering royalty or the higher nobility travelling through Europe. Such people had known him very well and would easily be able to recognise him.

From Sluis to Avignon is at least 600 miles to the south, and Normandy, towards where the Fieschi Letter says Edward 'turned his steps', is out of the way to the west; depending on which part of Normandy he visited, it might have been several hundred miles out of the way, in fact, and would have made his journey nearly half as long again. The well-established pilgrim route leading from England to Italy, the Via Francigena, did not lead from Flanders anywhere near Normandy, and if Edward had followed the route he would have remained to the east of Paris, but Normandy is west and north-west of the city. Even if Edward desired to see the holy relics held in the Norman towns of Caen and Rouen, his journeying there hardly suggests that he was in any urgent hurry to reach Avignon and talk to the pope. The Fieschi Letter then specifies that Edward passed through the region of Languedoc on his way to Avignon from Normandy, and while this is accurate and he certainly would have had to travel this way, it is not clear why Manuele Fieschi felt the need to mention it when he does not specify the route taken by Edward on any other occasion. A popular pilgrim route would have taken Edward south from Normandy through Chartres, with its magnificent cathedral; Tours, which had a shrine to St Martin, Bishop of Tours (d. 397) and a very popular saint; and Poitiers in central France. From there a journey through Limoges and Rocamadour would have been a viable route to Avignon through Languedoc, as the Fieschi Letter states. Rocamadour was and is a major pilgrim site, where one of Edward II's own household staff went on pilgrimage to the church of the Blessed Virgin Mary in June 1308 having made a vow that he would not cut his beard until he had gone. Edward's great-uncle Simon de Montfort, Earl of Leicester, great-great-grandparents Henry II and Eleanor of Aquitaine, father-in-law Philip IV and his brother Charles de Valois, and brother-in-law Charles IV and his second wife Marie of Luxembourg had also worshipped in Rocamadour. Philip VI visited in 1336.[17]

At Avignon Edward gave a florin to a servant of the pope to announce him, which oddly enough is an accurate detail: about half-way through the papacy of John XXII, which ran from August 1316 to December 1334, the papal court switched from using pounds of Tours (*livres tournois*) as their currency and began minting their own coins, which were called florins.[18] The Fieschi Letter says that John XXII received Edward 'secretly and honourably'. Although the two men had communicated frequently by letter from 1316 to 1326, they had never met in person. There were, however, plenty of men at the papal court who did know Edward II personally, and would have been able to recognise him. One of them was Cardinal Luca Fieschi, a second cousin once removed of Manuele Fieschi and a rather more distant kinsman of Edward himself. Edward and Luca had met and spent much time together when Luca visited England in 1317–18, during which visit Luca and his fellow cardinal Gaucelme Jean suffered the indignity of being attacked, stripped naked and robbed by the renegade English knight Gilbert Middleton, who swas executed by hanging, drawing and quartering in January 1318 for it. John XXII died on 4 December 1334 and was succeeded sixteen days later by Benedict XII, years before Edward III could have read the Fieschi Letter, so the king would have been unable to verify with the pope directly whether the story was true or not. It may have been at this point that Manuele Fieschi himself met Edward, and heard his 'confession' as he states in his own letter, though he does not say so directly.

The Fieschi Letter ends:

Finally, after various discussions, all things having been considered, permission having been received, he went to Paris, and from Paris to Brabant, from Brabant to Cologne so that out of devotion he might see The Three Kings, and leaving Cologne he crossed over Germany, that is to say, he headed for Milan in Lombardy, and from Milan he entered a certain hermitage of the castle of *Milascio*, in which hermitage he stayed for two years and a half; and because war overran the said castle, he changed himself to the castle of Cecima in another hermitage of the diocese of Pavia in Lombardy, and he was in this last hermitage for two years or thereabouts, always the recluse, doing penance and praying to God for you and other sinners. In testimony of which I caused my seal to be affixed for the consideration of Your Highness. Your Manuele de Fieschi, notary of the lord pope, your devoted servant.

This final part of the letter implies considerable debate at the papal court as to what Edward should do next: 'various discussions'; 'all things having been considered'; 'permission having been received'. Presumably this means John XXII's permission, and it sounds as though much discussion took place over the pros and cons of Edward's next moves. Travelling to Paris was risky, and it is difficult to explain why the letter states that Edward had feared to be recognised in Ireland yet was perfectly happy to visit Paris. He had spent several weeks there with Queen Isabella in June 1313, when they attended the knighting of her three brothers and cousin Philip de Valois. The three brothers, Louis X, Philip V and Charles IV, were all dead, but plenty of people at the Parisian court in *c.* 1331 would have known Edward and been able to recognise him, not least Philip de Valois, now King Philip VI of France. Philip may even have been knighted by Edward personally; Edward, his father-in-law Philip IV and oldest brother-in-law Louis knighted the several hundred young men who attended the ceremony in June 1313. Edward had also visited France in June 1320, when he paid homage to his brother-in-law Philip V at Amiens 70 miles from Paris, though did not visit the capital on that occasion. As for Edward's motives in travelling to the city, we can only speculate, but perhaps as he was now in the guise of a hermit or pilgrim and had always been a more than usually devout Christian, he wished to see the shrine of St Denis, the patron saint of Paris, or the holy relic held at Sainte-Chapelle. This was a thorn from the Crown of Thorns, though he had already seen it and made an offering there in 1313. It should be noted that Cardinal Luca Fieschi was a canon of Paris, perhaps a relevant point.[19] Given that the Fieschi Letter states that Edward feared to be recognised in Ireland, his passing through Sandwich and visiting Paris seems oddly provocative.

We are on firmer ground regarding Edward's visit to the duchy of Brabant, a large territory now mostly in Belgium and partly in the Netherlands, whose most important city was Brussels. Edward's sister Margaret, widow of Duke John II of Brabant, may still have been alive (the date of her death is not known), and the duchy was ruled by his nephew John III, who in 1329 had supported the Earl of Kent by allowing him to meet several of the men plotting with him to free Edward in the duke's Paris chamber. Edward may have known or guessed that he would find a safe haven in his nephew's territories.[20] There was a connection between the ruling house of Brabant and the Fieschi family: Margareta of Brabant, sister of Edward II's brother-in-law Duke John II and aunt of John III, married Henry of Luxembourg, Holy Roman Emperor, and died in Genoa on 14 December 1311. She was buried in the church of San Francesco di Castelletto in the city, where several members of the Fieschi family including Cardinal Luca's parents Niccolo and Leonora, great-uncle Andrea and uncle Federico, and perhaps others, were also buried.[21]

Edward may also have wished to see the holy oil of St Thomas Becket (the Archbishop of Canterbury killed on the orders of his great-great-grandfather Henry II in 1170) which his sister Margaret and her husband Duke John II had brought to his coronation in February 1308, though on the advice of his counsellors Edward decided not to use it. In 1317, Duchess Margaret's confessor Nicholas de Wisbech persuaded Edward that he should have himself re-anointed with the oil as a means of ending his troubles. The whole thing ended in political embarrassment for the king and he wrote to John XXII to apologise for his naïveté, but may never have let go of his reverence for the oil, which was associated with a belief that the king who used it would be a good man and a champion of the Church.[22] And although the Fieschi Letter does not mention it, another of Edward II's nephews, Edouard I, was Count of Bar east of Paris in the direction of Strasbourg, and it would not have taken Edward too far out of his way to go there on the route to Brabant. Count Edouard was alive until November 1336, when he drowned off Cyprus on his way to a crusade; he was the son of Edward's eldest sister Eleanor, and the Via Francigena, one of the most-used pilgrim routes in Europe, passed through his county.

Probably in the 1310s, around the time that Edward III was born, a political prophecy was made and written down, and became known as the Prophecy of the Six Kings. The six Kings of England who succeeded King John – Edward II's great-grandfather, who died in 1216 – were characterised as beasts. Henry III was a lamb, Edward I a dragon, Edward II a goat, and Edward III a boar or a lion (the next two kings, Edward III's grandsons Richard II and Henry IV, would be a second lamb and a mole). One version of the prophecy, now in the British Library, says that Edward II would die overseas.[23] The 'boar of Windsor', Edward III, would 'whet his teeth upon the gates of Paris' and conquer France and then the Holy Land, and ultimately would be buried at the shrine of the Three Kings in Cologne, a city in the west of Germany on the River Rhine. Edward II may have known of this prophecy, though it only began circulating in *c.* 1330 after his deposition and official death; if he had heard of the prophecy, this would explain his interest in visiting the city and the shrine where it was claimed that his son would later be buried (Edward III was in fact buried at Westminster Abbey in 1377).[24] Even if Edward was unaware of it, he surely knew of the Three Kings in Cologne, which was one of the great shrines and pilgrim destinations in fourteenth-century Europe: in 1305/06 near the end of his life, his father Edward I sent an offering to the Three Kings, i.e. the Magi or Wise Men of the Gospels, in Cologne.[25]

The feast of the Three Kings in the Christian calendar is 6 January, otherwise known as the Epiphany, and although he could not have known it, Edward II's great-grandson Richard II of England would be born in Bordeaux, southern France on this date in 1367. Mere months after he had visited Berkeley Castle with Edward Despenser to inquire into Edward II's fate there, the chronicler Jean Froissart was in Bordeaux at the time that Richard was born. Froissart commented that Richard's mother Joan of Kent (who was married to Edward II's grandson the Prince of Wales and was also Edward's niece, daughter of his half-brother the Earl of Kent executed in 1330) 'was delivered of a fair son on the day of the three kings of Cologne'. This demonstrates how closely the three Magi were associated with the city in the fourteenth century.[26] The precious relics of the Three Kings were, and still are, housed in a spectacular golden shrine dating from 1191, which depicts the men presenting their offerings to the baby Christ.[27] This reliquary and its precious contents were moved to the choir of Cologne Cathedral after it was consecrated by the archbishop Heinrich II von Virneburg on 27 September 1322, only a few years before the Fieschi Letter alleges that Edward of Caernarfon saw them. Pilgrims were led in through the south entrance of the (as yet unfinished) cathedral, past the shrine of the Three Kings and the famous Gero Cross – a crucifix almost 10ft high dating from the late tenth century – then left by the north door.[28]

Also in Cologne, mere hundreds of yards from the cathedral, stood a basilica dedicated to Saint Ursula and the 11,000 virgins, which may also have interested Edward of Caernarfon: the remains of some of these women were among the holy relics he had inherited from his father and passed on to his son. His wife Queen Isabella also owned a head of one of the 11,000 virgins, which their son Edward III inherited on her death in 1358.[29] Even by the standards of medieval Europe, the city of Cologne was particularly rich in religious houses and holy relics, to the point where it was known as the 'German Rome'. Of special interest to Edward might have been the presence of a house of Dominican friars in the city which had existed since 1232.[30] The shrine of the Three Kings was and is situated in Cologne Cathedral, seat of the Archbishop of Cologne, and it may or may not be significant that on 27 January 1332 a new archbishop of the city was elected. If Edward travelled from Sluis via Normandy to Avignon, then all the way back up France to Brabant and then to Cologne, he may not have reached the city until 1332; he had already walked far in excess of 1,000 miles since landing at Sluis probably in early 1331 or thereabouts and thus may not have arrived in Cologne much before early 1332, especially if he spent some time in Paris and Brabant rather than just passing through (which the Fieschi Letter does not specify) and if the winter of late 1331 was a hard one and he chose to spend the period in one location rather than pushing on through the cold. Edward may only have reached his penultimate destination, a hermitage near Mulazzo in Italy, around the end of 1333, so there is no reason to suppose that he was hurrying.

The new Archbishop of Cologne in January 1332, succeeding Heinrich II von Virneburg who died on 5 January and who was the man responsible for placing the reliquary of the Three Kings in the choir of the cathedral where Edward of Caernarfon would have seen it, was Walram von Jülich. Walram was a nobleman; his mother Elisabeth was a first cousin of Duke John II of Brabant, and he was the younger brother of Wilhelm, Count, then Margrave and later Duke of Jülich, who was married to Johanna of Hainault, sister of Edward III's queen Philippa. Johanna and Philippa's other sister Margareta of Hainault was married to the Holy Roman Emperor Ludwig of Bavaria, whom Edward III met in Germany in the late summer of 1338. Margareta and Johanna married Ludwig of Bavaria and Wilhelm of Jülich in a joint wedding in Cologne on 26 February 1324, though owing to the vicissitudes of German politics, Archbishop Heinrich II von Virneburg did not officiate at the ceremony but pointedly stayed away.[31] One of the predecessors of Walram von Jülich and Heinrich von Virneburg as Archbishop of Cologne, Siegfried von Westerburg, lost the Battle of Worringen in 1288 to Duke John I of Brabant (father of Edward II's brother-in-law John II and of Margareta of Brabant) and Archbishop Walram's uncle and namesake Walram, Count of Jülich. Westerburg was imprisoned and thereafter Cologne technically became a free imperial city, though this did not really take hold until the late fifteenth century and Walram von Jülich as the archbishop still controlled the city from 1332 to 1349. A man who claimed to be Edward II was arrested in

Cologne in the late summer of 1338, and Archbishop Walram must surely have known about it. It is also not inconceivable that he knew about Edward's visit to his city in 1331 or 1332, if the Fieschi Letter is to be trusted on this point.

In late May 1332 Edward II's elder daughter Eleanor of Woodstock, aged almost 14, married Reinhoud II, Count and later Duke of Guelders, in the town of Nijmegen (now in the Netherlands near the German border). One of Eleanor's attendants, a man called William of Cornwall, was given expenses to travel to the shrine of the Three Kings in Cologne. Manuele Fieschi, meanwhile, had become provost of Arnhem near Nijmegen on 29 February 1332.[32] Eleanor of Woodstock and her retinue were in Sluis in the county of Flanders on 9 and 10 May 1332, where she gave a penny each in alms to forty paupers; the same port where her father had supposedly landed fifteen or so months earlier. Among the English noblemen who accompanied Eleanor from England to her wedding in Nijmegen were her cousins the twins Edward and William de Bohun, brothers of the Earl of Hereford and sons of Edward II's sister Elizabeth, and William la Zouche, who two years previously had joined the Earl of Kent's plot to free Edward. Another was Edward III's close friend William Montacute, whom he sent to talk to John Maltravers in this part of the world two years later.[33] Professor Roy Martin Haines has suggested, not altogether seriously, that Edward of Caernarfon may have been a clandestine guest at his daughter's wedding to Count Reinhoud.[34] This is, as of course Professor Haines well knows, taking speculation a little too far, but given the possible speed of Edward's travelling after originally landing at Sluis and the timing of his arrival in Brabant and Cologne, it is not inconceivable that he was in the same general area at the same time as his daughter, and also that he travelled from Brabant to Cologne at around the same time as her attendant William of Cornwall made the journey to the shrine of the Three Kings in Cologne. Eleanor and her retinue crossed the duchy of Brabant on the way from Sluis to her future husband's lands farther to the north and west for about two weeks from 10 May 1332.[35] Sir John Maltravers was probably also living in Flanders at this time, whether Edward of Caernarfon knew it or not.

Cologne to Milan in Lombardy, northern Italy, the next stage of Edward's journey, is a distance of at least 500 miles, and we have no information as to the route he took and where he might have gone on the way except that he 'crossed over Germany'. The most obvious way south from western Germany to northern Italy is to follow the Rhine, which would have taken Edward past or through Bonn, Koblenz – where another piece of evidence places him or someone claiming to be him in 1338 – Mainz, Worms and Speyer. A large part of the area south of Cologne was ruled by Rudolf, count palatine of the Rhine, nephew of the Holy Roman Emperor Ludwig of Bavaria whose wife Margareta was Edward III's sister-in-law. Another prominent person in the area was the Archbishop of Trier, who from late 1307 until his death in early 1354 was Balduin or Baldwin of Luxembourg, younger brother of Henry of Luxembourg (d. 1313), Ludwig of Bavaria's predecessor as Holy Roman Emperor. Balduin of Luxembourg was thus the brother-in-law of Margareta of Brabant, buried in the same church in Genoa in late 1311 as many of the Fieschi family, and, like Edward II himself, was the uncle (albeit only by marriage) of Duke John III of Brabant.

Balduin had accompanied his brother Henry on the latter's long campaign in Italy from 1310 to 1313 and probably attended Margareta's funeral at the church of the Fieschis in Genoa. He was certainly familiar with Cardinal Luca Fieschi: Luca was with Henry of Luxembourg and thus also with Balduin for most of the emperor's Italian campaign, and travelled to Naples on Henry's behalf in May 1312 to seek a marital alliance between the houses of Luxembourg and Naples.[36] Luca Fieschi was one of the three men who crowned Henry of Luxembourg as emperor in the basilica of St John Lateran in Rome on 29 June 1312.[37] Balduin and Emperor Henry's other brother, Walram of Luxembourg, died on 21 July 1311 during Henry's siege of Brescia, a town in Lombardy where Manuele Fieschi's first cousin Percivalle Fieschi was appointed bishop in 1317. As well as his ties to the Fieschis and the ruling house of Brabant, there was a family connection between Balduin and Edward II's queen Isabella: in May 1323 he visited Paris for the coronation of his niece Marie of Luxembourg, daughter of Emperor Henry and Margareta of Brabant, as Queen of France (she was the short-lived

Caernarfon Castle, Edward II's birthplace in 1284. (Author's Collection)

Llanthony Secunda Priory, Gloucester, where Edward spent the night when being transferred to Berkeley Castle in April 1327. (Craig Robinson)

Berkeley Castle, Gloucestershire; inner courtyard. (Craig Robinson)

The room at Berkeley Castle where Edward was supposedly kept. (Craig Robinson)

The covered walkway leading to Edward's purported room, Berkeley Castle. (Craig Robinson)

The effigy of Edward's custodian Thomas, Lord Berkeley (d. 1361) and his second wife Katherine Cliveden, in St Mary's church next to Berkeley Castle. (Craig Robinson; reproduced by kind permission of Richard Avery, vicar of Berkeley)

Floor tiles on the south side of Edward's tomb, cracked and broken, apparently evidence of excavation, though when this happened is not clear. (Craig Robinson)

King Edward's Gatehouse, Gloucester. (Craig Robinson)

Edward II's effigy in Gloucester Cathedral, from the south side; the effigy once depicted Edward holding his staff of office, but this has been broken over the centuries. (Craig Robinson; reproduced by kind permission of the Very Reverend Stephen Lake, Dean of Gloucester)

The spectacular golden shrine of the Three Kings in Cologne Cathedral, which the Fieschi Letter says Edward visited in *c.* 1331. (Reproduced by kind permission of the Dombauarchiv Köln, Matz und Schenk)

The empty reliquary of the Three Kings in the church of Sant'Eustorgio, Milan, looted by Frederick Barbarossa in 1164. (Author's Collection; reproduced by kind permission of the dean of Sant'Eustorgio and the office of cultural heritage in Milan)

The hermitage of Sant'Alberto south of Milan, where the Fieschi Letter says Edward stayed in the 1330s. (Author's Collection)

Oramala Castle near Sant'Alberto, owned in the 1330s by Cardinal Luca Fieschi's nephew. (Daniele Marioli)

The Fieschi Letter of *c.* 1338, addressed to Edward III by Manuele Fieschi in Latin, discovered in a French archive in 1877. (Archives départementales de l'Hérault (France), G 1123/28; photo by the Auramala Project and reproduced by kind permission of the Project and the Archives départementales)

The Church of Saint Castor, Koblenz, Germany, where Edward III met Emperor Ludwig of Bavaria and six of the seven electors in September 1338. While in Koblenz, Edward also met a man who claimed to be his father. (Author's Collection)

The Sanctuary of the Madonna of Coal Mountain, Mulazzo, probably the hermitage of *Milascio*. (Ivan Fowler)

Edward of Caernarfon in his 'afterlife' at Sant'Alberto di Butrio, by artist Joanne Renaud.

second wife of Isabella's third and youngest brother Charles IV) and for the wedding of his great-nephew Wenzel a.k.a. the future Holy Roman Emperor Charles IV, son and heir of John 'the Blind', King of Bohemia, to Isabella's cousin Blanche de Valois (the newlyweds were both children). Balduin and Henry of Luxembourg were also the first cousins of Queen Philippa's father Willem, Count of Hainault and Holland, whose mother was Philippa of Luxembourg.[38]

Archbishop Balduin was a great territorial magnate as well as a churchman and a high-ranking nobleman by birth, and administered, among others, the dioceses of Worms and Speyer along the Rhine, and Liège in modern-day Belgium, where Manuele Fieschi held a benefice. From 1328 to 1336 Balduin also controlled the archbishopric of Mainz, and ruled the town of Koblenz between Cologne and Mainz, where in early September 1338 a man who claimed to be Edward II was taken to meet Edward III. A bridge in Koblenz was built by Balduin and is named after him to this day, the *Balduinbrücke*, and he also founded a Carthusian monastery in the town in August 1331. Balduin has been described by one German historian as 'one of the most important politicians in the western empire' in the fourteenth century.[39] He must have heard about the man who claimed to be Edward II in his town of Koblenz in 1338, and if Edward was crossing his territories approximately six or seven years earlier as well, perhaps with a safe-conduct issued by Cardinal Luca Fieschi – a man Balduin knew well – there is every chance that Balduin knew about it.

It is possible that, if Edward was following the Rhine south, he crossed from Germany back into the territory of France, as the Rhine flows through Strasbourg and then onto Basel, a town on the border of Germany, France and Switzerland. From Basel the Rhine flows east and into Lake Constance, which would have taken Edward out of his way, as he needed to head south or south-west through Switzerland towards Italy. A pilgrim route ran this way, along the Rhine from Cologne (controlled by Archbishop Walram from 1332 to 1349) to Koblenz to Mainz to Worms to Speyer (these last four towns were controlled by Archbishop Balduin in the 1330s) to Strasbourg to Basel. In the imperial cathedral of Speyer stood the tombs of some people Edward had vaguely known: Rudolf von Habsburg, King of Germany and an ally of Edward's father, who had died in 1291 when Edward was 7 and whose son Hartmann had been betrothed to Edward's sister Joan of Acre; and Albrecht, another of Rudolf's sons and his successor as king, who had attended Edward's wedding to Isabella in 1308. Although in French territory, Strasbourg, 70 miles along the river from Speyer, then belonged to the Holy Roman Empire and had been declared a free imperial city some decades before. A revolution took place in the city which began on 20 May 1332 and ended on 12 August that year, when a group of burghers openly opposed the nobility-dominated city government and violence and unrest broke out. This might have persuaded Edward to avoid Strasbourg if he came to hear it and if he was travelling anywhere near the vicinity in the summer of 1332, and an alternative route would have left the Rhine at Mainz, Worms or Speyer and struck deeper into the south of Germany. A pilgrim route from Trondheim, Norway to Rome passed through the Bavarian city of Würzburg about 90 miles south-east of Mainz, Augsburg not far from the Bavarian capital of Munich, and Innsbruck in Austria, which was ruled by Emperor Ludwig of Bavaria's son (with his first wife) the Margrave of Brandenburg and Count of Tyrol, and then into Italy.

Edward would have had to cross the Alps, perhaps either via the Brenner pass on the border of Austria and Italy, or the Great St Bernard pass further west in Switzerland near the Italian border. The latter, known as the Mons Jovis or Mont Joux in Edward's time, was the oldest route through the Alps, and it and the Brenner were the most commonly used passes through the Alps in the Middle Ages.[40] Other possibilities are the Col du Mont Cenis pass, which would have brought Edward into Italy not far from Turin (but which, beginning in Savoy in France, may have been too far west), or the St Gotthard, Splügen or Septimer passes which led the traveller from Switzerland into Italy north and north-east of Milan. The Septimer especially was frequently used between the ninth and the sixteenth centuries, often crossed by pilgrims, merchants and Holy Roman Emperors travelling between their northern and southern domains, and on its summit stood the oldest Christian hospice which opened to Alpine travellers, first mentioned in 831.[41] The passes through the

Alps might not have been open to travellers in winter, depending on the weather conditions, and if Edward traversed them at any time other than the height of summer it is likely to have been an unpleasantly cold and hard journey. It is basically impossible that Edward could have entered Italy without crossing the Alps. It would be possible to travel to the south of France and take a ship from there to Italy, but would plainly be absurd for Edward to retrace his steps all the way from Cologne back to the south of France not far from Avignon in order to do so. The only other way would have been to take a massively long detour through Austria, Hungary and Serbia, and sail across the Adriatic to the east coast of Italy; hardly a viable option either.

Three men close to Manuele Fieschi held benefices in Lausanne in modern-day Switzerland, and Luca Fieschi later became a canon of Constance also in Switzerland and a Hector Fieschi already was, which may give us a clue as to the route taken by Edward after he left Germany; his later itinerary in Italy took him from one Fieschi stronghold to another. During this period, there were nine points of contact between the Fieschi family and the town of Constance.[42] The remains of the Three Kings had originally lain in Milan at the Dominican church of Sant'Eustorgio, but were looted by the Holy Roman Emperor Frederick Barbarossa when he invaded Italy, and in July 1164 were taken to their new home of Cologne Cathedral by the then archbishop of the city, Rainald von Dassel.[43] Barbarossa himself had often crossed the Alps, taking either the Brenner pass or the Great St Bernard; more than 500 years before Edward II's time, the emperor Charlemagne also crossed the Alps into Italy via the Great St Bernard, and, nearly 500 years after Edward, so did Napoleon.[44] It is perhaps revealing that Edward is said to have gone to Milan, where an empty sarcophagus of the Three Kings stands to this day in the church of Sant'Eustorgio and was also there in the early 1330s. Sant'Eustorgio was an important pilgrim site for this reason, and was the main seat in Milan of the Dominican order of friars; Edward II could always expect a warm welcome from the Dominicans, and had been in touch with chapters in various European cities throughout his reign when he asked them to pray for him, his wife and children and his kingdom.

(Although the Dominicans of Milan had not been asked to do this, Edward had contacted the order in Venice and Florence to request their prayers in 1321 and 1325.)[45]

The lord of Milan at this time and until his death in 1349 was Luchino Visconti, whose wife Isabella Fieschi was Cardinal Luca Fieschi's niece, one of the children of his brother Carlo, the *capitano del popolo* or elected ruler of the important port of Genoa. Luchino's brother and co-ruler of the city of Milan from 1339, Giovanni Visconti, was a cardinal and future Archbishop of Milan; he was chosen as archbishop in 1317 but John XXII refused to confirm him and elected Aicardo da Intimiano instead. Giovanni had to wait until 1342 to gain his archbishopric officially, though on 1 August 1331 was made bishop and lord of the town of Novara between Milan and Vercelli, where Manuele Fieschi was appointed bishop in 1343. Intimiano, meanwhile, did not manage to take possession of his archbishopric until shortly before his death in 1339, and lived in exile for more than twenty years because Luchino Visconti would not allow him into Milan. Giovanni Visconti was later also lord of Pavia, Genoa and Bologna. As a cardinal and as a man who held much influence in northern Italy, Giovanni must have known Luca and Manuele Fieschi well, and perhaps also knew about Edward of Caernarfon's visit to the papal court in Avignon. His brother Luchino was also closely connected to the Fieschi family via marriage, and Luchino's father-in-law Carlo Fieschi was a man with whom Edward II had been in fairly regular contact. One of the many secular possessions of the archbishopric of Milan was the Three Valleys of Canton Ticino, which lead to the St Gotthard and Lukmanier passes over the Alps. This was a common route to Germany, via Constance and Zurich, for Milanese merchants, and may have been the route taken by Edward coming in the other direction.[46]

The identification of *Milasci* or *Milascio*, which Manuele Fieschi named as the next place on Edward's itinerary, is a little more difficult. In the late nineteenth century it was identified by Count Costantino Nigra of Vercelli, a diplomat and gentleman scholar, as Melazzo, a town in Piedmont 50 miles north-west of Genoa in the direction of Turin. So sure were Italian historians of the late nineteenth and early twentieth centuries of this identification that the town erected a sign declaring that Edward II had been there, which exists to this day. (It is a fairly common belief in northern Italy that Edward II died in that country.) Melazzo stands 4 miles from the town of Acqui Terme, which is a bigger town and seat of a historic bishopric, and is thus far more likely to have been the name used in the Fieschi Letter than the obscure Melazzo. There were no Fieschi interests in or near Melazzo, and also no hermitage, abbey or priory in the vicinity where Edward might have stayed in the 1330s, as detailed in the Fieschi Letter.[47]

Milascio is in fact far more likely to be the town of Mulazzo near Pontremoli, now in the province of Massa-Carrara in the far north of Tuscany, south-east of Genoa and in a broad river valley called the Lunigiana.[48] The area around Mulazzo was controlled by the Malaspina family, another noble family into which Cardinal Luca Fieschi's sisters Fiesca and Alagia married. The Marquis of Giovagallo near Mulazzo, Manfredi Malaspina, was the son of Alagia and was thus Luca's nephew. He would also have been a distant kinsman of Edward II himself, probably a fourth cousin, and was a third cousin of Manuele Fieschi.[49] The lord of Mulazzo itself was a Malaspina cousin. Another family member, Niccolo Malaspina, the Marquis of Oramala and a nephew of Cardinal Luca via Luca's other sister Fiesca, controlled the other side of the river Magra from Mulazzo. Niccolo Malaspina was married to the sister of the Marquis of Mulazzo, and his brother Bernabo was appointed Bishop of Luni, the diocese where Mulazzo lies, in 1321, succeeding another of their brothers, Gherardino. Bernabo's successor on his death in 1338 was Antonio Fieschi, brother of Isabella, lady of Milan and yet another of Luca's nephews, and the co-executor of Luca's will in 1336 with Manuele Fieschi. The area was thus dominated by the Fieschi family and their close relatives the Malaspina: in the early to mid-1330s, Cardinal Luca Fieschi's nephews were substantial lords in the area and closely related by blood and marriage to the lord of Mulazzo himself, and the local bishop was another nephew.

The Fieschi Letter talks of 'a hermitage of the castle of Milascio' where Edward stayed. There is and was no hermitage in the vicinity of Melazzo near Acqui Terme. Above Mulazzo, however, on the same mountain and overlooking the town, stands a hermitage called Santuario della Madonna del Monte Carbone, the 'Sanctuary of the

Madonna of Coal Mountain'. The Mulazzo hermitage was a dependency of the abbey of *Sant'Andrea di Borzone*, Saint Andrew of Borzone, and for 200 years the abbots of Sant'Andrea were members of the Fieschi family or of a cadet branch of their family.[50] The letter also says that Edward stayed for two and a half years at the hermitage of *Milascio*, 'and because war overran the said castle, he changed himself to the castle of Cecima in another hermitage of the diocese of Pavia in Lombardy'. Ian Mortimer has suggested that the 'war which overran the said castle' might have been the siege of the town of Pontremoli, which is about 5 miles from Mulazzo. The lord of Pontremoli at this time was Pietro Rossi of Parma, whose wife Ginetta was a niece of Cardinal Luca Fieschi and the sister of Isabella, wife of Luchino Visconti, lord of Milan, and of Antonio Fieschi, future Bishop of Luni; the town of Pontremoli had once been partly held by Luca himself, shared equally among himself and his brothers. Ginetta, Isabella and Antonio were all children of Luca Fieschi's brother Carlo, whom Edward II appointed as a member of his royal council in August 1315.[51]

Edward wrote to Carlo Fieschi in January 1318 rejoicing that he had been elected *capitano del popolo* or 'captain of the people' of Genoa, acknowledged him as his kinsman as he also had when appointing him to his council in 1315, and told him that he 'may confidently make requests to the king for matters touching his honour, as the king wishes that he may acquire greater honours'.[52] Carlo Fieschi's son-in-law Pietro Rossi and his family were involved in a long-running feud with the da Correggio family, and although they reached a peace settlement in June 1335, this broke on 8 May 1336 and Rossi fled to Pontremoli. On 13 June 1336, Simone da Correggio and his ally Spinetta Malaspina began laying siege to the town, a siege which lasted until late October that year. A contemporary chronicler refers to the soldiers attacking Pontremoli as 'countryside wreckers'. Of course an army needs to be fed, and as they were there for four and a half months, it is likely that the besiegers of Pontremoli ransacked the surrounding countryside for provisions. The town of Mulazzo and its hermitage were an easy day's raiding from Pontremoli, being only 5 miles away, and thus were at risk.[53] It is possible that this was the war which drove Edward of Caernarfon, or members of the Fieschi and Malaspina families controlling him, to seek refuge elsewhere. Given that soldiers were 'wrecking the countryside', the possibility of his discovery and capture may have been seen as an issue, and the siege of Pontremoli seems to have been the only armed conflict in this area at the right time.

If we assume that Edward was moved from Mulazzo around the time the siege began, or shortly before or afterwards, he would have travelled or been sent to his next location, a hermitage 100 miles or so from Mulazzo, sometime in about May to July 1336. The Fieschi Letter says 'he was in this last hermitage for two years or thereabouts', *fuit in isto ultimo heremitorio per duos annos vel circa*, in the past tense. As it happens, we have another piece of evidence which would place Edward in Cologne and Koblenz, Germany, in early September 1338. This would mean that he left Mulazzo around June 1336, spent two years at the next hermitage, and by September 1338 had retraced his footsteps and travelled the 550 or so miles north to Cologne. The timing thus fits extremely well. In the meantime, Cardinal Luca Fieschi died in Avignon on 31 January 1336, and his kinsman Manuele Fieschi and nephew Antonio Fieschi were executors while his nephew Bernabo Malaspina was a witness to the will.[54]

The identification of 'the castle of Cecima in another hermitage of the diocese of Pavia in Lombardy' poses considerably fewer problems than *Milascio*: it is the hermitage of Sant'Alberto di Butrio in the Staffora valley, half a dozen miles from the town of Cecima. Cecima and Sant'Alberto lie within a pocket of the diocese of Pavia, surrounded by the diocese of Tortona, so this description in the letter is correct and accurate. The Bishop of Tortona at this time and since 1325 (when he was transferred from the bishopric of Brescia) was Manuele Fieschi's first cousin Percivalle Fieschi, and the town of Tortona itself is 20 miles from the hermitage. Also within the Staffora valley, a couple of miles from the hermitage of Sant'Alberto (though the two places are not visible from each other), lies the castle of Oramala, which in the 1330s was held by Cardinal Luca Fieschi's nephew Niccolo Malaspina, the area's powerful secular lord. He was known as *il Marchesotto* and was the son of Luca's sister Fiesca Fieschi and Alberto Malaspina, also held lands in the vicinity of Mulazzo, and was married to Beatrice, sister of the Marquis of Mulazzo.

Edward of Caernarfon would thus appear to have been travelling from one destination controlled by the Fieschi family or their close relatives to another. The hermitage of Sant'Alberto lies in the hills and was – and is – quite remote, but the Staffora valley and the town of Cecima stood in the middle of communication routes and trade routes from Genoa and Milan to the centre of Italy. This may be a reason why Manuele Fieschi mentioned 'the castle of Cecima in another hermitage of the diocese of Pavia in Lombardy', as Cecima would be a location far better known than the hermitage which stood in the hills some miles from it. There was a castle in Cecima in the fourteenth century, now ruins on a hill.[55] Manuele Fieschi states that Edward of Caernarfon spent two years at Sant'Alberto, 'always the recluse, doing penance and praying to God for you [Edward III] and other sinners'. This may not be as strange as it might seem: Edward II was always pious, and had always enjoyed the company of religious men and debating with them. One of his close personal friends was an abbot, William of Langdon in Kent. It is therefore not too implausible that Edward might have taken to a contemplative existence of prayer, and he had also loved hard physical work and the outdoors for much of his life, much to the bafflement and disdain of many of his contemporaries. It is therefore perhaps not quite as implausible that Edward II would take to a life of work than it would be for almost any other King of England.

11

THE KING IN FRANCE, GERMANY AND ITALY PART 2

Edward travelled, assuming that the Fieschi Letter is correct, considerable distances. From the port of Sluis to Normandy would be approximately 200 or 250 miles, depending on where in the duchy he went. Normandy to Avignon is about 500 miles, and Avignon to Brabant via Paris close to 600; when he finally reached Brabant, Edward was only a few miles from where he had originally landed at Sluis, and had walked all the way through France, the second largest country in Europe after Ukraine, twice. From the duchy of Brabant he went to Cologne, a city which is 120 miles to the east of Brabant's main city Brussels and was then ruled by Emperor Ludwig of Bavaria and Archbishop Walram von Jülich, both of whom had family connections to Edward. The journey from Brussels to Cologne would probably have taken Edward through or near the city of Liège where Manuele Fieschi held a benefice, and then through the county of Jülich, ruled by his son Edward III's brother-in-law Wilhelm, brother of Archbishop Walram. From Cologne Edward travelled south through Germany and Switzerland (or possibly Austria or eastern France) to Milan, a journey of a good 500 miles which necessitated travelling over the highest range of mountains in Europe after the Caucasus, from there presumably to *Milascio* or Mulazzo which is about 125 miles from Milan, and finally from Mulazzo to the hermitage of Sant'Alberto, almost another 100 miles. Edward's journeys on the Continent, from Sluis to

Normandy to Avignon to Brabant to Cologne to Milan to Mulazzo to Sant'Alberto, represent a total distance of at least 2,000 miles, and other evidence indicates that he returned to Cologne and Koblenz in 1338, and so made the journey of more than 500 miles in reverse. Given that he had become a hermit or pilgrim, he must have made all his journeys on foot, or at the very least perhaps he rode a mule on occasion; he certainly was not galloping over the Continent on a fast and expensive horse, which would have made him extremely conspicuous.

Putting together the timing as detailed in the Fieschi Letter with the evidence that he was in Cologne and Koblenz again in early September 1338 implies that Edward probably arrived at the hermitage near Mulazzo at the end of 1333 or beginning of 1334. He had departed from Ireland at the end of 1330 or beginning of 1331 – Manuele Fieschi says that he left Ireland nine months after the Earl of Kent's execution on 19 March 1330 – so this gives us three years for his travels around the Continent, excluding the final leg of his journey to Sant'Alberto and the return journey to Cologne. It is hardly a wonder if it took Edward several years to complete such a huge distance, especially as the European weather must have been inclement on numerous occasions and he may have spent winters, or long rainy periods, resting in one place. Crossing the Alps, when travelling from Cologne to Milan, would have been considerably easier in the summer months. Possibly Edward travelled over the Brenner pass, the Septimer, the St Gotthard or the Great St Bernard in 1332 or 1333. From the Brenner he would still have had over 200 miles to travel to Milan, from the Great St Bernard about 140, and from the Septimer and St Gotthard passes about 100. If he had passed through Lausanne, a Swiss town with Fieschi connections, he would have picked up the Via Francigena pilgrim route again, which would have taken him over the Great St Bernard pass and through the town of Vercelli in Piedmont, where Manuele Fieschi was elected bishop in 1343. The Via Francigena also passes through Pontremoli near Mulazzo, and Luni, where Cardinal Luca Fieschi's nephew Bernabo Malaspina was bishop in the 1330s, on its way to Rome.

The pilgrim route from Trondheim to Rome, which Edward could have joined in the south of Germany, passed over the Brenner. If

Edward crossed the Alps into Italy in *c.* late 1332 or the first half of 1333, this would have given him a few months to travel to Milan and spend some time there before arriving at the hermitage of Santa Maria del Monte above Mulazzo around the end of 1333 or beginning of 1334.[1] The Fieschi Letter says he stayed at Mulazzo for two and a half years, probably until the siege of nearby Pontremoli which began in June 1336 forced him or those in charge of him to move him to Sant'Alberto, where he stayed for another two years until the summer of 1338. At this point, according to other evidence, he returned to Cologne and was taken to his son at nearby Koblenz in the late summer of 1338.

Seventy years later, the chronicler Adam of Usk made a very similar journey to Edward when he travelled from England to Rome: from Brabant, he went east through Maastricht and into Germany, then followed the Rhine south through Cologne, Koblenz, Worms, Speyer, Strasbourg and Basel. Finally he crossed the Alps via the St Gotthard pass, which brought him to Milan via Lake Como and then down to Rome. On the way back to England, Usk passed through Pontremoli and Genoa and used the Col du Mont Cenis pass through the mountains into Savoy, eastern France. Usk left England on 19 February 1402 and arrived in Rome on 5 April, a very fast journey given the distance and the time of year; evidently he had few problems traversing the Alps in March.[2] Clearly Usk was travelling much faster than Edward, though something of the perils of journeying through the mountains in late winter is apparent from Usk's comment about the St Gotthard: 'I was drawn in an ox-wagon half dead with cold and with my eyes blindfold lest I should see the dangers of the pass.'[3] A Premonstratensien monk from near Groningen now in the Netherlands also made a pilgrimage to Rome in 1211/12. On the journey there he travelled through France, but made his way home past Milan and Lake Como, probably over the Splügen pass, then north through Basel, Strasbourg, Speyer, Worms, Mainz and Cologne.[4] In 1489, a rich Hainaulter merchant named Jehan de Tournay went on pilgrimage to Rome, and followed the Rhine through Cologne and Koblenz until Speyer. He then followed a route through rural Württemberg and Bavaria and through Switzerland before entering Italy via a much more obscure Alpine pass called the Reschen in South Tyrol.[5] Edward was certainly travelling well-worn routes; numerous other people in the Middle Ages made their way from Germany down into Italy.

It seems quite clear that Edward of Caernarfon, at least once he arrived in Italy in or around the summer of 1333 and perhaps even in the places he had visited before he arrived in Italy, was spending time at places closely associated with the Fieschi family and their relatives the Malaspinas. All the places he visited on the Continent, with the possible exception of Brabant, were pilgrim sites, but were also, for the most part, places where the Fieschi family held some influence. Edward did not, for example, travel to the most famous pilgrim site in Europe, the burial place of St James in Santiago de Compostela in northern Spain, a place visited by numerous English people throughout his lifetime (and long before and afterwards). Perhaps surprisingly, he did not travel anywhere near his mother's homeland of Castile in Spain, where he had numerous cousins, and for all his long journeys through France also did not go to Gascony in the south-west of that country, the large territory he had once ruled over and where his beloved Piers Gaveston came from. The author of the *Scalacronica* chronicle says that Gascony was the 'country and nation which he [Edward] loved best'.[6]

As he was an extremely devoted supporter of the Dominican order of friars, it seems reasonable that Edward II in the guise of a man who had dedicated himself to religion might have wished to visit Caleruega in northern Castile, the birthplace in *c.* 1170 of the order's founder St Dominic, or Burgos not far from Caleruega where his parents had married as teenagers in 1254 and which stood on the long-established pilgrim route to Santiago de Compostela. Edward could have passed through Piers Gaveston's native Béarn in Gascony on his way to Caleruega, Burgos and Santiago, and through the lordship of Biscay in northern Spain which in the early 1330s was ruled by his kinswoman Maria Diaz de Haro, with whom he had been on excellent and familiar terms as king; yet he did not. This is perhaps explicable by the fact that the Fieschi family had virtually no interests, influence or even contacts in Spain or Gascony. Assuming that the Fieschi Letter is a viable piece of evidence and not an invention with poorly chosen details, it therefore seems entirely probable that Edward met his kinsman Cardinal Luca Fieschi when visiting John XXII at the papal court in Avignon and that Fieschi took over responsibility for the former king's movements, via his nephews and trusted agents in Italy and other parts of Europe.

Edward II had had little contact with Italy during his reign, except that he had Italian servants and money-lenders at his court, and it seems a little peculiar that he would choose to go there of all places rather than Gascony and Castile, if he was acting entirely under his own agency; the choice otherwise seems a little random and unlikely. While in Italy, Edward did not even take the opportunity to visit Rome, Assisi or any other well-known pilgrim destination, perhaps also because the Fieschi sphere of influence did not extend to these places. Instead, he spent a total of four and a half years at two obscure hermitages which were not dedicated to saints he had previously shown any interest in, and it can hardly be a coincidence that both of them lay in parts of Italy dominated by the Fieschi and Malaspina families.

Ian Mortimer has written a detailed account of the Fieschi family, their possible involvement in the continued existence of Edward II in the 1330s, and their dealings with Edward III, in his *Medieval Intrigue*.[7] He draws particular attention to Niccolinus or Niccolino Fieschi, a member of the family whose place in the family tree is uncertain but who was certainly a relative of Manuele and of Cardinal Luca, perhaps even Manuele's uncle. Mortimer considers that Niccolino may have been the man who delivered the Fieschi Letter to Edward III in April 1336, when he was appointed as a member of the king's council.[8] Although this seems be too early for Edward II's wanderings around the Continent to have been completed and for the Fieschi Letter to have been written in its entirety, it is certainly possible that an earlier version of it was delivered to Edward III in 1336, or that at least Niccolino Fieschi informed Edward III of his father's whereabouts from 1327 until his visit to the papal court in Avignon presumably sometime in 1331. Cardinal Luca Fieschi's nephew Antonio Fieschi, made Bishop of Luni in 1338 and already a chaplain of the pope, also visited Edward III in the summer of 1337.[9] Antonio and Manuele Fieschi were only fairly distantly related – third cousins, meaning they had a set of great-great-grandparents in common – but were both executors of Cardinal Luca's will in 1336, so clearly knew each other. It is possible that Cardinal Luca Fieschi gave Edward letters of protection at the papal court when Edward went there to meet John XXII, probably in 1331. Merchants from Genoa, the great port city where the Fieschis came from, were active in much of Europe, so that the letters would be helpful to Edward in getting around, and would be less conspicuous than letters of protection issued by the pope himself.[10] Perhaps John XXII and Luca came to the conclusion that Edward would be safest in Italy, though the decision may not simply have been altruistic: custody of the former King of England, who was believed to be dead, would give the Fieschi family a powerful bargaining tool to hold over his son the present king.

So who were the Fieschis? They were a powerful noble family of northern Italy who in the thirteenth and fourteenth centuries wielded considerable influence in both the religious and the secular worlds. Two Fieschi men, Sinibaldo and Ottobuono, were elected as pope in the thirteenth century (Innocent IV and Adrian V respectively), and many other members of the family became cardinals and bishops. Innocent IV was Cardinal Luca Fieschi's great-uncle and Manuele Fieschi's great-great-uncle, and Adrian V was Luca's uncle. Outside religion, some of the Fieschis were counts of Lavagna, and intermarried often with the Malaspinas, another powerful noble family of the region. Manuele Fieschi was a second cousin once removed and a member of the retinue of Luca Fieschi, who was born in the early 1270s and made a cardinal in 1300.[11] Edward I and his son Edward II always addressed Cardinal Luca Fieschi in letters as their cousin or kinsman; the relationship was acknowledged for the first time in October 1300, a few months after Luca became a cardinal when still only in his late 20s, when Edward I called him 'his dear cousin and friend Luke'.[12] Edward I also called Luca 'the king's kinsman and dear friend' in October 1301 when he granted Luca 50 marks a year from the English Exchequer 'in consideration of his good offices in the king's affairs'.[13] Edward of Caernarfon, the future Edward II, addressed Luca as his kinsman when he wrote to him in 1305, two years before he became king; the men were in contact for many years.[14]

Luca's brothers Federico and Carlo and his nephews were also acknowledged as Edward I and II's kinsmen, but his father Niccolo, Count of Lavagna, and uncles (who included Ottobuono Fieschi, elected Pope Adrian V shortly before his death in 1276) were not. The family connection to the English royal family therefore must have come from Luca's mother, whose name was Leonora or Lionetta but whose family background is uncertain. Manuele Fieschi, a cousin of Luca but not descended from Luca's mother, was thus not related to the English royal house; neither was he Luca's nephew, as some English historians have claimed.[15] Luca Fieschi also claimed kinship to Jaime II, King of Aragon in Spain (born 1267, reigned 1291 to 1327), and the only family relationship which would connect him to both Edward II and Jaime II came via the houses of Savoy and Geneva.[16] Edward I's mother Eleanor of Provence, Queen of England and wife of Henry III, was the daughter of Raymond-Berenger V, Count of Provence, and her mother was Beatrice of Savoy, daughter of Thomas, Count of Savoy (Edward II's great-great-grandfather) and granddaughter of William, Count of Geneva.

Ian Mortimer has suggested that Luca Fieschi's mother Leonora/Lionetta was a daughter of the Italian nobleman Giacomo del Carretto, marquis of Savona, Noli and Finale (d. 1268), who was a grandson of William, Count of Geneva and the first cousin of Edward II's great-grandmother Beatrice of Savoy, and was also related to Jaime II of Aragon (another descendant of William, Count of Geneva). Giacomo del Carretto's daughter Brumisan addressed Edward I as her kinsman in 1278.[17] Del Carretto's second wife Caterina da Marano (c. 1216/18–72) was one of the many illegitimate children of the Holy Roman Emperor Frederick II (1194–1250), and was the full sister of Enzo, King of Sardinia and a half-sister of Konrad, King of Germany and Manfredi, King of Sicily. It is possible, though still only speculative, that Giacomo del Carretto and Caterina da Marano had another daughter, Leonora or Lionetta, who married Niccolo Fieschi and was the mother of Cardinal Luca Fieschi. If Luca was indeed the grandson of Giacomo and Caterina, he would have been the third cousin of Edward I (they would both be great-great-grandsons of William, Count of Geneva) and the third cousin once removed of Edward II. Luca's Malaspina nephews Manfredi, Bernabo and Niccolo, who may have been in charge of Edward II in Italy on the cardinal's behalf, would have been the former king's fourth cousins. This family link would make Luca a second cousin of Jaime II of Aragon, who was a grandson of Manfredi, King of Sicily and great-grandson of Emperor Frederick II, and also his third cousin once removed via common descent from William, Count of Geneva. There was certainly a blood connection between Luca Fieschi and his brothers and nephews, and Edward I and II; although one of Edward I's great-uncles from Savoy married a Fieschi woman, a mere marital connection would not be enough for the Kings of England to address several of the Fieschi men as their relatives. Neither Edward I nor his father Henry III ever addressed any of the Fieschis before Luca and his generation as their kinsmen.

To be acknowledged as a cousin of the King of England was a very great honour and one which Edward I and II would only have bestowed on people they knew for certain were their blood relatives, not only people connected to them by marriage, which would have included most of the nobility of Europe. If Luca Fieschi and his brothers were great-grandsons of an emperor, Frederick II (whose much younger third wife Isabella of England was Edward I's aunt, another possible marital connection between the Fieschis and the English royal family) as well as relatives of the English royals, this would certainly go a long way to explaining the honour, respect and affection shown to them by Edward I and II.[18]

As for Manuele Fieschi himself, he held benefices in England, though it is not certain that he ever visited the country; quite possibly he did, but there is no direct evidence. Among others, he was a canon of Salisbury, York and Lincoln and an archdeacon of Nottingham. John Walwayn, the English clerk sent to John XXII to explain the Earl of Kent's plot in March 1330, was also a canon of Salisbury, as were the Wyvill brothers, parsons of Kingsclere in Hampshire.[19] Manuele Fieschi was a long way from being a humble, ignorant, illiterate priest who knew nothing of England or European politics or anything beyond his local Italian valley. He was educated and cosmopolitan, and became a notary of Pope John XXII in the late 1320s; the pope only had six notaries, so Manuele held an important position and was one of a small handful of men who had the ear of the pope and access to his correspondence. Fieschi came from a wealthy, highly influential noble family, some of whom were related to the English royal family, worked with no less a figure than the pope himself on a daily basis, and thus was not a man who would have needed to blackmail anyone for privilege and position by fabricating implausible stories about the King of England's father surviving Berkeley Castle.[20]

Manuele Fieschi became Bishop of Vercelli in 1343, and held the position until his death in 1348, perhaps of the plague which had then begun ravaging Europe. Manuele died in Milan while acting as an ambassador of the pope to Luchino Visconti, lord of the city and of a rapidly expanding state in northern Italy, who was married to his third cousin Isabella Fieschi, Cardinal Luca's niece. Manuele was succeeded as bishop by his nephew and later by three more Fieschi bishops, making the rich and strategically placed diocese of Vercelli essentially a Fieschi fief for over a century. This is some indication of the sway the Fieschi family and their relatives the Malaspinas held over much of northern Italy in the fourteenth century and how certain bishoprics were almost hereditary, passing from one Fieschi or Malaspina to another. Both Manuele and his kinsman Cardinal Luca Fieschi knew William Melton, Archbishop of York, and probably also Thomas Dunheved, the friar who had temporarily freed Edward of Caernarfon from Berkeley Castle in the summer of 1327; Dunheved had spent a few months at the papal court in 1325 and been made a papal chaplain. Edward II's half-brother the Earl of Kent had visited John XXII in the summer or autumn of 1329 and asked his advice about freeing Edward from captivity. Manuele surely also knew of the visit of John Walwayn, his fellow canon of Salisbury, to Avignon in 1330, bringing details of the Earl of Kent's plot and execution to John XXII. There is therefore every reason to suppose that certainly Manuele and probably Luca as well knew a great deal about the plots to free Edward and the belief among many influential men in England and elsewhere that he had not died in 1327, long before the man claiming to be Edward arrived in Avignon.

There were plenty of men at the papal court in Avignon in the 1330s who knew Edward II and could have recognised him, although the pope himself had never met him. Manuele Fieschi's first cousin Percivalle Fieschi, Bishop of Tortona, was one of them; he had accompanied their kinsman Cardinal Luca Fieschi to England in 1317–18.[21] Luca himself was another, and certainly spent considerable time with Edward in England at that time. Yet another was Cardinal Gaucelin or Gaucelme Jean, who lived until 1348 and was a nephew of John XXII himself, and had accompanied Luca on his visit to England in 1317–18 and also spent much time with Edward; he was the other cardinal attacked and robbed by Sir Gilbert Middleton.[22] One of John XXII's two envoys to England in the summer of 1326, when he was trying to reconcile Edward II and Queen Isabella, was the Dominican Guillaume Laudun, then Archbishop of Vienne and from 1327 Archbishop of Toulouse. Laudun lived until 1352 and had met Edward II face to face in May 1321, September 1324, and at Saltwood Castle, Kent in early June 1326. In 1345 he retired to a Dominican convent in Avignon.[23] Laudun's fellow envoy to Edward II in the early summer of 1326 was Hugues Aimery or Adhémar, son of the lord of Rochemaure, in 1326 Bishop of Orange and from 1328 Bishop of Saint-Paul-Trois-Châteaux, both of which are towns just north of Avignon. Aimery would therefore certainly have been close at hand when the man claiming to be Edward II visited the papal court at Avignon, and he lived until 1348. Both he and Guillaume Laudun spent a few days with Edward II at Saltwood Castle at the beginning of June 1326, and talked to him privately when they asked him and Hugh Despenser the Younger questions about Queen Isabella's refusal to return to her husband and the reasons behind it. Laudun and Aimery had spent considerable time in the company of the King of England not many years before 'Edward' arrived at Avignon and thus were in an excellent position to be able to identify him, not only physically but by asking questions only Edward II would be able to answer.

Manuele Fieschi thus simply had to ask his own first cousin, a cardinal who was a rather more distant cousin of his, the pope's nephew, an archbishop or a bishop, men who would also have been present at the papal court at Avignon, to identify the man he met claiming to be

Edward II. Another man well known to Manuele Fieschi who may have been in Avignon in the first half of 1331 was Master John Arundel, brother of the Earl of Arundel who remained loyal to Edward II after Queen Isabella's invasion. John Arundel, born in about 1290, was a canon of Lichfield, York, Lincoln and, as so many others including Manuele Fieschi himself, of Salisbury. The Arundel siblings were half-Italian through their mother Alesia di Saluzzo, daughter of Tommaso I del Vasto, Marquis of Saluzzo (in northern Italy not far from the places mentioned in this book). Edward II himself was related to the Saluzzos, and if the identity of Cardinal Luca Fieschi's mother Leonora as discussed above is correct, so was Luca himself; Alesia di Saluzzo was, like Edward and perhaps Luca, yet another descendant of William, Count of Geneva.

In August 1310, Master John Arundel travelled to the papal court in the company of his uncles Giorgio and Bonifacio di Saluzzo – the former was a clerk of Edward II and acknowledged by him some years later as his relative, being his third cousin – and Manfredi Malaspina, presumably Luca Fieschi's nephew of this name though Malaspina was a secular lord, not a cleric.[24] Manuele Fieschi acted as John Arundel's executor in October 1329 regarding John XXII's promise of several benefices to him.[25] This was the month in which the Archbishop of York William Melton, who was also well known to Manuele Fieschi, received news of Edward II's survival at Corfe Castle. Some of the lands of John Arundel's brother Edmund, Earl of Arundel passed after Edmund's execution in November 1326 to Edward II's half-brother the Earl of Kent, including the castle of Arundel in Sussex; it was to this castle where Kent intended to take Edward after the latter's release, according to his confession of March 1330. John Arundel's nephew Richard was also involved in the Earl of Kent's plot, and fled from England in June 1330. Master John Arundel died in June 1331, so depending on how long Edward took to reach Avignon after his long journey through France, it is just possible that Arundel was able to confirm to Manuele Fieschi that his brother Edmund the earl had indeed been with the king in South Wales in October 1326, weeks before his beheading, as the Fieschi Letter states. John Arundel would be another man able to confirm the identity of the man presenting himself to Pope John XXII as Edward II, and to confirm one of the details of his story.[26]

Although we have no way of knowing what, if any, attempts Manuele Fieschi made to confirm the identity of the man presenting himself at the papal court as Edward II, it seems likely that he must have made at least some before he rushed off a letter to the King of England with an incredible and seemingly wildly implausible story about his father living years past his official death. The survival of Edward II in another country and well beyond Edward III's control was a serious potential threat to the English king, and it seems unlikely that Manuele Fieschi, a well-educated and well-connected notary and associate of the pope, would have written such a letter without considering the implications of what he was doing and checking the identity of the man he met. Although it is not certain that Manuele Fieschi ever saw Edward II in person during his reign – he may well have done, but we cannot prove it – it seems extremely likely that his first cousin Percivalle did, in 1317–18. And in the 1330s, when Manuele wrote his letter telling Edward III that his father had escaped from Berkeley and travelled to Italy, Percivalle was Bishop of Tortona, a town about 20 miles from the hermitage of Sant'Alberto di Butrio, where Manuele claims Edward had gone. Indeed, the hermitage lay in a pocket of the diocese of Pavia within the diocese of Tortona, and the Fieschi Letter states that it lies in the diocese of Pavia, a statement which required good local knowledge. Not only would men who knew Edward II personally have been present in Avignon, Manuele Fieschi could easily have sent people to Sant'Alberto di Butrio to check if Edward had ever been there. The hermitage, as well as being close to his cousin Percivalle's diocese, lay about 60 miles south of the town of Vercelli, his own future diocese. The Bishop of Pavia, the diocese where Sant'Alberto lay, from 1328 to 1343 was Giovanni Fulgosi, a native of the town of Piacenza 40 miles from Sant'Alberto, which had many Fieschi connections.[27]

It is possible that Manuele Fieschi wrote the bulk of the letter in c. 1331/32 having recently met Edward II, or at least the man claiming to be Edward II, at Avignon, and updated it years later after he was informed by members of his family where Edward had been ever since. Hearing the account of Edward's escape from Berkeley and sojourns in Corfe and Ireland from Edward himself enabled Fieschi to write a relatively rather more detailed description of this period, but he had only a general outline of the former king's movements after leaving Avignon. The expression in the letter that Edward 'came' to Avignon, not 'went' (*venit Avinionem* in Latin), might imply that the former king was still there when Fieschi wrote the first part of his letter – though equally might simply mean that Fieschi was in Avignon when he wrote it.[28] The rest of the letter could have been completed in *c.* 1338, after Manuele was informed of Edward's later movements and that he had spent two and a half years at the hermitage of *Milascio*/Mulazzo and another two at the hermitage of Sant'Alberto near Cecima. The past tense used in the letter for Edward's sojourn at Sant'Alberto shows that when Manuele wrote that part of the letter, Edward had already left the hermitage. The Fieschi Letter does not state directly, however, that Manuele Fieschi met Edward at the papal court when Edward visited John XXII there in *c.* early 1331, and it is not impossible that he met him in Italy some years later.

The French scholar Alexandre Germain discovered the Fieschi Letter in an archive in Montpellier, southern France in 1877, and presented it in Paris on 21 September 1877, which, whether by chance or design, was the 550th anniversary of Edward II's supposed death.[29] It appears in Register A, the first of six volumes of a cartulary begun by Arnaud Verdale, Bishop of Maguelone from 1339 to 1352, and finished by Gaucelm Deaux, bishop from 1367 to 1373. The Fieschi Letter appears on folio 86 recto, and is written in the middle of a series of unrelated documents referring to certain property rights of Bishop Verdale in a small town near Montpellier. It is thirty-eight lines long and the word *vacat*, vacant or cancelled, is written in the margin. There is no reason at all to think that the letter is a later forgery; the handwriting and decorated initials are consistent with the rest of the register in which it is located, and there are no blank pages in the document which might suggest that the Fieschi Letter was written into the cartulary later in a conveniently empty space. All the documents in the cartulary, with the exception of the last one which dates from 1387 and is a later addition, date from between about 1176 and 1347, though are not in chronological order. The Fieschi Letter is found among the personal documents of Bishop Arnaud Verdale, which strongly implies that he was in possession of a copy of the letter.[30] In 1901, the Italian scholar Costantino Nigra wrote a paper about the Fieschi Letter, identifying *Milascio* (almost certainly wrongly) as Melazzo near Acqui Terme and Cecima as the town of this name south of Voghera, near the hermitage of Sant'Alberto di Butrio (almost certainly correctly). Anna Benedetti, another Italian scholar, claimed in 1924 that Edward II had not only sought refuge at Sant'Alberto but had been buried there.[31] Indeed, an empty tomb at the hermitage is claimed as Edward's first tomb to this day, though in fact there is no evidence that Edward returned there after he apparently met his son in Germany in the autumn of 1338, or that he died there. A skull fragment found at Sant'Alberto has sometimes been thought to be his, but until such time as it can be examined and compared to a DNA sample, this is incapable of proof.

The researchers of the Auramala Project in Italy believe that the copy of the Fieschi Letter which still exists in a Montpellier archive was taken to the Holy Roman Emperor (the ruler and overlord of Germany, large parts of eastern and southern France, parts of Italy, and the Low Countries) Ludwig of Bavaria in early 1339 by the new Bishop of Maguelone near Montpellier, Arnaud Verdale, who had it copied into Register A of his cartulary. Verdale was a papal legate who in 1338–39 was trying to persuade Ludwig to broker peace between England and France, Edward III having claimed the French throne from his mother's cousin Philip VI in 1337 and begun what much later would become known as the Hundred Years War. On 13 September 1338, just eight days after Ludwig met Edward III at Koblenz in western Germany and also just a few days after the King of England's wardrobe clerk recorded the appearance in Koblenz of a man who said that he was the king's father (of which more later), Pope Benedict XII – who had succeeded John XXII on 20 December 1334 – appointed Verdale as an envoy to Ludwig.

Some months later in January 1339, Benedict sent Verdale two secret letters to show the emperor, marked Letter A and Letter B.[32] Possibly one of these was the Fieschi Letter. This is only speculation, but Arnaud Verdale was certainly an envoy of the pope sent to Ludwig of Bavaria in 1338–39, and the Fieschi Letter certainly ended up in a cartulary created on Verdale's orders and was copied into the middle of other documents relating to himself personally. It is difficult to explain otherwise how the Fieschi Letter came to exist in a document created by the Bishop of a town near Montpellier, of all places; neither Verdale himself nor Maguelone/Montpellier had any connections to Manuele Fieschi or any direct connections to Edward III of England. There must be an explanation as to how and why a scribe of the Bishop of Maguelone near Montpellier managed to get hold of a letter sent from an Italian papal notary to the King of England and copy it into the bishop's register, and this theory seems as good as any.[33] It is possible that Verdale showed the letter to Emperor Ludwig on the pope's orders to demonstrate to him that Edward III's occupation of the English throne might be deemed shaky, with his father alive and at large on the Continent, which would have a profound effect on his claim to the French throne. Perhaps Verdale's aim was to show to the emperor that his alliance with England was not in his best interests, and indeed, Ludwig broke off his alliance with Edward III and by the beginning of 1340 was allied with Philip VI of France instead, and in June 1341 revoked the title of imperial vicar which he had bestowed on Edward in September 1338.[34]

A French historian has pointed out that Arnaud Verdale had 'wrought the dissolution of an alliance' between England and the empire which 'would have been catastrophic for the history of France'.[35] Benedict XII's aim may have been to prevent war between England and France, and to this end sought to persuade the King of England's new ally the emperor that Edward III was vulnerable because of the continued existence of his father on the Continent. If Ludwig broke off his alliance with Edward III, this might have persuaded Edward to abandon his claim to the French throne and his war against Philip VI (though in fact he did not).

Although Edward III was crowned King of England on 1 February 1327 while his father was certainly still living, and Edward II remained officially alive for the first nine months of his son's reign, the older Edward was kept in captivity so that he could not threaten his son's position and authority as king. The plots to free the former Edward II in 1327 were a danger both to Edward III and to his mother the dowager queen Isabella, and to her favourite and co-ruler Roger Mortimer. The usual explanation for the pair's assumed murder of Isabella's husband in September 1327 is that they needed to safeguard the young king's position and their own, and that Edward II had to die so that no-one else would be able to attempt to free him and perhaps try to restore him to the throne. To Edward III, the thought of his father wandering around freely in England or, even worse, in a foreign country where he had no possible control over him and his actions, must have been a serious threat. Edward II had been the crowned and anointed King of England, chosen by God as it was then seen, and there would always be people who believed that his deposition or forced abdication had been invalid and that, whatever Edward's many flaws and mistakes, only death could stop a king being the rightful king.

Edward II was the first King of England deposed from his throne or forced to abdicate, and there were doubts over the legality of the procedure. The Fieschi Letter was addressed to Edward III and presumably was sent to him (though we have no direct evidence of this as no copy of it has ever been found in England to prove that he received it), but may also have been recycled and sent to Emperor Ludwig of Bavaria in order to sway his decision about allying with Edward III and England against Philip VI and France. The notion that the Fieschi Letter was intended as some form of high-level political blackmail has been suggested by various modern historians. If Edward II was under the control of the Fieschi and Malaspina families in Italy, with the knowledge of Cardinal Luca Fieschi and the popes John XXII and Benedict XII, to be used as potential leverage against Edward III, the young King of England had no means of returning his father to England so that Edward II could publicly renounce his throne again and thus make Edward III's throne more secure. The idea that Edward II in Italy was not free, wandering around wherever he pleased, but was under the control of a powerful noble Italian family, would also answer the question many people have when faced with the notion of the former King of England's survival in Italy: why would he not return to England and try to reclaim his throne? If Edward II was not acting under his own agency, and Edward III was not able to gain control of his father either, the question is answered.

So to sum up, the Fieschi Letter may have been originally written in *c.* 1331/32 after Manuele Fieschi met Edward II, then updated and completed in *c.* September 1338 with Edward's later movements on the Continent as a diplomatic tool for the pope's envoy Arnaud Verdale to use in his dealings with Emperor Ludwig of Bavaria which also began in September 1338. This was shortly after Edward II had supposedly left the hermitage of Sant'Alberto and perhaps met his son in Koblenz on or a little before 6 September 1338. Not too long afterwards, Ludwig broke off his alliance with Edward III and England. The Fieschi Letter was then copied into Verdale's cartulary, perhaps by accident but to the extreme good fortune of historians centuries later, though it is even possible that it was copied deliberately by a scribe in a kind of fourteenth-century WikiLeaks action, in order to preserve it.[36]

Arnaud Verdale became Bishop of Maguelone in early 1339, some months after Edward III met Ludwig of Bavaria at Koblenz in early September 1338 and after Verdale himself met the emperor. The bishopric of Maguelone was subsumed into the archbishopric of Montpellier in 1536; Villeneuve-lès-Maguelone is a small community just outside the city of Montpellier, and in the early fourteenth century the area was controlled by the Kings of Aragon in Spain and only came under French control in 1349. The town and bishopric of Maguelone came under increasing pressure from the Kings of France in the thirteenth and fourteenth centuries, via their seneschals in the towns of Nîmes and Beaucaire.[37] The latter place, a town on the River Rhône near Avignon, was presumably the home town of William Beaukaire, the sergeant-at-arms who guarded Edward II's body at Berkeley Castle for a month in 1327 alone and then with a group of others in Gloucester.

The very existence of the Fieschi Letter implies some doubt as to whether Edward II had really died in 1327 or not. Had Manuele Fieschi known for certain that Edward was dead, he would not have been taken in by an impostor, and he had close ties to England and was in a good position to know what was happening there. He must have known about Edward II's deposition, his alleged murder and his funeral; John XXII, whose notary he was, was kept well informed about events in England. And yet, even knowing of Edward's official death and funeral, Fieschi was still convinced enough that the man he met was Edward himself to write to Edward's son about it. If he was lying and knew that the man he met was not Edward II, and yet he told Edward III that he was, what would be his motive to lie to the King of England? Manuele Fieschi of all people did not need to blackmail anyone for influence; from a noble, influential family and working at the papal court with the ear of the pope. If we assume blackmail as his motive for writing the letter to Edward III, it makes far more sense that the blackmail was related to Edward III's new war with France and claims to the French throne, and that the pope was trying to force peace between the two powerful kingdoms (if so, Edward III ignored the threat, and carried on with his war). But still, trying to blackmail the King of England with the news that his father was not dead at the very least implies that Manuele Fieschi thought Edward III was not entirely sure if his father was dead or not. To make a comparison, attempting blackmail on Edward II by telling him that his father was still alive would never have worked; Edward II had certainly seen his father dead near Carlisle in July 1307 and would never have been vulnerable to claims that Edward I was still alive.

If the man was not Edward II, then why would he lie and claim that he was? The lie could easily be exposed, after all, as soon as someone who had known Edward II saw him. Perhaps he was simply a madman, or looking for attention; if this man was a pretender, he was certainly not the only royal pretender of the era. If the man Manuele Fieschi met was not in fact Edward II, then it must have been someone extremely well informed; there are details in the letter, particularly Edward sailing from Chepstow in October 1326 and his heart being sent to Isabella, which the vast majority of people in England and Europe could not have known. If the man who met Manuele Fieschi was not Edward II, it must have been someone close to Edward in order for him to be aware of such details. And if the man who met Edward II was a madman or an impostor, it is hard to imagine why he spent a full fifteen days or more with the pope; an impostor could have been spotted well before fifteen days had passed, and it would not take John XXII this long to realise that he was dealing with someone deluded or insane who could not possibly be the former King of England.

Historian Seymour Phillips points out correctly that John XXII 'would have needed little persuading that his strange visitor was an impostor, and so have sent him on his way', but does not comment on why or how the visitor needed to spend more than two weeks with the pope for it to be ascertained with 'little persuading' that he was an impostor.[38] The Fieschi Letter also does not say as such that the pope sent the impostor on his way, but that 'after various discussions, all things having been considered, permission having been received', the man at the papal court went on to Paris, Brabant and so on. Nowhere does the Fieschi Letter state that John XXII believed the man he met to be an impostor. If John XXII had accepted the man he met as Edward II, as apparently he did, but Manuele Fieschi knew he was an impostor, it would have been peculiar and highly disrespectful for Fieschi not to set the pope straight but to allow him to continue believing that an impostor was the former King of England, and to treat him 'honourably'. There seems no particular reason for the pope to treat a deluded madman pretending to be a dead king 'honourably' for more than two weeks. Historian Andy King says that the Fieschi Letter was written by 'an Italian who, as far as is known, had never laid eyes on Edward II during his reign, and whose account was written perhaps a decade after his funeral'.[39] This is true, but ignores the fact that there were plenty of other men at the curia who did see Edward II during his reign even if Manuele Fieschi did not, some of whom were Fieschi's own relatives, and that identifying the former King of England was not simply a matter of recognising his appearance. There were questions the man could be asked which only Edward II would know the answers to; if he could not answer them he would easily be exposed, and this would not take as long as fifteen days.

The language the 'impostor' used would also be a giveaway. Edward II's first language was Anglo-Norman, a dialect of French. The use of Anglo-Norman in England, where the vast majority of people spoke only English, was restricted to a small percentage of the population: royalty, nobility, knights and their families, high-ranking lawyers, bishops, sheriffs, probably some abbots, wealthy merchants, a few royal clerks; in short, the rich and powerful and those who had frequent contact with them. Being able to speak it fluently would severely limit the number of people who 'Edward' could possibly be, if he was not Edward II. Plenty of men at the papal court would know Anglo-Norman and would be able to differentiate it from other French dialects such as the Francien spoken in Paris and the Île de France. John XXII, born Jacques Duèse, came from Cahors in south-west France and thus was himself a native speaker of French, presumably the Occitan dialect of that region, and his successor Jacques Fournier or Benedict XII also came from the south of France. Fournier was made a cardinal in 1327 and may have been one of the men who knew of Edward II's visit to the papal court in *c.* 1331. Guillaume Laudun, the archbishop who had met Edward II in person in England several times, came from the village of Laudun l'Ardoise near Avignon and was yet another native speaker of French who would be able to assess the linguistic ability of the man passing himself off as Edward, and who would also be able to ask him thorough questions.

It was thus well within the pope's own power to check the man's identity, as well as asking the many people at the papal court who had met Edward II personally to meet and talk to him. The Fieschi Letter says that the pope met Edward 'secretly' yet Manuele Fieschi himself also evidently met him, perhaps at Avignon, and if Manuele Fieschi met him, the pope's other notaries might have done so, too, and some of the cardinals or other members of the curia. John XXII died on 4 December 1334, years before Edward III could possibly have received Manuele Fieschi's letter, and was succeeded a few days later by Benedict XII, Cardinal-bishop of Mirepoix. Cardinal Luca Fieschi died on 31 January 1336. Although Edward III, had he wished to do so, could therefore not have asked John XXII or Luca Fieschi directly if they had met his father at Avignon, there were many members of the two men's households whom he could have asked, including Luca's nephew and executor Antonio Fieschi, who met Edward III in the summer of 1337.

12

WILLIAM THE WELSHMAN

In September 1338 Edward III (then aged almost 26) was in Koblenz, south of Cologne on the River Rhine in western Germany, where he met the Holy Roman Emperor Ludwig of Bavaria, who was married to the sister of Edward's queen Philippa of Hainault. Ludwig made Edward a vicar of the Holy Roman Empire on 5 September in a grand ceremony in the town, an appointment which gave the English king the right to summon princes of the Empire to aid him militarily against France.[1] On his way there Edward III spent 22 August 1338 in Jülich, whose ruler Wilhelm was married to his queen Philippa's other sister Johanna and whose brother Walram was Archbishop of Cologne. He spent the next two days, 23 and 24 August, in Cologne itself. He worshipped at the shrine of the Three Kings in the cathedral, which his father was said by the Fieschi Letter to have visited some years before – whether Edward III was yet aware of this or not – and made a very generous donation of more than £67. He promised, though it did not happen, that he would one day be buried at the cathedral church (he must have known of the Prophecy of the Six Kings which foretold this).[2]

Edward III had left England in mid-July 1338, sailing from Orwell in Suffolk where he and his mother had arrived with their invasion force a dozen years before, and was at anchor off Sluis on 17 and 18 July, the port where his father had supposedly landed in c. early 1331 and where his sister Eleanor of Woodstock also arrived on 9 May 1332 prior to her wedding.[3] Queen Philippa accompanied her husband to the Continent, and gave birth to their third (but second surviving) son Lionel in Antwerp on 29 November 1338. On 22 August Edward III sent Wilhelm, formerly Count and now Margrave of Jülich, south to arrange a meeting with Emperor Ludwig as soon as possible. Almost immediately, however, he set off behind Wilhelm without waiting for Ludwig's reply, taking only eleven companions with him and ordering the rest of his entourage to follow behind him. What prompted Edward to send Wilhelm of Jülich to Ludwig and to travel south himself with such haste was his being made aware that on 1 September, an embassy from France was due to meet delegates from the emperor's side and that Ludwig was showing some interest in what Philip VI had to offer him, which seriously threatened the Anglo-German alliance. Ludwig had convened a *Reichstag* to meet in the town of Koblenz at the start of September, and thus Edward III travelled there.[4]

Edward III arrived in Koblenz, 60 miles along the Rhine south of Cologne, and on the confluence of the Rhine and Moselle rivers, at the end of August or beginning of September 1338 and stayed there until 6 September; Ludwig of Bavaria had travelled there in the other direction from Frankfurt and arrived some days earlier on 27 August. The King of England's wardrobe clerk William Norwell made two entries in his account book relating to a man called William le Galeys, 'who asserts that he is the father of the present lord king' and 'who calls himself King of England, father of the present king'. The first, undated entry is a payment of 25s 6d to a royal sergeant-at-arms called Franciscus Lumbard who had brought William le Galeys to the king; William had been 'recently arrested' (*nuper arestati*) in Cologne. The second entry, dated 18 October 1338, records a payment of 13s 6d to one Francekino Forceti for William's expenses for three weeks in his custody in December, seemingly a payment being made months in advance.[5] The medieval French name 'le Galeys' can be translated as 'the Welshman' and can also be spelled 'le Waleys' (the modern French word for 'Welshman' is *Gallois*), and is the origin of the modern names Wallace and Walsh. The Scotsman Sir William Wallace, executed by Edward I in 1305 and hero of the 1995 film

Braveheart, was called 'William le Waleys' in English documents of the era, presumably because his family's origins lay in Wales.[6] In 1328, Edward III had a household squire called Guillelmus (a Latinised form of William) Galeys, and the name was not an uncommon one.[7] A William le Galeys was given permission by Edward III in November 1347 to build a chapel in honour of the Virgin Mary at Queen Isabella's manor of Cheylesmore in Coventry, and to have prayers said there daily for himself, Isabella and Edward III and for the souls of Edward II and his second son John of Eltham, who died in September 1336.[8] Edward II was of course born in Wales, in Caernarfon in April 1284, and was made Prince of Wales by his father in February 1301, which, if this man were truly he, could explain the name.

What is interesting about the appearance of William le Galeys in 1338 is the involvement of two Italians called 'Franciscus Lumbard' or Francesco the Lombard, i.e. a man from northern Italy, and 'Francekino Forceti', better known as Francesco Forcetti, who was an agent of the banking firm the Peruzzi of Florence and may have been a relative of Dino Forcetti, an agent in England of another Italian banking firm, the Bardi, also of Florence.[9] 'Dyno Forcetti and his three companions' were named as squires of Edward III's household in 1330, as was Simon Swanland, mayor of London and the recipient of the Archbishop of York's letter that year saying that Edward II was alive.[10]

The two entries in the account book of William Norwell do not state outright that William the Welshman spent time with Edward III, or even necessarily that the king met him; it is only stated that the Welshman was taken by Francesco the Lombard *apud regem*. This might mean 'taken into the king's presence' or 'before the king' or even simply 'near the king'. It seems likely that Edward III was curious to see a man claiming to be his father, although William the Welshman is said in the king's wardrobe account to have spent three weeks in the custody of Francesco Forcetti (who may or may not be the same person as Francesco the Lombard) but not necessarily three weeks in the company of the king himself. It is striking that William the Welshman *nominavit se regem Angliae patrem regis nunc*, 'called himself the King of England, father of the present king', as though he was still the king. The first entry in Norwell's account book simply says that he 'asserts that he is the father of the present lord king' and the second that he spent three weeks in the custody of Francesco Forcetti 'because he called himself the King of England'. Judging by the first entry William was apparently not 'arrested' because of his assertion to be the King of England's father, but did spend three weeks in the custody of Francesco Forcetti (a banker) because of his claim. The Latin word *arestare* in variant forms appears in other entries in the same account book of Edward III, and does not mean 'arrested' in the modern sense or necessarily imply that William the Welshman had committed a crime. Two entries after the one relating to William the Welshman and Francesco Forcetti, we find a payment of 20*s* to an Athelard of Middlesbrough for bringing military equipment from Middlesbrough to Antwerp. It says that Athelard had *arestatis* the equipment, in this sense clearly a reference to 'picking up' or 'collecting' it and bringing it to the Continent for the king's use. In the sense used in Edward III's account it probably simply means that Francesco had collected William the Welshman in Cologne and brought him to Koblenz. It is not clear how, where, when and to whom William asserted that he was the king's father.[11]

The clerk William Norwell had served Edward II himself from 1313 onwards and therefore would have been able to recognise and identify him if he saw him, though it is not clear if he did or not.[12]. Francesco Forcetti appears to have been paid on 18 October for William the Welshman spending three weeks in his custody the following December; to what purpose is uncertain. Nor is it clear why this payment to Forcetti was being made a few weeks in advance If Edward III met William le Galeys at all, the meeting presumably took place between 1 and 6 September, the period the king spent in Koblenz (as the first entry relating to William in Norwell's account book says he was taken from Cologne to Koblenz), presumably on the island of Niederwerth just outside the town where Edward III was staying. The English king's last day in Koblenz before he returned north was 6 September: on 8 September he was in Bonn, and arrived in Antwerp on 21 September 1338, the eleventh anniversary of his father's supposed death at Berkeley Castle on 21 September 1327.

Edward III attended Mass for the soul of his father at the conventual church of St Andrew in the city on that day, and other churches and religious orders of Antwerp including the Dominican friars also celebrated Mass in Edward II's memory.[13] If William le Galeys did spend three weeks with the king or at least was in his retinue in the custody of the banker Francesco Forcetti, he may have accompanied him on this trip. This raises the intriguing possibility that Edward II was somewhere nearby when his son attended a Mass for his late soul. There is also the intriguing possilibity that 'Edward II' or William the Welshman met or saw Edward III's queen, Philippa, in Antwerp, and the royal couple's second surviving son Lionel was born there on 29 November. Edward II and Phillipa of Hainault hadnever previously met.

Emperor Ludwig met Edward III in the *Kastorkirche* or Church of Saint Castor in Koblenz on 5 September 1338, and then in the square in front of the church, the *Kastorhof*, made him a vicar of the Holy Roman Empire. This grand ceremony was attended by numerous German bishops and noblemen and six of the seven electors (in German, *Kurfürsten*). These were three archbishops and four princes who had the right to elect the Kings of Germany who were then crowned as Holy Roman Emperors by the pope; almost uniquely in Europe, Kings of Germany were elected and it was not a hereditary position (Edward II's great-uncle Richard of Cornwall was elected King of Germany in 1257). The missing elector was John 'the Blind', King of Bohemia, who would be killed fighting for Philip VI of France against Edward III at the Battle of Crécy eight years later. Those present were three archbishops and three secular lords. The archbishops, all of them noblemen by birth, were Walram von Jülich of Cologne, who was the brother of the Margrave of Jülich; Balduin von Luxembourg of Trier, who was the uncle of John 'the Blind' and brother of the late Holy Roman Emperor Henry; and Heinrich III von Virneburg of Mainz. He was the brother of Robert, Count of Virneburg west of Koblenz, and his uncle Heinrich II von Virneburg had been Walram von Jülich's predecessor as Archbishop of Cologne. The secular lords were Emperor Ludwig's nephew Rudolf, Count Palatine of the Rhine; Ludwig's son from his first marriage, Ludwig the younger, Margrave of Brandenburg and Count of Tyrol; and Rudolf, Duke of Saxony-Wittenberg, a first cousin of the emperor.[14]

These half-dozen men had met in the town of Rhens, just south of Koblenz, some weeks earlier, and on 16 July 1338 issued the Declaration of Rhens, which stated that the electors alone had the independent right to choose the King of Germany and the future emperor regardless of the pope's approval or interference. Ludwig of Bavaria proclaimed the Declaration as imperial law at a formal session of the *Reichstag* in Koblenz on 5 September, at which Edward III was an honorary guest. On this day, Ludwig also appointed Edward III and the archbishops of Cologne, Mainz and Trier as his mediators to seek reconciliation with the papal court.[15] The Declaration, Ludwig's appointment of Edward III as an imperial vicar which represented his public announcement of an alliance with Edward against France (despite his men meeting Philip VI's delegates mere days earlier), and his appointment of mediators to deal with the curia, were probably the factors that prompted Benedict XII to send his close associate Arnaud Verdale as an envoy to Ludwig shortly afterwards, perhaps bearing a copy of the Fieschi Letter. Ludwig of Bavaria was still in Koblenz on 6 September, when he appointed Edward II's nephew Duke John III of Brabant as an imperial vicar as well. On this day the emperor was still negotiating with Edward III about their alliance, and Edward promised to pay him the remaining 320,000 gulders of the 400,000 he owed him in two instalments in early 1339. Ludwig must therefore have come to hear of William the Welshman and his claim to be Edward II. The ruler of Koblenz, Balduin of Luxembourg, the powerful and nobly-born archbishop-elector of Trier, and the ruler of Cologne from where William was brought to Koblenz by Francesco the Lombard, the archbishop-elector Walram von Jülich, surely also came to hear about William. If the emperor read the Fieschi Letter some months later when he met Arnaud Verdale, he and the two archbishops must have been most interested in Edward II's alleged afterlife, and they may previously have been aware of the situation given that Edward supposedly passed through Cologne and probably Koblenz in *c.* 1331/32 as well. The emperor, overlord of much of Italy and the Low Countries as well as Germany, had the ability to check the veracity of the story with people on the ground if he wished to do so. At least four of the seven electors – the three archbishops and the count palatine of the Rhine – ruled territories which would have been crossed by Edward of Caernarfon in the travels the Fieschi Letter claims he took through Europe, and perhaps the Count of Tyrol as well.

William the Welshman had previously been in Cologne, from where he was taken the 60 miles to Koblenz by Francesco the Lombard. This journey would have taken at least two days, so William must have arrived in Cologne by early September 1338 at the latest. If we can put together the appearance of William the Welshman with the details of Edward II's movements as described by the Fieschi Letter, Edward must have travelled 550 or more miles from the hermitage of Sant'Alberto in northern Italy to Cologne, a journey which required a good few weeks. How did Edward II, if it really was he, know so early that his son would be in the vicinity of Cologne or Koblenz in late August or early September 1338, and travel there in time to meet him? Edward III had asked Parliament in February 1338 to support his visiting the Low Countries, and on the 24th of that month gave orders for his fleet to assemble and to be ready to sail from Orwell in May, though in the end did not leave until 16 July 1338.[16] Although the king had been attempting to build relations with Ludwig since 1335, and in 1336 and 1337 those attempts intensified, Edward III could not have known that he would meet Ludwig in Koblenz in early September 1338 until mere days before he did.[17]

It is extremely improbable that Edward of Caernarfon would just happen to be in the same part of Germany as his son and at the same time by chance. He must have travelled there, or been taken there, specifically in the hope of seeing his son, and the news of Edward III's wish to visit Germany and the emperor must have reached Edward II or those who controlled him in Italy some months previously in order for Edward and his guards or guardians (or whatever they were) to reach western Germany in time. Luckily, it was late summer and thus the Alpine passes could surely be crossed without too much difficulty, or perhaps Edward was taken by ship from the port of Genoa to Marseille or Nice in the south of France and from there by land to Cologne. Ian Mortimer thinks that Edward was taken by a Fieschi galley from Italy to Britain then to Germany, and so was coming from the south to Cologne, not from the north. This is also a lengthy journey which would have taken months, but it is perhaps interesting that Cologne is north of Koblenz, which might suggest that Edward was travelling south rather than north and thus arrived in Cologne before he came to Koblenz.[18] On the other hand, travelling north by land from Italy to Germany in late summer, when there must have been numerous pilgrims from northern Europe who had been visiting Rome and other sites making the journey home, perhaps makes more sense. The difficulty would lie in co-ordinating Edward of Caernarfon's return to Germany with his son's visit there, months in advance, and Edward III set off from England in mid–July 1338 almost two months after he had originally planned to do so. The king passed through Cologne on 23 and 24 August, the city where William the Welshman was 'arrested' probably only a few days later, but William apparently did not attempt to see Edward III on this occasion or make his claim to be his father. This may simply be because William had not yet arrived in the city, and thus missed Edward III there by some days.

Edward III had originally intended to make a high–profile journey from Antwerp to Cologne and ordered special robes made for this journey for himself and the noblemen accompanying him, before he was forced to change his plans and travelled directly and hastily to Koblenz with only a few attendants. Ian Mortimer has suggested that this may be significant and may demonstrate that there had been prior communication, allowing William or his keepers to know where the English king would be and on what date.[19] We might also consider the possibility that William's appearance in Koblenz in early September 1338 at the time when Edward III was meeting the emperor was not a coincidence but was done deliberately so that William could be shown to Ludwig and other powerful figures. This is only speculation, but there is a very good chance that men such as Balduin of Luxembourg and Walram von Jülich already knew of the existence of the man who was either a very convincing impostor or who really was Edward II.

Edward III perhaps wished to present William/Edward II to the emperor and the electors, presumably in private rather than at the session of the *Reichstag* which he attended, in order to demonstrate to them that the man was under his control rather than the pope's or anyone else's, and that the emperor had no need to worry about the pretender trying to reclaim the English throne and thus no need to worry about making an alliance with him against France. Whoever had been guarding or looking after Edward II in the previous few years, in September/October 1338 he, as William the Welshman, was under Edward III's control at least temporarily, as the two entries in the royal account book make clear. If Edward III's aim was simply to see the impostor in order to ascertain his identity (or even just to have members of his household look at him for the same purpose), he could have done this anywhere and at any time, and it seems odd that he had William brought to Koblenz at exactly the time when he was taking part in probably the most important and far-reaching negotiations of his entire fifty-year reign. It would have been hugely risky and also foolish to have an impostor brought to a town ruled by the powerful politician and archbishop-elector Balduin, when almost all the great men of the Holy Roman Empire were present, if he wanted to keep the impostor's existence secret. This whole curious situation of a seemingly plausible impostor who had, or least could pretend to have, a strong claim to the English throne could have caused the emperor and the electors to rethink and even abandon the whole alliance with England.[20] Edward III was many things but he was not foolish, and it is therefore hard to imagine that he did not know what he was doing, and likely that he had William the Welshman brought to Koblenz at this time deliberately. On 15 September 1338, ten days after the ceremony at the *Kastorkirche*, Emperor Ludwig officially recognised Edward III's claim to the throne of France.[21] Just two days before this, on the 13th, Pope Benedict XII in Avignon appointed Arnaud Verdale (in whose cartulary the Fieschi Letter was discovered centuries later) as his envoy to Ludwig with a mission of reconciling the pope and the emperor and attempting to prevent imperial involvement in the war between England and France. This strongly suggests that Benedict had already heard about the events in Koblenz a few days before, events which had the potential to change the shape of Europe.

William the Welshman was not punished for claiming to be the King of England's father, at least not that we know of; if he was executed or imprisoned in Koblenz in the autumn of 1338, no record of this has yet been found. Royal pretenders of this era were often executed, however. In July 1318, Edward II himself met a man named John of Powderham, who claimed that he and not the king was the real son of Edward I. Powderham was hanged shortly afterwards. A woman from Lübeck, Germany who claimed to be Margaret 'the Maid' of Norway, young Queen of Scotland in her own right, cousin and first fiancée of Edward of Caernarfon in 1289–90, was burned alive in 1300 in Norway on the orders of Margaret's uncle King Haakon V, and is known to history as 'False Margaret' (the real Margaret died at the age of 7 in 1290 before she and Edward could marry).[22] On the other hand, just before he and Isabella left England for an extended visit to France in May 1313, Edward II met a man named Richard de Neueby or Newby, who said he was from Gascony — though this is an oddly English name for a Gascon — and that he was Edward's brother. Far from having him executed as an impostor, Edward gave his 'brother' a generous gift of £13.[23] Either Edward was distracted by his impending departure from his kingdom (he sailed from Dover the next day) and had no mind to deal with the impostor, or he thought that Newby was insane and not worth the bother of dealing with, or he simply laughed at him, or Newby convinced him that he was an illegitimate son of Edward I and thus truly his half-brother; it is not clear. Newby is never heard of again. This rather peculiar situation does show that royal pretenders were not inevitably executed, and according to one chronicle Edward II had even been unwilling at first to execute the impostor John of Powderham in 1318, preferring the idea of making him his court jester. Edward III's biographer Mark Ormrod believes that the king treated William the Welshman as 'a deluded simpleton.'[24] There is no real reason to assume that Edward III was in any way threatened by the appearance of the man who said that he was his father, but it is rather hard to understand why the king paid expenses for three weeks for a man he considered a deluded simpleton rather than sending him packing. Some of Edward III's actions in the 1330s, trying desperately to track down Thomas Gurney, sending his closest friend William Montacute to meet John Maltravers and meeting William the Welshman, might imply that he was unsure whether his father had really died in 1327, and if he had not, that the king wished to learn his present location.

Returning now to the Fieschi Letter, academic opinion of it has varied.[25] Roy Martin Haines thinks it was a forgery written by an unknown Genoese person with Manuele Fieschi's name attached to it to give it more plausibility, and was intended to promote the cause of Edward II's canonisation, i.e. being made a saint, by claiming that he lived a pious prayerful life in Italy as a means of expiating his sins and the disaster of his reign.[26] The letter does not in fact come close to fitting the contemporary template of promoted canonisations. This would have required a claim that miracles were being performed at Berkeley Castle or St Peter's Abbey in Gloucester, the sites of Edward's death and burial, and would also require holy relics for pilgrims to visit and pray to, such as the late king's bones or a part of his body. This was how Thomas of Lancaster's brother Henry and their cousin Edmund of Woodstock, Earl of Kent, attempted to promote Thomas's sainthood in the late 1320s, not with a peculiar story that Thomas had in fact survived his execution and moved to another country. The Fieschi Letter does not even say that Edward II was dead at the time that it was written, and precisely how a letter stating that to all extents and purposes the former King of England was still alive in Italy was intended to promote his sainthood is unclear. Only dead men (or women) could be canonised. According to the letter, Edward II had committed murder – the killing of the innocent sleeping porter at Berkeley Castle before his escape – which makes it even more unlikely that it was intended to push him as a candidate for sainthood.

Paul Doherty thinks that the letter was a clever forgery and a piece of blackmail intended to embarrass Edward III and stir up unhappy memories of his mother Isabella's actions during his minority, and for Manuele Fieschi to wheedle favours out of the king.[27] As noted above, it is absurd to imagine that a man such as Manuele Fieschi would need to blackmail anyone for favours, and blackmail could only possibly work if Edward III knew or suspected that his father was not really dead. Otherwise he would have laughed at the gullible Italian lawyer bringing silly stories to him and ignored him (as perhaps he did; we have no evidence of his reaction to the Fieschi Letter, assuming he ever knew about it). The chronicle of Geoffrey le Baker and one version of the French *Brut*, which claim that Edward nobly and patiently suffered the abuse of the malicious 'satraps of Satan' who had him in their keeping and who performed miracles at Gloucester, are a far better example of how candidates for sainthood were promoted in the fourteenth century than the Fieschi Letter.

Ian Mortimer thinks the letter was genuine and that Edward II was in the custody of Cardinal Luca Fieschi's relatives in Italy, and that it was intended to make Edward III pay off outstanding debts to Genoese merchants. Edward III did indeed pay the 1321 debts of Hugh Despenser the Younger to various merchants of the port city in July 1336.[28] Seymour Phillips says 'there is little doubt that Manuel Fieschi did meet someone who either claimed to be or thought that he was Edward II' and that the Fieschi Letter is 'almost certainly genuine', but ultimately finds the story it tells 'superficially plausible, but ultimately unbelievable'. He suggests that 'Edward II' was an impostor so seemingly credible that he was causing embarrassment to the Church and even to Edward III's legitimacy as king, and so was sent to two places in Italy under the control of the Fieschi family in Italy whose discretion could be counted on and until it could be decided what should be done with him.[29] Andy King notes that the letter is 'certainly puzzling' but that 'in the total absence of any supporting evidence, it cannot be taken as proof of Edward's survival'.[30] This is correct; there is, to date, no direct corroborating evidence that what the Fieschi Letter says is true.

The curious appearance of William le Galeys in Koblenz in the autumn of 1338 is the last reference to Edward II, assuming that it really was he, in any document discovered so far. What became of him after meeting his son is unknown: perhaps he was taken back to Italy by his guardians acting for the Fieschi and Malaspina families, perhaps his son took over his custody, or perhaps he was even murdered and his body disposed of somewhere, if it was thought that he was no longer of use. His kinsman Cardinal Luca Fieschi, who may have taken an interest in his welfare and been his protector, had died in Avignon in early 1336. With Luca gone, it is possible that his Fieschi and Malaspina nephews were no longer interested in the former king, especially if it had become clear that Edward III would not allow himself to be blackmailed by them by their custody of his father; or perhaps they saw him as a useful weapon to continue to hold over his son the present king and therefore did take him back to Italy. Until such time as further evidence comes to light, if it ever does, Edward II's continued existence past the autumn of 1338 can only remain a matter for speculation. Although the hermitage of Sant'Alberto di Butrio in Lombardy has, for a few decades, presented an empty tomb there as Edward II's resting place, we do not know if he returned there after meeting his son in Germany. If the tomb in St Peter's Abbey, Gloucester, now Gloucester Cathedral, which has been assumed to be Edward II's for 700 years, does not in fact contain the king's body but someone else's, we do not know who that person is, or where King Edward II really lies.

There are some other possible pieces of evidence, though only speculative, about the date of Edward II's death, and Ian Mortimer suggests that Edward in fact died in late 1341 or early 1342 when he would have been 57.[31] Edward III gave his eldest son and heir Edward of Woodstock the title of Prince of Wales, and the lands that came with it, on 12 May 1343, a month before the boy's 13th birthday. Mortimer has suggested that this was because Edward III had only fairly recently heard that his father had finally died, in late 1341 or early 1342, and at the next session of Parliament finally made his son Prince of Wales, the one title Edward II had never given up to his son. Edward II made the future Edward III Earl of Chester just after he was born in November 1312, Duke of Aquitaine and Count of Ponthieu in September 1325, and conceded his titles of King of England and Lord of Ireland to him in January 1327. The argument goes that the only title he still held but never gave to his son was Prince of Wales, and thus, Edward III could never give it to his own son until he knew that his father was dead. This is possible, though there are other potential reasons for Edward III's delay. He may have thought that his son was too young to receive and hold such a massive landed endowment until he was almost 13, and Edward III himself had never been Prince of Wales, perhaps also because Edward II thought he was too young; the last time father and son (officially) met each other was in September 1325, when the future Edward III was still only 12, and it may be that Edward II intended to give him the title when he returned from France later that year or the following year.

It should also be noted that Edward II never called himself Prince of Wales again after he succeeded to the throne in July 1307; his official address was 'Edward by the grace of God King of England, Lord of Ireland and Duke of Aquitaine'. Occasionally, when he was dealing with business in his northern French county of Ponthieu, he appended the title 'Count of Ponthieu and Montreuil' to his other titles, but did not do so otherwise, and never again used the name Prince of Wales even with dealing with issues in the principality. It is therefore debatable whether either Edward II or Edward III thought that Edward II, in his 'afterlife' post-1327, was in fact still Prince of Wales or whether only the heir to the throne could hold the title (as has been the case ever since) and automatically gave it up on becoming king. The man who appeared in Cologne and Koblenz in September 1338, William le Galeys or 'the Welshman', if this really was Edward II, may simply have chosen the name because Edward was born in Caernarfon, not because he was still believed to be Prince of Wales.

Isabella of France, the dowager Queen of England, knew by 22 October 1341 that her husband was dead, when she petitioned for two chaplains to say divine service daily in the chapel of Leeds Castle, Kent for herself and her son Edward III and for their souls after death, and for the souls of Edward II and their late second son John of Eltham, Earl of Cornwall.[32] Isabella would hardly have done this had she not been sure that her husband was then dead. It may be interesting, however, that in the fourteen years since Edward's alleged death, she had not had prayers said for his soul (at least, not that we have a record of), but did so regularly from the early 1340s onwards. Edward III made a pilgrimage to his father's tomb in Gloucester, the first time he had done so, in March 1343. Ian Mortimer has speculated that the purpose of Niccolino Fieschi's visit to Edward III's court in November 1341 was to inform the king of his father's death.[33] But if Edward II did not die in September 1327, we have no real way of knowing when and where he did, or where he was buried if his body was not placed in the tomb at St Peter's Abbey in Gloucester. The mystery remains.

PART IV

ARGUMENTS FOR AND AGAINST EDWARD II'S MURDER AND SURVIVAL

IS IT PLAUSIBLE THAT EDWARD WAS KILLED WITH A RED-HOT POKER?

The usual argument for the use of this method is that Edward's murderers could kill him without leaving an obvious mark on his body, so that nobody would know or guess that he had been murdered and his sudden death could be passed off as natural. This is contradicted by the statement in Geoffrey le Baker's chronicle that the inhabitants of nearby Berkeley village heard Edward's screams: one does not kill a man in a deliberately internal manner to disguise the fact of his murder and at the same time inflict such agony on him that people can hear his screams and know that he is being murdered. And if a man died in such terrible pain that he screamed loudly, the agony might be easily visible on his face after death, and would thus seem to defeat the whole object.

Another modern assumption, one which is not found in any fourteenth-century source, is that Edward was killed by having a poker inserted inside his anus because he had been the passive partner in sexual acts with men, therefore was 'penetrated' by the poker as punishment for allowing his male lovers to penetrate him. Ian Mortimer has referred to this story as the 'anal rape' narrative of Edward's death.[1] We do not, of course, know that he ever was the passive partner in sexual acts with men, and it seems doubtful that his alleged murderers knew whether or not he was, either. There is sometimes a tendency in the twenty-first century to portray Edward as a martyr of his sexuality, to state that he and his lovers were killed because of the homophobia of their enemies. If Edward had been a competent king who had won military victories in Scotland and France, if he had been more balanced with his favour and patronage, if he had been a stronger ruler who did not let himself be swayed by the biased opinions of those close to him, and so on, his male lovers (assuming they were his lovers) would not in fact have been such an issue. Stating or assuming that Edward was the victim of homophobia or some kind of hate crime, or of the jealousy of his wife because she was unable to deal with his love for men, is far too simplistic. Isabella did tolerate the presence of Edward's male favourites without complaint for many years, and it was only when Hugh Despenser the Younger's influence grew so great that her position as Edward's wife and queen was undermined that she moved into opposition to Despenser and by extension her husband. The idea that Edward was killed by a poker as an act of revenge by his wife or as punishment for his sexual acts by homophobic haters is simply a modern invention.

In the 1990s, one writer suggested ingeniously that the chronicler Adam Murimuth's statement that Edward was 'killed by a trick', *per cautelam occisus*, might have been misinterpreted by later writers as *per cauterem occisus*, 'killed by a branding-iron'.[2] Murimuth's word *cautela(m)* for 'trickery' is most unusual in this context and more usually means 'caution', and might easily have been misunderstood by later writers as *cauter(em)*, a far more common word and the origin of modern English 'cauterise'.[3] It is unclear exactly how the poker method would kill someone, and it might have taken several days for the subject to die of shock or infection or peritonitis. Then again, the stress and agony might have caused a heart attack, or the massive internal damage might have killed him quickly. The point is that Edward's murderers would not and could not have known how quickly this method would kill Edward, or even if it would at all. There seems no reason why they would have experimented with such a pointlessly sadistic method when far easier methods were at hand, and experienced soldiers such as Thomas Gurney would have known how to kill men efficiently. Suffocation or smothering, for example, would have had few visible signs – possibly congestion, slight bruising or petechial haemorrhages, which could easily be covered up – or they could simply have given him sedatives strong enough that he would never wake up or enough that he would not struggle when he was suffocated or strangled or smothered or crushed or pushed downstairs or another method which would be vastly easier and faster than a red-hot poker. Roger Mortimer had escaped from the Tower of London on 1 August 1323 by feeding his guards sedatives in their wine (the constable of the Tower was still ill from the after-effects a few days later), so he obviously knew how to procure them. Geoffrey le Baker's description of the weight of fifteen men being used to hold Edward down before using the red-hot poker on him is absurd; if Edward's murderers had the weight of fifteen men they could simply have smothered him to death without needing a poker at all. As well as the agony on his face, the red-hot poker method would probably have left a foul smell which would have been difficult to disguise, even if the body was washed. The abbots, burgesses and knights who saw Edward's body 'superficially', according to Adam Murimuth, could hardly have failed to notice a strong and vile smell.

SURELY CHRONICLERS COULDN'T HAVE MADE UP SUCH A BIZARRE STORY ABOUT A RED-HOT POKER OUT OF NOTHING, THEREFORE IT MUST HAVE SOME TRUTH TO IT?

One idea, found sometimes online and in an episode of the TV show *Medieval Murder Mysteries* which focused on Edward II's death, is that the story of the red-hot poker is too ridiculous, bizarre and implausible to have been made up, and therefore must have some truth to it.[4] This is a peculiar argument: people make up bizarre untrue stories all the time, or we wouldn't have such a thing as novels. It is somewhat akin to claiming that the popular tales about a boy who learns that he is a wizard and plays Quidditch on a broomstick and fights Dementors and Voldemort are too ridiculous to be invented, and that therefore Joanne Rowling was not making up entertaining fiction about a youth named Harry Potter but narrating his true life story. Simply because something sounds weird and implausible does not point to its truth; there is nothing so strange that a person could not invent it. To assume otherwise is a logical fallacy. Fourteenth-century chroniclers were the tabloid newspaper writers of their day, and just as we would not (or at least should not) automatically believe everything we read in *The Sun* or *Daily Mail*, we should not take everything chroniclers say as gospel truth. Besides, they most probably did not make up the poker story out of nothing. In and after the twelfth century, rumours circulated that the real cause of the sudden and rather mysterious death of Edmund Ironside, who was briefly King of England in 1016 and who was only in his 20s when he died, was a spear through the anus while he was using the privy. These rumours were certainly still around in the late thirteenth century and probably in the fourteenth. Duke Godfrey IV of Lower Lorraine was also said to have been murdered this way in 1076.[5] During the Battle of Boroughbridge on 16 March 1322, Edward II's brother-in-law Humphrey de Bohun, Earl of Hereford, died a horrible death when he was skewered in the anus with a pike by a man under the bridge. There was therefore some precedent for the idea of a man being killed by a skewer or pike or metal implement in the anus, and the chroniclers who give this as the cause of Edward II's death did not make it up out of thin air. It is also unfortunately the case that lurid tales of torture stick in the mind far more easily than more prosaic means of death, and perhaps the poker narrative represents a general willingness to believe a more gruesome story in preference to a far less 'interesting' narrative of suffocation or strangling or poisoning. If Edward II died at Berkeley Castle, however, it is vastly more likely to have been via one of these methods. It is even possible, though perhaps rather improbable, that Edward died of illness, or perhaps suicide. He had lost everything, his crown, his freedom, his family and his beloved Hugh Despenser, and it would not be too surprising if, in the depths of despair, he decided to take his own life. The cause of Edward's death at Berkeley Castle, if he died there, can never be known for sure, but there are very good reasons for rejecting the tale of the red-hot poker.

EDWARD MUST HAVE BEEN KILLED, BECAUSE DEPOSED KINGS ALWAYS WERE, AS THEY THREATENED THE POSITION OF THEIR SUCCESSORS

It is often assumed that Roger Mortimer and perhaps Queen Isabella as well had Edward II killed in order to safeguard their position and her son's. Edward's continued survival was a threat, especially given the plots to free him in 1327: Edward, once freed, might try to reclaim his throne, which imperilled his son and his own occupation of it; and if he could become king again he would have Mortimer grotesquely executed and Isabella imprisoned, and probably try to have his marriage to her annulled. The pair certainly did have a seemingly strong motive to kill him, or at least what we 700 years later perceive as a motive, though an assumed motive is not evidence. Edmund of Woodstock, Earl of Kent, knew Isabella (his sister-in-law and first cousin) and Roger Mortimer extremely well, as did Archbishop William Melton and others, and evidently they thought the pair had not had Edward killed.

The idea goes that deposed kings were a threat to their successors, and therefore were always murdered. It is certainly true that Richard II was murdered by his first cousin and usurper Henry IV (both of them grandsons of Edward III) at Pontefract Castle, Yorkshire in 1400, and that Henry VI was killed in the Tower of London on the orders of his rather more distant cousin Edward IV in 1471. Edward IV's son Edward V is also often presumed to have been killed in or soon after 1483 by his uncle Richard III, or by the victor of Bosworth Field, Henry VII, or by someone acting on behalf of one of these men. At any rate, the three later deposed kings of medieval England lost their freedom and subsequently their lives after their depositions at the behest of those who replaced them in power, as did Charles I in 1649 when he was executed after losing the civil war. Therefore, it has seemed inevitable to many commentators that Edward II must also have been murdered by the people who pushed through his forced abdication; not by his son Edward III, who was no patricide, but by Roger Mortimer and his allies, perhaps including Edward's wife Isabella. And there is certainly plenty of evidence that the majority of his contemporaries believed that Edward died at Berkeley Castle in September 1327.

However, Edward II's deposition was a new and revolutionary act in England, a fact we must not lose sight of in the knowledge that it later became reasonably common. People in 1327 did not yet have a concept that deposed kings must be murdered in order to safeguard the position of their successors, and Edward II's deposition was unique in that he was succeeded as king by his son, which none of the other three deposed kings of the Middle Ages were. Edward's son, whatever he might have thought of his father and his disastrous reign, would not simply allow the murder of his royally born parent to go unpunished. Henry IV and Edward IV could have their predecessors Richard II and

Henry VI killed with considerably more impunity, as the deposed kings had no surviving royal children who one day would have the power to avenge them and punish those who had killed them. Edward II's supposed murderer was not his successor, but a nobleman who had no claim to the throne himself nor any prospect that a child of his might succeed to the throne, and whose political influence and position at court depended entirely on his personal relationship with the young king's mother.[6] Roger Mortimer must have realised that one day in the not-too-distant future Edward III would come of age and take over the rule of his own kingdom, on which day Mortimer would be edged out of power whether he had had Edward II killed or not. He therefore had considerably less motive to kill the former king than Henry IV or Edward IV, who needed to secure their own position, and that of their sons, on the throne.

DID EDWARD DIE AT ALL IN 1327?

One of the biggest arguments in favour of Edward's death in 1327 is that no chronicler of the age so much as hinted that they believed he did not die at Berkeley Castle. The *Annales Paulini* and the *Brut* note the widespread belief that he was still alive in 1329–30 but do not suggest that they themselves believed this was the case; Lanercost notes that a friar told the Earl of Kent that he had raised a demon who told him Edward was alive, but calls it lies; Geoffrey le Baker calls this whole idea a fantasy. Apparently not one of them had ever heard any evidence which convinced them that Edward truly had survived; not one of them heard of the Fieschi Letter or William Melton's letter to the mayor of London or William le Galeys; not one of these is mentioned by any chronicler. Nor did the execution of the Earl of Kent in 1330 convince them that Edward II was truly alive then. The idea that Edward died at Berkeley was never questioned at all until the late nineteenth century, five and a half centuries later, when the Fieschi Letter was discovered in an archive in France in 1877. Edward's family (with, of course, the exception of his half-brother the Earl of Kent) also behaved as though they believed he had died in 1327, by keeping the anniversary of his death on 21 September and so on. With the exception of those mentioned above, chroniclers had never heard any story other than Edward's death in September 1327, and the notion that Edward II died then came from seemingly the most reliable and authoritative source there possibly could be: his son the king. Edward III stated in late 1330 that Edward II had been murdered, and kept the anniversary of his death every year. Yet Edward III immediately began disseminating news in September 1327 that his father had died before he could possibly have checked that it was true, and his only source was Lord Berkeley's letter brought to him by Thomas Gurney (who probably also told the young king more details by mouth). Three years later, Lord Berkeley came before Parliament and stated that he had not heard of Edward II's death until this Parliament, and in the early 1330s Edward III pursued Gurney relentlessly in Spain and Italy and wanted him brought back to England alive rather than have him summarily executed in southern Europe – Gurney was under sentence of death for regicide, after all – as he was desperate to question him or hear his confession.

BUT WHAT WOULD BE THE POINT OF KEEPING EDWARD ALIVE? HIS ENEMIES, ESPECIALLY ROGER MORTIMER, HAD NO GOOD REASON TO KEEP EDWARD ALIVE AND EVERY REASON TO KILL HIM

If Edward II was not murdered in September 1327, but his death was reported to his son the young king, it is likely that there was a deliberate plan to keep him alive but to pretend publicly that he was dead. This was, presumably, done by Roger Mortimer and Queen Isabella, perhaps because Isabella did not wish for her husband's death, or because they both feared the consequences when Isabella's son came of age and decided to punish those responsible for his father's murder. On the other hand, the three or four, perhaps even more, plots to free Edward in 1327 and the risk that he would be released from captivity was a great risk to the pair, as noted above. Pretending that Edward was dead gave them the benefits of killing him without having to do so, without having to commit regicide and, in Isabella's case, mariticide (the murder of one's husband). The announcement of Edward II's death in September 1327 did indeed put an abrupt end to the plots to free him, until news of his survival began to seep out in late 1328 and 1329.

The idea that Roger Mortimer and his allies had little choice but to kill Edward in 1327 is, as noted above, based on the assumption that deposed kings must always have been killed because the later medieval deposed Kings of England were. If, however, Edward II could be kept alive in a secret location months and even years after his supposed death had been publicly announced, under the guard of a handful of men closely associated with and trusted by Roger Mortimer, the threat of his release and possible restoration to the throne was averted without committing regicide. Roger Mortimer was charged with the murder of Edward II in November 1330, and until the twenty-first century few historians thought to question whether he was truly guilty of this crime or not. Perhaps Edward III, in September 1327 – when he was still not even 15 years old and little more than a child – was tricked into believing that his father was dead, and having made the news public and attended his father's funeral, could hardly admit later that he was wrong and that Edward II was alive after all. After he began to rule his own kingdom in October 1330, it suited the young king's purposes to pretend that his father was dead as much as it had suited his mother and Mortimer, and for the same reasons: there would be no more plots to free his father, no attempts to help him regain his throne, no threat of civil war as father and son fought over the rightful ownership of the throne.

Given Edward II's disastrous reign, there cannot have been many people who would genuinely prefer him as king over the son who showed vastly more promise as a ruler, but loyalty to a king died hard, and there would certainly be people uncomfortable with Edward II's forced deposition who felt that he should be the rightful ruler of England as long as he lived. Even in January 1327, after the astonishing success of Queen Isabella's invasion and when Edward II's power base had collapsed, there were still many at the London Parliament unenthusiastic about his deposition, and events of that year showed that he still had many supporters. Meanwhile, Edward III would always have enemies, who would be only too glad to hold the return of his father over his head as leverage. Therefore it was entirely in Edward III's own interests to continue to state in public that his father was dead, whether he was or not, and the execution of Roger Mortimer reinforced this idea in people's minds. Edward III, furious that his mother's favourite had exercised royal power to which he had no right, was always going to execute Mortimer; the king issued thirteen other charges against him in November 1330, so may have thought that the murder of Edward II might as well be added to the long list. Arrest warrants for Thomas Gurney and William Ockley, also convicted of Edward's murder at this time, were not issued until 3 December, four days after Mortimer's execution and a week after Parliament began. It hardly seems that Edward III was in any desperate hurry to have them found and captured.

If there really was a plot in and after 1327 to keep Edward II alive secretly but to tell the world that he was dead, the question as to who knew of the plot arises, and how much of it they knew. The plan would require only a small number of people; everyone else would believe that Edward truly was dead. Thomas, Lord Berkeley's words to Parliament in November 1330 suggest that he knew Edward had not been killed in his castle in September 1327, but had no idea what had befallen Edward after he left Berkeley Castle; in other words, it is likely that members of the plot were told only a small part of it, only what they had to know. After 1330, Thomas Berkeley remained in England and at liberty for the remaining thirty-one years of his life, but in 1331/33 Edward III still wanted desperately to talk to Sir Thomas Gurney and to take down his written confession 'concerning the sedition and conspiracy [to kill Edward II] aforesaid and the assent, instigation and procuration made concerning it, and by whom and in what manner they were made'. The young king also sent his closest friend and ally William Montacute to the Continent to talk to John Maltravers in 1334, as Maltravers 'was desirous to reveal to him many things concerning his honour and the estate and well-being of his realm'. It seems as though Edward III thought Gurney and Maltravers had information regarding the death or otherwise of his father which

Thomas Berkeley did not have. William Ockley, the man-at-arms, disappeared in late 1330 and was never heard of again; if Edward III made any attempts to find him, they are not recorded. Perhaps the king assumed Ockley would be unable to answer any questions about what really happened to Edward II in 1327 and let him go, or perhaps he was even secretly killed by the king's agents.

There are still numerous questions which cannot be answered. If Edward II was deliberately kept alive, was Queen Isabella aware of it, and was it done by her instigation because she could not tolerate the murder of her husband and lord? When did Edward III find out that his father was not dead? Did Edward II's younger children John, Eleanor and Joan ever know that he was not dead, or his sisters Margaret and Mary, or his niece Eleanor Despenser? Margaret's son Duke John III of Brabant allowed the Earl of Kent to meet his adherents in his Paris chamber in 1329, which might imply that he and his mother believed in Edward's survival, but we cannot know for sure. There is also the question of the Fieschi Letter's statement that Edward had an unnamed guardian at Berkeley Castle who helped him escape and who travelled with him to Corfe Castle and then to Ireland, but who then vanishes from the story. His identity is unknown. According to the Fieschi Letter, Edward of Caernarfon met Pope John XXII and presumably Manuele Fieschi himself at Avignon, and if we take this as true, it seems likely that Manuele's and Edward's kinsman Cardinal Luca Fieschi took over responsibility for him via his relatives and associates.

WAS ISABELLA OF FRANCE RESPONSIBLE FOR THE MURDER OF HER HUSBAND?

For centuries, Isabella of France has had a dire reputation as a 'she-wolf' because of the assumption that she committed adultery with her husband's enemy and had her husband killed, or at the very least stood by in silence and allowed her lover to kill him, and continued living with him for years in the full knowledge of what he had done. It is often assumed that Isabella and Edward II's relationship was an unhappy, tragic disaster for many years, which it was not, and that Isabella hated Edward and felt repulsed by him, which she did not. Even weeks after her invasion force landed in England in 1326, there is evidence that she was trying to reconcile with Edward and begged him to forgive her, and there is every reason to suppose that Isabella sought the downfall of Hugh Despenser the Younger, a man she detested and feared, but not of her husband. There is no reason whatsoever, except hindsight, to think that she was at all involved with Roger Mortimer's escape in 1323 or was aiding him in any way before his escape or afterwards; no reason to think that she and Mortimer fell into a passionately sexual affair in late 1325 or 1326, which is modern romanticising; no reason whatsoever to think that Isabella ever hated or despised Edward or wished him dead. Isabella herself declared in late 1325 and again in early 1326 that she wished to return to Edward but dared not because of her fear of Hugh Despenser, and she behaved at all times like a woman who wished to resume her married life without the interference of a third party, not like a woman desperate for revenge on the husband she hated.[7]

On the other hand, the Fieschi Letter states that Isabella and Roger Mortimer sent two men, Thomas Gurney and Simon Bereford, to kill Edward, and that she would have been so angry that they had failed to do so that they sent her a fake heart claiming that it was Edward's. According to the Fieschi Letter, Isabella did think that her husband was dead. Edward III never accused his mother of any complicity in his father's death, and although this may mean that either he did not think his father had been murdered or that Isabella had anything to do with it, there were also political reasons for the king's actions. Edward III claimed the throne of France via Isabella, and to imprison or punish her for involvement in the murder of his father might jeopardise that claim. There were probably also sound psychological reasons for Edward not to examine too closely the notion that his mother had been partly responsible for the death of his father. All in all, Edward III's reaction in and after 1330 was to forgive and forget the difficulties of his father's reign and his mother's regency, and he was not a vindictive man, as his later treatment of the Mortimer family (Roger Mortimer's great-grandson Edmund was married to the king's own granddaughter some decades later) demonstrates. The idea that Isabella wanted her husband dead is not borne out by any other reliable source, and may simply be the assumption of a man who never met her, Manuele Fieschi.

IS EDWARD II'S SURVIVAL PAST HIS 'DEATH' SIMPLY TOO IMPLAUSIBLE?

Edward's survival is often said by modern historians of the fourteenth century to be 'implausible' or 'unlikely' or even 'bizarre', which is not in itself an argument but an expression of the logical fallacy of personal incredulity. Implausible and bizarre things can and do happen. To take just one fairly random historical example, it is entirely implausible that Empress Matilda might escape from her cousin King Stephen's siege of Oxford Castle by dressing in white clothes and walking right through his army in the snow during their struggles over the English throne in the 1140s, but it happened. If an intelligent and astute archbishop believed in 1330 that his friend Edward II was alive and so strongly believed this that he started putting a plan into action to help him, it is not 'implausible' that he was indeed alive. If an English archbishop, an Italian bishop, an English earl and a Scottish earl and many hundreds of other men of all ranks right across England, Wales, Scotland and the Continent believed that Edward had survived past his alleged death and acted on this belief despite the threat of imprisonment, loss of lands and even execution, then commentators writing almost 700 years later are in no position to dismiss their belief as 'implausible' or 'bizarre'. It is still not automatically the case that their belief in Edward's survival is necessarily true, of course, and there were plenty of other important people in 1329–30 who seemingly did not share this belief, but it should not simply be dismissed out of hand.

IF EDWARD WAS ALIVE AFTER 1327, WHY DID HE NOT MAKE HIMSELF KNOWN PUBLICLY AND TRY TO RECLAIM HIS THRONE? HOW WOULD A FORMER KING BE ABLE TO LIVE AS A HERMIT?

Edward, if he truly was alive after 1327, never tried to claim his throne or even identify himself publicly as the former king (William le Galeys, 'arrested' in Cologne in September 1338, seems not to have made his assertion that he was Edward III's father publicly or to have done so with any ambition of regaining his throne). It is very easy to understand why the secret survival of a king for years in Italy is impossible for many people to understand or believe. Why would the former King of England, so used to power, wealth, good living and deference, choose to become a penniless hermit in Italy and not try to regain his throne or at least demand that his son keep him in the royal style to which he was accustomed? Even if we accept that Edward II was a most unconventional king who enjoyed the company of his common subjects and taking part in activities such as digging ditches, thatching roofs and metalwork, which makes it rather more plausible that he would be able to live on for years in a hermitage than it would be for almost any other King of England, it still seems a strange concept for many people. It is highly likely, however, that if Edward II was still alive, wandering around the Continent and spending years at two Italian hermitages in the 1330s, that he was not acting under his own agency but was under the control of others, specifically his distant kinsmen the Fieschi and Malaspina families. It can hardly be a coincidence that the two hermitages both lay in areas firmly under Fieschi/Malaspina control, and that the evidence we have which places Edward II in Italy in the 1330s was written by a Fieschi. Under this model, Edward did not have a choice: he spent almost the entire period from 1327 until 1338, with the possible exception of his journey from Ireland to Sandwich to Avignon in *c.* late 1330 and 1331, under the control of others.

The Supposed Survival of a King or Even of a Celebrity Past Their Death is a Common Cultural Event; Why is Edward II Any Different?

Critics of the idea that Edward II survived past 1327 often invoke other kings, royals or even celebrities thought by some to have lived past the date of their official death. Louis XVII of France (son of the guillotined Louis XVI and Marie Antoinette), who died at the age of 10 in 1795 after the French Revolution, was thought by some to have escaped; Edward II's great-grandson Richard II, murdered in 1400, was supposedly seen in Scotland a few years later. Anna Anderson or Franziska Schanzkowska claimed for much of the twentieth century to be Grand Duchess Anastasia Romanova, assassinated with her family in 1918 after the Russian Revolution; there were claims that Elvis Presley did not die in 1977. These have all been brought up as examples of some people's refusal to believe or accept that a king or a famous person can truly be dead. None of these later examples are relevant because the people in Europe in the late 1320s and 1330s who believed in Edward II's survival could not possibly have been influenced by the centuries-later claims that Louis XVII or Elvis Presley or Anastasia was still alive. We know that many people in England in 1329–30 did think that Edward II was alive because they were being arrested for saying so, and because several contemporary chroniclers commented that a large part of the population believed it. Mentioning Elvis Presley in this context is a rather cynical move, intended to be a statement on the ridiculousness of the concept that Edward II could have lived past 1327 without dealing with the rather inconvenient fact that many people of Edward's own era genuinely believed that he did. Simply because some people in the twentieth century wrongly believed, or wanted to believe, that one of the most famous men in the world did not die in 1977 has no bearing on Edward II's survival or otherwise.

Although people in England in the late 1320s could not possibly have known that some of their descendants 650 years later would believe they had seen a dead American singer after his death and that believing in the supposed afterlife of a famous dead person would become a cultural phenomenon, several other kings were said to have lived on after their deaths before and during Edward II's time. One of them was Edward's own nephew King John I of France, posthumous son of Edward's brother-in-law Louis X, who died when he was 5 days old in November 1316. John was said to have been secretly sent away to Italy and to have grown up there unaware of his real identity.[8] Emperor Heinrich V of Germany, who died in 1125, was believed by some of his subjects to have lived on after his death either in England (near Chester) or France, and a hermit in Burgundy years later claimed to be the late emperor. People had hated and feared Heinrich; the belief that he was alive seems to have been a fear that a despised tyrant was not dead and gone after all, but might come back to oppress and harm his people even more. There was also a legend in England that Harold Godwinson, the king killed at the Battle of Hastings in October 1066, was not dead in battle but merely sleeping and would return to England when his people needed him. This has nothing to do with a belief that a king had not truly died, but positions Godwinson as a heroic figure in the mould of King Arthur, a great warrior-king who would return at his kingdom's hour of need even if many centuries in the future. Edward II, who failed miserably as a war leader, emphatically does not fit this tradition, a dream of a conquered people. And although unpopular and an incompetent ruler, Edward was not harsh, brutal and tyrannical enough to be deeply feared by his people even years after his death, so the Heinrich V of Germany example does not fit him either. John I and Louis XVII of France were children when they died, so this is also a different tradition, perhaps an unwillingness to accept the death of a prominent, royally born child.

In his book *The Death of Kings*, Michael Evans has claimed that the Fieschi Letter detailing Edward II's later life in Italy 'fits too neatly into the folklore tradition'.[9] Other than the belief in Harold Godwinson's return to save his people in the manner of a superhero, there was no folklore tradition in England in the early fourteenth century regarding the survival of a king (and certainly not one as ineffectual and unpopular as Edward II), nor any reason to think that an Italian notary and future bishop had any reason to write to Edward III and promulgate this myth, if he had ever even heard of Godwinson or the supposed afterlife of the German ruler Heinrich V 200 years previously. It has also been claimed that 'it was a common occurrence in the late Middle Ages, after the violent death of a king, for the enemies of his successor to spread reports that he was still living'.[10] This is, as so often happens, looking at history backwards. Edward II was the first ever King of England to be deposed, and the only 'violent death' of a predecessor was William II Rufus in 1100 (unless one counts Richard I in 1199, dead of gangrene in France a few days after being struck with an arrow). No-one seems to have claimed that Rufus lived on after his accident in the New Forest or that Richard lived into the reign of his brother and successor John. There were, no doubt, people in the early 1400s who thought they could gain some kind of advantage by claiming that Richard II was still alive in the reign of his successor and murderer Henry IV, but this has no bearing on an Italian noble-man or an English archbishop in the 1330s committing their belief in Edward II's survival to letters.

The 'afterlives' of other kings such as Richard II of England, Heinrich V of Germany and John I and Louis XVII of France were not attested to by an archbishop, several bishops and earls, or other high-ranking and influential individuals. An archbishop did not write a letter ordering provisions for Heinrich V of Germany years after his death and stating that he was alive and in good health; a bishop did not write a long letter to his successor explaining in detail how he had survived; and a close member of his family was not executed for trying to free the supposedly dead former emperor from captivity. Even if we dismiss the Fieschi Letter as implausible and unreliable, we still have the Melton Letter, the Earl of Kent's execution, considerable evidence that Kent and Melton's followers were subject to legal process, the evidence of two near-contemporary chronicles which say that belief in Edward II's survival years after his death was widespread in England, and entries in the chancery rolls in 1330 ordering the arrest of anyone who stated publicly that Edward II was still alive. Whether we believe that Edward II was alive after 1327 or not, there is considerably more to the tale than 'folklore tradition'.

THE EARL OF KENT ONLY BELIEVED EDWARD WAS ALIVE IN 1329–30 BECAUSE HE WAS STUPID

The frequently alleged 'stupidity' and 'gullibility' of the Earl of Kent is a twentieth-century invention by historians trying to fit his belief in his brother's survival into their belief that Edward II was dead. It relies to a great extent on examining Kent's short life with the notion in mind that he was stupid and trying to make his career fit that supposed fact, which is nothing more than confirmation bias and cherry-picking, and relies on circular logic: Kent only believed his brother was alive because he was stupid, and we know he was stupid because he believed his brother was alive. In his article 'The Captivity and Death of Edward of Carnarvon', published in 1934, Professor T. F. Tout invented the notion of Kent's stupidity, and ever since, historians have indulged themselves in remarkably negative judgements about Kent: that he was 'gullible, inconsistent and foolish', 'stupid and unpopular', 'strangely credulous' and 'an unstable young man', that he 'demonstrated a predisposition for gullibility and inconsistency', that his 'stupidity and credulity make him a poor witness', that he was 'a famously stupid man', that 'no-one could have been more gullible than Kent' and that he was 'a weak character, easily duped and politically ineffectual'.[11] None of these writers cites any primary source for their assertions, which is not surprising, as there is none.

Besides his belief in Edward II's survival, the other central plank of the 'Kent was stupid' argument rests on his failure during the War of Saintt-Sardos in the autumn of 1324, when he was appointed Edward II's commander in Gascony and allowed Charles IV of France's uncle Charles de Valois to box him in at the town of Agen, whereupon he was forced to conclude a truce with Valois. As Ian Mortimer has pointed out, this is evidence of inexperience, not stupidity.[12] It is not 'stupid' for a man who had only just turned 23 and who had no experience of military command to be outmanoeuvred by a man thirty years his senior. It is also perhaps evidence of a certain naïveté on Kent's part in expecting that Charles de Valois, who was his own uncle as well as the King of France's – Valois was the older half-brother of Kent's mother Queen Marguerite – would not try to trick him, but it hardly seems evidence of the high level of gullibility ascribed to him by many modern writers. Besides, believing that one's brother is still alive if you have seen his face after death and been able to identify him would not be mere stupidity or naïveté, but would seem to point to some kind of mental impairment, which Kent's contemporaries would surely have noticed and commented on. They did not. It is reasonable to assume that Kent did not see his brother's face either during his funeral of 20 December 1327 or before, had no chance to identify him, and did not talk to anyone else who had seen him either. Edward II and his son Edward III both trusted Kent and often selected him for important military expeditions or sensitive diplomatic missions in preference to his older brother Thomas of Brotherton, Earl of Norfolk (who genuinely does seem to have been viewed by contemporaries as incompetent, untrustworthy and not very intelligent, and perhaps not without good reason).

Edmund, Earl of Kent is also condemned as inconstant and emotionally unstable for his changes of allegiance in the 1320s. He was loyal to his brother Edward II until late 1325 or early 1326, when he joined Queen Isabella and Roger Mortimer and took part in their invasion of England, perhaps hoping to gain the position at the king's side to which his high birth and rank entitled him. Kent seems to have desired the downfall of the Despensers rather than Edward himself, which may also have been the case for Queen Isabella until late 1326. Although Kent seemingly supported the new regime until he participated in the rebellion of his cousin the Earl of Lancaster in late 1328 (or at least, we have no evidence that he did not support it), this may have been done out of self-preservation rather than conviction, and thereafter he tried to free his dead half-brother and thus acted against his sister-in-law and first cousin Isabella. Kent's allegiances in fact make perfect sense in the context of Edward II's turbulent reign and its aftermath: loyal to Edward for many years until Edward's behaviour pushed him into opposition, opposition which Kent seems to have found difficult, as in 1326 he wrote to Edward explaining that his actions in allying with Isabella were not intended to be treasonable. When he came to hear, probably in 1328, that Edward was still alive, his natural loyalty to and affection for his brother once again came to the fore.[13]

Numerous people switched sides several times during the 1320s; it was a political necessity given the conflicts and turbulence of the era, and those who failed to do so at the right time frequently ended up dead or in prison or in exile. Other people whose career followed the same trajectory as Kent's, for example his kinsmen Henry, Lord Beaumont and Beaumont's sister Isabella, Lady Vescy, have been praised for their political shrewdness in changing sides at the right time and saving their careers and lands and even their lives, not condemned as erratic and unstable as the unfortunate Kent has been .[14] John de Warenne, Earl of Surrey, also remained loyal to Edward II until after the 1326 invasion and then switched his allegiance to Queen Isabella, and thus saved his life; he died in his early 60s in 1347 and avoided the tragic fate of his brother-in-law the Earl of Arundel, who suffered a slow and terrible death for remaining firmly loyal to Edward II after the invasion. Neither did any chronicler of the fourteenth century even vaguely imply that the Earl of Kent was or was believed to be stupid, gullible or erratic. Adam Murimuth says that he was not widely mourned after his death because of his household's rapacity, probably a reference to his allowing his followers to plunder far and wide after the 1326 invasion, but that is not at all the same thing as calling him stupid, gullible and unstable.[15] The idea that he was is simply the invention of modern historians unable otherwise to explain his belief in his half-brother's survival.

The tired old argument that the Earl of Kent was foolish and credulous and that this was the only reason why he came to believe that his half-brother Edward II was still alive in 1329–30 no longer holds water. Besides, it contradicts another argument often expressed in an attempt to make Kent's plot fit the traditional narrative that Edward II died in 1327: that Kent was a leader of the opposition to Queen Isabella and her favourite Roger Mortimer, and that the two therefore deliberately lured him into treason by pretending that Edward was alive, so that they had an excuse to execute him and thus protect their position as the de facto rulers of the country. The notion that Kent was a leader of the opposition, and so dangerous to Isabella and Mortimer and their continued political survival that they needed to manufacture an excuse to kill him, sits oddly with the notion that the earl was stupid, unstable and gullible. This contradiction appears in, for example, Professor May McKisack's magisterial 1959 work *The Fourteenth Century 1307–1399*, where she describes Kent as both 'foolish' and guilty of 'weakness' yet also 'dangerous' to Mortimer and Isabella.[16]

It is not entirely clear why Isabella and Mortimer would think that an unstable and foolish man could lead a political movement against them and remove them from power, or that men such as William Melton, Henry Beaumont and so on would follow him. If they thought that Kent might become a figurehead of the opposition despite his presumed lack of intelligence, being the son, brother and uncle of kings, then his older brother Thomas, Earl of Norfolk would have made an equally plausible target. Neither is it clear why they would think that the best way to neutralise Kent's supposed threat was to spread rumours across the country that Edward II had not died. Pretending that Edward was still alive was the last thing Mortimer and Isabella would have wanted to do. The idea that they did so contradicts the popular notion that they had Edward killed to put a stop to all the plots to free him from Berkeley Castle, which plots also put their continued political survival at risk. The announcement of Edward II's death in September 1327 did indeed put an abrupt stop to all the conspiracies to free Edward and perhaps restore him to his lost throne. For more than two years Isabella and Mortimer had lived without this threat, and it makes no sense that they would wish it all to start up again, especially for no better reason than to have an excuse to execute a man who was allegedly stupid, weak and unstable. As Andy King says, in late 1328 after the rebellion of Henry, Earl of Lancaster, against Roger Mortimer and Isabella's regime, 'the last thing that he [Mortimer] needed was the emergence of rumours of Edward of Caernarfon's survival.' The Earl of Kent did briefly join Lancaster's rebellion with his brother the Earl of Norfolk at the end of 1328, but they soon returned to the side of Edward III and his mother Isabella, and by extension Roger Mortimer.

Even if Edmund of Woodstock, Earl of Kent, were stupid and gullible, which he was not, not all of his followers in 1329–30 can be condemned as such. Kent was supported by, at the very least, many dozens of men who are named in extant records and probably many hundreds: sheriffs across the country were ordered to search for his adherents after his execution, and they were believed to be particularly numerous in Wales and East Anglia. The Archbishop of York, William Melton, also strongly believed that Edward II was still alive in 1330, to the point of arranging money, clothes, shoes and other provisions for him. In my article 'The Adherents of Edmund of Woodstock, Earl of Kent, in March 1330', published in the *English Historical Review* in 2011, I drew attention to Kent's many supporters and their back-grounds: many of them had formerly been members of Edward II's household, while others had been adherents of the Despensers. Although we can never know their motives for certain, many of them came from backgrounds which betokened great loyalty to Edward II, or were, as former adherents of the Despensers, not natural allies of the Earl of Kent, one of the men who condemned both Hugh Despensers to death in 1326. Still, we must bear in mind that it is not necessarily the case that Edward II was genuinely alive in 1329–30 merely because some people thought so. The Earl of Kent's brother the Earl of Norfolk did not take part in his plot, and neither did their cousin Henry, Earl of Lancaster. If Lancaster's letter to London in November 1328 telling them that there were certain things he did not dare put in writing related to Edward II's survival, Lancaster took no further part in Kent's plot, and perhaps did not believe that his cousin was alive.

THE ARCHBISHOP OF YORK WAS DECEIVED INTO BELIEVING EDWARD WAS ALIVE

Professor Roy Martin Haines, when presenting the Melton Letter in the 2009 *English Historical Review*, simply assumed that Archbishop William Melton was 'deceived' and 'misled' and 'so easily convinced' into believing that Edward of Caernarfon was still alive in 1329–30, without even attempting to speculate who deceived him and why, and how they so easily deceived a highly intelligent, experienced and shrewd archbishop in his 50s.[17] Claiming that Melton was misled or deceived without further explanation is rather pat. Professor Haines, in an article published in 2008, also claimed that the men who aided the Earl of Kent and the Archbishop of York in 1329–30 were 'unduly credulous'.[18] Dozens or probably hundreds of men risked imprisonment, forfeiture of all their lands and goods, and even death, to aid Kent; to suggest that they were all credulous and unstable, or that they were foolish enough to follow a man who was himself stupid and gullible, is to do them a huge disservice. Some of the men involved were very wealthy and influential indeed. It also comes across as rather arrogant to assume 700 years later that we have better information as to whether Edward II had survived or not than men who were alive at the time and who risked a great deal to help him. It is absurd to imagine that so many men, a number of whom were decades older than Kent and highly experienced knights, administrators and politicians, would have followed him into treason against Edward III for no better reason than that they were 'unduly credulous'. It is likely that men of such calibre did not follow the Earl of Kent into treason on the basis of a friar raising the devil or on the silly story told by chronicler Geoffrey le Baker that Kent met a man who thought he had seen his half-brother at a feast in Corfe Castle. Professor Haines and Professor Seymour Phillips, both eminent modern historians of Edward II's reign, have said that 'The [Melton] letter does not prove that the king was alive; it does no more than confirm Melton's conviction that he was' and that it 'confirms that Melton had been led to believe that Edward was still alive in 1330 but provides no evidence that this was the case'.[19] This is true, though it is difficult to imagine what evidence could be provided in a letter beyond the archbishop's statement that Edward 'is alive and in good physical health' and his request for clothes and money for him. Professor Haines has also claimed that Kent's fellow plotters 'were mainly churchmen' and 'pre-eminently clerical in character', and that 'the alleged constituent members of the plot were clerical'.[20] As seen above, the men who followed the Earl of Kent in 1329–30, although they included the Archbishop of York, the Bishop of London and a few friars, were in fact mostly secular, and included the earls of Mar and Buchan, four sheriffs (John Hauteyn, Ingelram Berenger, Roger Reyham and William Orlaston), numerous secular lords and knights, squires and merchants.

The Earl of Kent's adherents did not truly believe that Edward II was alive, but were trying to bring down Isabella and Mortimer's regime

It has sometimes been speculated that many or most or all of the men who joined the Earl of Kent and the Archbishop of York in 1329–30 did not really believe that Edward II was still alive, but used the plot to express their dissatisfaction with the regime of Queen Isabella and Roger Mortimer, i.e. that they were 'desirous of producing a back-lash against a dictatorial and unpopular government'.[21] It is beyond doubt that by 1330 the regime of Isabella and Mortimer was highly unpopular, after they had proved themselves as greedy, incompetent and self-serving as Edward II and the Despensers had, and for sure we cannot know the private thoughts of Kent's adherents and whether they all genuinely believed that Edward II was alive or not. What is not clear is how claiming that Edward was alive, if the conspirators knew that he was not, would 'produce a backlash' or why a rebellion against the unpopular ruling pair needed to use the name of the dead and equally unpopular king. Henry, Earl of Lancaster, when rebelling against Isabella and Mortimer in late 1328, did not feel the need to invoke his cousin Edward II's name. Instead, he set out his grievances against them with a list of what he believed to be their wrong-doings. The 'contrariants' on the Continent planning an invasion of England in the summer of 1330, although the Earl of Kent's allies, also did not use the former king's name in their own rebellion against Mortimer and Isabella.

Archbishop William Melton certainly believed that Edward was alive, but he was not using his alleged survival as a rallying call for rebellion against Isabella and Mortimer; he begged Simon Swanland to keep the news that Edward was 'alive and in good physical health' secret, hardly the action of a man trying to incite a rebellion. Melton's aim seemingly was to help a man of whom he had always been extremely fond, and a month after Edward's official death Melton had asked for prayers for his soul, so clearly believed then that Edward was dead. If everyone knew in 1329–30 that Edward II was dead and in his grave at Gloucester and there was no doubt at all about this, it is unclear how pretending that he was alive was going to help bring down the regime of his wife and her favourite. Edward III's rapid forgiveness of all the men involved in his uncle's plot – he deemed them all 'guiltless' and restored them to their lands and goods within weeks of his mother and Mortimer's downfall – is also hard to explain if he believed that they were cynically using the potential restoration of his father as an incitement to rebellion, which would have been a weapon against him personally, not only against his mother and Mortimer. Some people claimed that Edward II's great-grandson Richard II was alive after his murder in 1400, but Richard was deposed and murdered by his cousin and enemy Henry IV, while Edward II was forced to abdicate his throne to his own son, so the situation is different. The plotters of 1330 did not seek the downfall of Edward III himself, but of the unpopular regime of his mother and her favourite. Using the name of the young Edward III as a rallying call against the pair running his kingdom into the ground in his name would have made far more sense than using the name of his deposed, disgraced and dead father.

DID THE ARCHBISHOP OF YORK AND THE EARL OF KENT REALLY KNOW IN 1329–30 THAT EDWARD WAS NOT DEAD?

Andy King has made the point that neither the Earl of Kent nor the Archbishop of York nor any of their adherents claimed that they themselves had seen Edward II alive after 1327, and that 'crucially, they all depended on information received from others … aside from the Fieschi letter, they are all based on second-hand information'.[22] Kent supposedly heard of his half-brother's survival either from a friar who had raised the devil, according to his own confession as recorded by chroniclers, or from a friar he sent to Corfe Castle who saw 'Edward' from a distance at a feast, according to the rather unreliable chronicle of Geoffrey le Baker. Archbishop Melton heard of Edward's survival from the mysterious messenger William of Kingsclere, who in July 1332 was supposedly arrested for involvement in Edward's murder, and who, King speculates, was therefore likely to have been an agent of Roger Mortimer. Melton is likely to have also heard the news from other sources, however, and was also in contact with the Earl of Kent via several messengers in 1329–30. It is probable that the men did not rush into treason against Edward III without thoroughly checking; but still, their belief that Edward II was not dead was based on information they had received from others and thus was indeed second-hand information, or hearsay evidence. It is probably revealing that Melton's letter to Simon Swanland on 14 January 1330 tells Swanland that Edward II was then 'alive and in good health', wording which repeats the message Melton had received three months previously from William of Kingsclere (according to the records of King's Bench in April 1330). One might therefore question whether Melton really knew that Edward was alive, though he was an intelligent and astute politician probably then in his 50s, and is unlikely to have believed the tale without asking numerous questions of the messenger William of Kingsclere.

On the other hand, if the belief of the Earl of Kent and the Archbishop of York in Edward's survival can be dismissed because they did not see Edward II in person after his official death in 1327 but only heard that he was alive from other people, then all fourteenth-century chroniclers who wrote that Edward died at Berkeley Castle can also be dismissed as second-hand information or hearsay evidence, as none of them saw Edward's dead body or were present at Berkeley when he was killed. The great variation given by chroniclers as the cause of Edward's death, from natural causes to grief to suffocation to a fall to a red-hot poker and so on, also indicates that few if any of them had any real idea what happened to Edward and were only speculating or repeating rumours.

The statement in the records of King's Bench that William Melton heard of Edward II's survival from William of Kingsclere on 10 October 1329 is not even second-hand information: it was passed from an informant called John of Lincoln (a man whose name was, perhaps rather conveniently, extremely common and whose identity is therefore almost impossible to determine) either directly to Roger Mortimer or Queen Isabella, or much more likely via intermediaries to Mortimer or Isabella, and then from Mortimer to the lawyers of King's Bench who indicted Melton, probably also via intermediaries. There is also the question of whether John of Lincoln was an eyewitness to Kingsclere informing Melton, or whether he heard it from yet another person or persons. It is at best fourth- or fifth-hand information, yet has been accepted as true and accurate by modern historians who wish to claim that Melton was being deliberately deceived and lured into treason by an agent of Mortimer. Even Edward III's statement at the Parliament of November–December 1330 that his father had been falsely and treacherously murdered, could, if one wished, be dismissed as mere hearsay evidence, given that the young king was not at Berkeley Castle on 21 September 1327 and only heard that his father had been murdered from someone else. Edward III may not even have seen Edward II's dead body. He never heard evidence from the men he accused of killing his father, Thomas Gurney and William Ockley, who did not appear at Parliament to answer the charges against them and never admitted to the murder, and were condemned to death unheard. Their conviction by Parliament and the notion that they were responsible for Edward II's murder – or even that Edward was murdered at all – is thus also 'information received from others'.

If proponents of the idea that Edward II died at Berkeley Castle in 1327 can dismiss most of the evidence that he was alive after this date as hearsay, then most of the evidence in favour of Edward's dying at Berkeley should also be dismissed as hearsay unless it came directly from someone present at the castle on the day of Edward's death. The only person at Berkeley Castle on 21 September 1327 who ever spoke about it in public was Thomas, Lord Berkeley, when he apparently made the curious comment to the Parliament of late 1330 that he 'had not known of Edward's death' until he arrived there. If the 'second-hand information' argument is used and deemed to be 'crucial' but is not applied equally to both sides of the debate, it is not a reasonable point but only confirmation bias.

The only person who made the direct claim that he had seen Edward II in person after his alleged death was the Italian papal notary and future bishop, Manuele Fieschi. Andy King points out that Fieschi wrote his letter a decade or so after Edward's 1327 funeral (though may have met 'Edward' at Avignon in 1331) and that we cannot know for sure if he ever saw Edward in person and if he would therefore have been able to recognise him.[23] This is true, but as noted, there were plenty of men at Avignon who did know Edward well, as Seymour Phillips has also noted, with whom Fieschi could have checked. Identifying a man as the former King of England was not only a question of recognising him physically, and indeed the appearance of a man in his 40s and 50s would have changed a great deal in a decade, especially if we assume that Edward spent years in captivity at Corfe. It could have involved asking him questions to which only Edward would know the answers, and was also a matter of language and his manner of speaking. Anyone claiming to be 'Edward II' would need to be fluent in Anglo-Norman. If he was not, he could not be the former king; if he was, this fact would drastically restrict the potential number of people who could pretend to be him, as Anglo-Norman was spoken by only a tiny percentage of the English population. The Fieschi Letter says that 'Edward II' spent fifteen days with Pope John XXII, which would be more than enough time for John to realise that the man could not possibly be the former King of England; yet John apparently did not realise this. There is nothing in the Fieschi Letter which presents 'Edward II' as an impostor.

ISABELLA AND MORTIMER MADE UP THE CHARGE OF ADHERENCE TO THE EARL OF KENT AS AN EXCUSE TO ARREST THEIR POLITICAL OPPONENTS

It has sometimes been claimed that, as well as luring the Earl of Kent into treason by making him believe that Edward II was alive in order to have an excuse to execute him, Queen Isabella and Roger Mortimer invented a charge of adherence to the earl in order to arrest and imprison their opponents and thus protect themselves and their regime, or adjusted the earl's confession to implicate their enemies.[24] If this was indeed their aim, it failed miserably, as they were overthrown by Isabella's son the king and his allies a mere seven months after the Earl of Kent's execution (or judicial murder). Although many of

the men named as Kent's adherents in 1330 were wealthy and influential, others were lowborn and so obscure that they appear in no
record before or after that year and are thus impossible to trace. Others
were mere squires, one was a glover, one was a resident of Fowey in
Cornwall, a handful were friars or clerks, and so on. Even so, these men
were ordered to be arrested in the days, weeks and months after the
Earl of Kent's execution. It is difficult to imagine the thought process
which would have led Isabella and Mortimer to conclude that they
simply had to arrest a group of such men who wielded no political
influence in order to protect their own political position, and decided
that the best way to achieve this was to pretend that Isabella's husband
was still alive, spread rumours to that effect in the hope that their
enemies would believe them and try to free Edward, and thus have an
excuse to arrest such dangerous men as a glover, some clerks and an
unknown Cornishman.

Many of the Earl of Kent's adherents had been released and restored
to their lands and goods by the time of Mortimer and Isabella's arrest
and downfall on 19 October 1330, which hardly suggests that the pair's
aim was to find an excuse to keep their enemies locked up. William
la Zouche, lord of Ashby, for example, was freed and restored to his
lands as early as 10 April 1330, and John Pecche, lord of Hampton-in-
Arden, on 9 August.[25] Roy Martin Haines has said that the Earl of Kent
was used by Mortimer and Isabella as a 'cat's paw' for them to 'flush
out' the opponents who most threatened their regime.[26] What in fact
happened was that the most dangerous of their enemies fled abroad
and planned an invasion of England in the summer of 1330, and thus
Mortimer and Isabella's situation became more precarious than if they
had done nothing and ensured that their enemies remained in England
where they could keep an eye on them. Their judicial murder of the
Earl of Kent also most probably hastened their downfall, as Kent's
nephew Edward III was so furious at his uncle's fate that he arrested
Mortimer only seven months after Kent's death, and hanged him some
weeks later.

Andy King has suggested that Roger Mortimer would have been
anxious to neutralise the threat to himself and the queen mother
caused by the Earl of Kent putting about rumours of Edward II's

survival and sharing them with Mortimer's enemy Henry, Earl of Lancaster, and that Kent was 'vulnerable, lacking resources and armed strength. It was probably this that motivated Mortimer to put Kent on trial.'[27] If Kent was vulnerable and lacking resources, he cannot have been such a threat to the regime that his trial and death was deemed necessary, unless executing him was meant to send a message to his cousin, the far more wealthy and powerful Henry of Lancaster (who in late 1328 led a failed rebellion against Mortimer and Isabella). Yet by the time of Kent's execution in March 1330, Lancaster had been effectively neutralised as a threat anyway, since the beginning of 1329 when Mortimer sacked his main power base of Leicester and forced him and his supporters to submit and acknowledge massive debts to the Crown as a way of keeping them in line. If Henry of Lancaster was thought to be the real threat, it is unclear why he was not the one whom Roger Mortimer attempted to lure into a treasonous plot. Edward II had had Henry's elder brother Earl Thomas beheaded for treason in March 1322, after all, so executing a Lancaster was not unprecedented. There is no real explanation as to why anyone pretending that Edward II was alive in the late 1320s, if he was dead, would have been a 'serious threat' to Roger Mortimer and his regime, or to the stability of it. The judicial murder of the king's own uncle, a man of whom Edward III was very fond, constituted a far greater threat to the stability and very existence of Roger Mortimer's regime than false rumours of Edward II's survival. The theory goes that executing the Earl of Kent was intended to take the sting out of the contemporary rumours that Edward II was still alive, but rumours would not matter if Edward truly was dead.[28] Rumours alone could not bring down the regime of Isabella and Mortimer. We are also told that the Earl of Kent 'obligingly provided evidence sufficient to secure his own conviction' by writing a letter to his half-brother at Corfe Castle, which was passed to Mortimer by John Deveril and was evidence of an active conspiracy, and thus the evidence Mortimer needed to press charges against Kent.[29] If this is true, it might have made more sense to allow Kent to continue and make a fool of himself by trying to storm an empty Corfe Castle, and catch him far more involved in an act of treason against his nephew Edward III than by a mere letter (which Kent could have claimed was a forgery and nothing to do with him).

THE EARL OF KENT WAS EXECUTED BECAUSE HE COMMITTED TREASON AGAINST EDWARD III

Why exactly was Edmund of Woodstock, Earl of Kent, executed in March 1330? At his trial in Winchester, the *Brut* chronicle says that he was accused of plotting to help Edward II that he 'should have been king again, and govern his people as he was wont before times, impairing our liege lord the king's state, that is now', i.e. Edward's son Edward III.[30] Ian Mortimer suggests that Kent's crime was to be genuinely on the verge of releasing Edward II, and that the plot was a real one and therefore Kent had to be hurriedly tried and executed before he could put it into action; Andy King says that plotting treason was as serious a crime as committing it in medieval England and that therefore Kent's execution does not in any way prove that Edward II was indeed still alive, citing Bracton's thirteenth-century *On the Laws and Customs of England*.[31]

The laws of treason, however, were silent on the issue of pretending that a dead former king was still alive and plotting to restore him to the throne now occupied by his son and successor. We also run into the thorny issue of Edward II's deposition or forced abdication in 1327 and whether it was lawful or not; it is possible that legally Edward II was still the rightful King of England from January 1327 until his death. There was no precedent for deposing a king and no provision for it in English law, and lawmakers had not considered the possibility of anyone pretending that a deposed and now dead king was still alive and trying to restore him to the throne, and thus had made no laws against it. William Melton, Archbishop of York, was charged with treason in April 1330 on the grounds that he had invited an army from Scotland, an enemy country, to invade England; not because he had tried to restore Edward II to the throne. Edward II himself had never been convicted of any crime, and therefore it could be argued that the lifelong imprisonment imposed on him in January

1327 (comfortable though it may well have been) was itself unlawful and against Magna Carta, and that freeing a man who from a legal perspective was entirely innocent from unlawful lifelong captivity could not be a crime. Edward III pardoned the Earl of Kent for his treason as soon as he was in a position to, at the Parliament which began in November 1330, and restored Kent's son to his inheritance. Although Andy King does not mention it in this context, we once again run into the issue of 'second-hand information': no official record survives of Kent's trial in March 1330, and only an account in the *Brut* chronicle exists to tell us what happened. The author of the *Brut* was almost certainly not personally present at Kent's trial, and was generally more interested in writing dramatic and creative stories than necessarily accurate accounts of events. We therefore do not really know what was said or not said at the trial.

DID LORD BERKELEY REALLY TELL PARLIAMENT IN 1330 THAT HE DID NOT KNOW ABOUT EDWARD'S DEATH?

Thomas, Lord Berkeley was Edward of Caernarfon's custodian at Berkeley Castle in 1327, and sent a letter to Edward III via Thomas Gurney to inform the young King of his father's death. Three years later at the Parliament of November–December 1330, Lord Berkeley told his audience *nec unquam scivit de morte sua usque in presenti Parliamento isto*, that he 'did not know about his [Edward's] death until this present Parliament'. His words to Parliament have often been over-elaborately translated so that they fit into historians' belief that Edward II died at Berkeley Castle in 1327; usually, that what Berkeley meant to say was that he did not realise Edward had been murdered (and it is true that the former king's death was presented as murder in this Parliament for the first time), or that he knew nothing of the circumstances of or details about Edward's death, even though it had taken place in his own castle. Historians' certainty that they know what Lord Berkeley really intended to say or should have said sometimes takes on an air of mental telepathy: 'What Berkeley meant to say, and he should have expressed himself more clearly, unless the recording clerk is to blame, is that he knew nothing about the circumstances of Edward's death'; 'He claimed that he did not know about the death until the present Parliament ... by which we must understand him to mean that he had known nothing of the details'; when taken in conjunction with the preceding statement that Berkeley was not an accomplice to the death nor aided it, 'this can only mean that Berkeley knew that the death had occurred but that he claimed he had no part in it'.[32] David Carpenter, in a 2007 piece in the *London Review of Books*, states that 'the most natural meaning of *scivit de morte sua* is that Berkeley did not know anything about the circumstances of Edward's death, that is he didn't know anything about the murder, not that he did not know Edward was dead'. Other historians agree with this interpretation.[33] The modern translators and editors of the Parliamentary rolls, however, translate *nec unquam scivit de morte sua usque in presenti Parliamento isto* as 'nor did he ever know of his death until the present Parliament'.[34] Presumably if Thomas Berkeley had wanted to say 'I did not know that the king's father was murdered until this present Parliament' or 'I did not know anything about the circumstances of the death of the king's father until this present Parliament', he was perfectly capable of expressing himself in this way.

I asked a well-known Latin scholar and translator to translate Lord Berkeley's words for me. Without the context and without any awareness of how he was 'supposed' to interpret the words to make them fit a pre-decided conclusion, he translated *nunquam fuit consentiens, auxilians, seu procurans, ad mortem suam, nec unquam scivit de morte sua usque in presenti Parliamento isto* as: 'He was never in agreement to his death, either by lending help or by direct involvement, and he never knew about his death until this present Parliament.'[35]

It should be noted that this stage of proceedings was recorded in Latin, though Lord Berkeley presumably spoke in French. It is therefore certainly possible that a clerk recorded the words wrongly, or misheard or misinterpreted or mistranslated, and with the translation of Berkeley's testimony into modern English, the problem is compounded. Berkeley's further untrue claim that he had been ill and suffering from amnesia and away from Berkeley Castle at the time of

Edward's death might be seen as confirmation that we should interpret his statement as meaning that he knew nothing of the circumstances of the death. Yet he did not say that, and as previously noted, we have to work with the evidence we have, not with the evidence we think we should have, and we should focus on what Berkeley actually said according to the record of a man who heard his speech, rather than providing over-elaborate translations or our own interpretations of what we think he should have said or meant to say, based on a belief that Edward II had died in Berkeley's castle. By itself, Berkeley's speech probably does not mean very much, but when taken with all the other evidence that Edward did not die in 1327, it forms part of a strong – though certainly far from watertight – case that he truly did not.

WERE THOMAS GURNEY AND WILLIAM OCKLEY REALLY RESPONSIBLE FOR THE KING'S MURDER?

It is curious that warrants for the arrest of these two men were only issued on 3 December 1330, four days after Roger Mortimer's execution. The records of Parliament are also oddly silent on the pair, stating only that they falsely and treacherously murdered and killed Edward without the slightest explanation as to how. William Ockley, the man-at-arms, is so obscure that we would have no clue as to why he was charged with Edward II's murder without the fortunate survival of a 1331 court case which states that Roger Mortimer sent him to Berkeley Castle in September 1327, bearing a letter from Mortimer's deputy justice of Wales, William Shalford. No chronicle names Ockley as one of Edward's murderers, or even mentions him at all. William Shalford himself, though he allegedly sent Mortimer a letter about the Welsh plot to free Edward of Caernarfon and asked him to find a solution to the ongoing Edward problem, and thus set Edward's murder in motion, was never charged by Edward III with any complicity in his father's death or even asked to appear at Parliament to explain himself. The role of Mortimer's ally Sir Simon Bereford, the only other man executed by Edward III in late 1330 for involvement in all Mortimer's felonies including presumably the murder of the king's father, is also

obscure and puzzling; no chronicle mentions Bereford at all in connection with the murder of Edward II. The Fieschi Letter, however,
names him and Thomas Gurney as the two men coming to kill Edward
before he escapes. The matter remains unresolved. It is notable and also
curious that of the many letters which Edward III sent to Alfonso XI
of Castile and his subjects, and his own subjects in Gascony, regarding
the capture and arrest of Thomas Gurney in Spain in the early 1330s,
not one states outright that Gurney had murdered Edward II or calls
him Edward's murderer, only that he had conspired to do so and had
thus committed sedition. As Gurney had been condemned to death for
killing Edward less than six months previously, this seems a little odd.

THE FIESCHI LETTER: IS IT A FAKE?

Could the Fieschi Letter be a forgery? Edward II scholar Roy Martin
Haines believes that although the letter was written by a Genoese
person, it was not written by Manuele Fieschi himself; he believes
it to be in excessively informal Latin with a distinctly Genoese fla-
vour, rather inappropriate for a notary of the pope to send to the
King of England. Haines also claims that the names of British people
and places in the letter are spelled in an odd and 'idiosyncratic' way.[36]
Edward's biographer Seymour Phillips thinks the Fieschi Letter is genuine (though not that the man Manuele met actually was Edward II),
and that Manuele Fieschi did indeed write it. Elena Corbellini of the
Auramala Project, an expert on Latin and medieval Latin manuscripts,
points out that the language of the Fieschi Letter only looks odd
in comparison with Classical Latin. Latin was the lingua franca of
Europe in the Middle Ages but was not anyone's native language, and
had changed and evolved considerably over the centuries since the
Romans spoke it. Lord Berkeley's words to Parliament in 1330 noted
above, *nec unquam scivit de morte sua*, would mean by the standards of
Classical Latin that Berkeley was saying that he did not know of his
own death rather than Edward II's, but clearly this was not the case in
the fourteenth-century form of the language used by the Parliamentary
clerk at Westminster.[37] The copy of the Fieschi Letter which now exists

in a Montpellier archive is just that, a copy, not necessarily exactly the same as the original version presumably sent to Edward III.

The British names as spelled in the Fieschi Letter look exactly like they would be written by an Italian with no access to a map or book of names to check the correct spelling, even if there were such a thing as 'correct spelling' in the fourteenth century: Ugone Dispenssario for Hugh Despenser; Berchelee for Berkeley; Gesosta for Chepstow; Henricus de Longo Castello for Henry of Lancaster; Maltraverse for Maltravers; Symon Desberfort for Simon de Bereford. Such spellings are not 'idiosyncratic' in an age when there was no standardised spelling; rather they represent a phonetic attempt at writing British names as they sounded to an Italian, and the letter was copied into the register of a French bishop by a French clerk, compounding the problem. To give just a handful of other contemporary examples, English scribes of the era often spelled the Welsh names Llewelyn and Llwyd as Thwellin or Thoellin and Thloyt which is how they sounded to English ears; French scribes, unfamiliar with Edward II's name (in the early fourteenth century, Edward's Old English name was still rare in Europe), spelled it as Edduvart or Oudouart. The Florentine chronicler Giovanni Villani called Edward II Adoardo, Hugh Despenser Ugo il Dispensiere, Ipswich Giepsivi, and Caerphilly Carsigli.[38] An order of 31 March 1330 recorded on the Fine Roll to arrest the adherents of the Earl of Kent gave the names Rhys and Ieuan ap Gruffudd as Res and Ivan ap Griffyn, because English scribes did not know the Welsh spelling and had no way of checking had they cared to do so. They also tended to anglicise Italian names, so that Giovanni Doria became John Dorie and Carlo Fieschi became Charles de Flisco, in the same way that Italian scribes made English names look Italian. Queen Isabella's name was spelled in many different ways in her own lifetime by both French and English scribes, including Yzabel, Ysabell and Isabele. In this context, to claim that names are spelled in an odd and idiosyncratic way in the Fieschi Letter makes little sense. And the letter is certainly not a fake document later inserted into the cartulary: it is in the same handwriting as the documents before and after it, the decoration of initials is the same as in the rest of the cartulary, and there are no other blank pages in the document that could have been written in later, and therefore there is no reason to think that this particular page was blank and that the Fieschi Letter was copied in later.

WAS THE 'EDWARD II' WHO MET THE POPE AT AVIGNON AND (A FEW YEARS LATER) EDWARD III AT KOBLENZ A CONVINCING IMPOSTOR?

Professor Seymour Phillips has postulated that the man who met Pope John XXII and Manuele Fieschi in Avignon in *c.* 1331 (Fieschi may have met 'Edward II' when the latter came to Avignon to see the pope on this occasion, though his letter does not say so directly) and Edward III in Koblenz in September 1338 was a clever and convincing impostor, the same man in both *c.* 1331 and 1338. He speculates that John XXII and his successor Benedict XII felt that the impostor's wanderings around the Continent were an embarrassment to the Church and even to Edward III's legitimacy as King of England, and therefore decided that Edward III had to be informed.[39] There is no real explanation as to why the impostor was allowed to travel around the Continent with John XXII's permission and after much debate at his court (the Fieschi Letter says that 'after various discussions, all things having been considered, permission having been received', 'Edward' moved on to Paris, Brabant and so on) and without informing Edward III at this point, or why John XXII appears to have been taken in by the impostor and spent more than two weeks with him, or why it took John XXII and Benedict XII so many years – at least five and perhaps more than seven – to decide to notify Edward III about the man claiming so plausibly to be his father. Phillips has also pointed out that there were many people at the papal court who had known Edward II, including the 1326 envoys to England the Bishop of Orange and the Archbishop of Vienne, who 'would readily have determined whether the traveller was genuine or not', and that the conclusion that the man 'was not the real Edward II could have been reached very quickly'.[40] This is absolutely true, yet he does not explain why 'Edward' would have needed to spend a full fifteen days with John XXII, as the Fieschi Letter states he did, for it to become apparent that the man was not Edward II. There is nothing in the Fieschi Letter which states that the man was an impostor or that John XXII or Fieschi thought he was an impostor, and the letter refers to the man as 'your father', i.e. Edward III's father. Phillips also postulates the existence of a covering letter which informed Edward III in effect that 'you had better know this following story'. A reply from Edward III is also postulated, stating that the king would be in Germany in 1338 and asking Fieschi and the pope to send his 'father' there so that he could meet him.[41] This notion cannot be proved or disproved as it speculates the existence of evidence which we do not have. The evidence we do have shows a notary of the pope telling the King of England about 'your father'.

WAS MANUELE FIESCHI A LIAR?

There are several possibilities. Fieschi told the truth and genuinely did meet Edward II; he met a plausible impostor and, taken in, thought the person truly was the former king; he was lying in some way, either by telling Edward III that he had met his father when nothing of the sort had happened, or he met an impostor who claimed to be Edward II, knew that he was not, but decided to present him as such to Edward III anyway; he met a convincing impostor and knew that he was not Edward II, but was worried that others might be taken in, so decided to inform Edward III. If he was deliberately lying, we would have to think of a good reason why he would do so. Blackmail is an obvious motive, but Manuele Fieschi was not a man who needed to blackmail the King of England in order to gain benefices and appointments when he saw the pope himself every day of his working life, and he was made Bishop of Vercelli in 1343 without needing Edward III's help or patronage in receiving it. Some kind of political blackmail at a higher level seems a much more plausible motive, if Manuele Fieschi knew that the man he met was not Edward II, though there is nothing in the letter to indicate that Fieschi thought the man was anyone but Edward. There are, however, some oddities in the letter which perhaps make it rather unlikely that it was Edward's true story, narrated by himself. It must be noted that as the matter currently stands, we have no other evidence that Edward II ever actually was in Italy and no confirmation that what the Fieschi Letter says is true, though the members of the Auramala Project are currently researching this, and searching Italian archives in an attempt to find a document or documents in support of the letter.

WAS WILLIAM LE GALEYS REALLY EDWARD II?

As with the Fieschi Letter and the Earl of Kent's plot, academic opinion is divided on the identity of the man who claimed to be Edward II in Germany in 1338. Ian Mortimer thinks he really was Edward II, that he spent time with his son, and even that the two men perhaps discussed Edward I, Edward II's father.[42] Paul Doherty has speculated that William le Galeys, 'the Welshman', was William Ockley, the man-at-arms convicted in late 1330 of Edward's murder, but Ockley was probably of Irish, not Welsh, origin, and it is unclear why he would choose to appear in front of Edward III as his dead father.[43] Ockley vanished after November 1330, and presenting himself in person to the King of England when he was still officially under sentence of death for murdering the king's father, and after he had managed to remain at large for eight years, seems extremely foolish and unlikely. Edward II's academic biographer Seymour Phillips, oddly, identifies William le Galeys as a William le Walsh of Woolstrop near Gloucester, despite admitting that Walsh had died in 1329, nearly a decade earlier; replacing one dead man with another hardly seems a satisfactory answer to this puzzle.[44] He also suggests that William le Galeys was the hermit claiming to be Edward II who met John XXII and (presumably) Manuele Fieschi in Avignon a few years earlier, and that he was brought to Germany specifically to meet Edward III by Francesco the Lombard, in whose custody he had been all this time. He does not deal with the issue of the long time period: if the hermit claiming to be Edward II was at the papal court sometime in 1331 and was so plausible that two popes were afraid he might damage the English monarchy, why was he not presented to Edward III until September 1338, seven years later?[45]

Assuming for a moment that this man really was Edward II, he might have chosen the name William because it did not belong to anyone in his family, but was borne by two of his closest friends and allies: William Melton, Archbishop of York, and William, abbot of Langdon in Kent, both of whom were still alive in 1338. Historian J. S. Hamilton has asked the rhetorical question 'William le Galys [*sic*] could be Edward II, or at least someone claiming to be him, but would Edward really choose William as his alias, not Piers?' after his beloved Piers Gaveston.[46] This is a fair question, though Edward calling himself 'Piers the Welshman' would surely have been too obvious that it was he, and the name William had the advantage of being a very common name not too closely associated with Edward.

It is difficult to ascertain Edward III's attitude towards William le Galeys and whether he believed him to be his father. It is also difficult to ascertain how much time, if any, the king spent with the man. We know that William was in the custody of the Italian banker Francesco Forcetti for three weeks in the early autumn of 1338, which does not necessarily mean that he spent this entire period with Edward III himself. Edward III did not have the man executed as a royal pretender, which might indicate that he did genuinely believe William was his father, or it might simply mean he thought the man was insane or deluded and not worth his time. In 1313 Edward II had met a man called Richard Newby who said that he was his brother and did not have him executed – indeed, he gave him a large sum of money – but in 1318 he did have the royal pretender John of Powderham hanged. There was no one way in which the English kings of the early fourteenth century behaved when confronted with men claiming to be their relatives or the rightful king, and therefore it is hard to determine Edward III's opinion on the matter or to assess what he 'should' have done when presented with a pretender.

The appearance of William le Galeys in Koblenz in early September 1338 does seem to fit quite well, however, with the details of the supposed former king's itinerary in Italy in the 1330s and with the appointment of Arnaud Verdale, who copied the Fieschi Letter into his bishop's register, as the papal envoy to Emperor Ludwig of Bavaria shortly after Ludwig met Edward III and made him a vicar of the

Holy Roman Empire. The appearance in the 1330s of a man claiming to be the King of England, the present king's father, alone would not necessarily mean very much, but in conjunction with the other pieces of evidence we have relating to Edward II's survival past 1327, it is perhaps significant.

IS IT POSSIBLE THAT EDWARD II WAS ALIVE UNTIL 1330, BUT THEN KILLED?

Given that so many influential men strongly believed that Edward was alive in 1329–30 and acted on that belief, is it possible that Edward was indeed alive until *c*. March 1330, but thereafter killed once it was realised that his continued existence was a huge threat to the status quo? This would mean that there was a plot to keep him alive but present his death to the public in September 1327 while he was secretly kept alive somewhere, and that the Earl of Kent, the Archbishop of York and all their allies were correct in thinking that he was concealed at Corfe Castle. After 1330, there is no real English evidence that Edward was still alive, unless we count the two entries in the wardrobe account of Edward III that he met William le Galeys/the Welshman, 'who asserts that he is the king's father', in Germany in September 1338. This theory would, of course, deny the validity of the Fieschi Letter. The letter states that Edward travelled to Ireland with his mysterious servant or keeper after the execution of his half-brother Kent in March 1330, presumably because it was deemed safer to send him out of England once many people had found out about his survival (though this is only speculation, as the letter does not give a reason for his journey to Ireland). It would seem to make sense to present Edward as dead in 1327 when really he was not, to put a stop to the many plots to free him without committing regicide, but why would he be kept alive in and after March 1330 when clearly it was so dangerous to do so and when his half-brother and others came close to releasing him? If this theory is correct, however, then the Fieschi Letter is untrue and we return to the points above: why Manuele Fieschi would lie to Edward III, or how he would be taken in by an impostor.

CONCLUSION

After 700 years it is frustratingly impossible to come to any firm con-clusions about Edward II's murder or survival, at least based on the evidence that we currently have. Occam's or Ockham's Razor – and William Ockham was a Franciscan friar from Surrey who was almost exactly Edward II's own age, so it is especially appropriate – states that 'among competing hypotheses, the one with the fewest assumptions should be selected'. The theory that Edward II did actually survive after 1327 explains all the evidence we have that he did, whereas the notion that he died in 1327 requires a number of explanations for the later evidence that he was not dead: that the Earl of Kent and his many fol-lowers were stupid and gullible; that the Earl of Kent and Archbishop of York were deceived into believing that Edward was still alive so that they would commit treason, as an excuse to arrest them; that Lord Berkeley was incapable of expressing himself properly to Parliament; that two popes and a papal notary were taken in by an impostor; that Manuele Fieschi was a liar and a blackmailer; and so on.[1]

The belief of all fourteenth-century chroniclers and the flow of information from the English government that Edward II died at Berkeley Castle in September 1327 were based on seemingly the most reliable source there could be: his own son, the king. And yet, Edward III immediately began disseminating news of his father's death in September 1327 before he could possibly have verified it, and his source, a letter from Lord Berkeley brought to him by Sir Thomas Gurney, was flawed in some way. Three years later, Lord Berkeley told Parliament a strange story that he had not previously known of the king's death or at least did not know how it had happened in his own castle, and Edward III pursued Thomas Gurney relentlessly in southern Europe in the early 1330s and ordered his man Giles of Spain to take down Gurney's confession and have it notarised and brought to him personally. This strongly implies that Edward III was desperate to hear what Gurney had to say about his father's fate in September 1327, who knew about it, and what role they played in it.[2] He had previously condemned Gurney and William Ockley to death for murdering Edward II without hearing them speak at Parliament. Who told him that these two men were responsible for the former king's murder is unclear: presumably Roger Mortimer and Thomas Berkeley, perhaps even Queen Isabella, though this information was never made public.

When so many influential people in 1330 strongly believed that Edward II was alive, and acted on this belief, then clearly it is entirely plausible that he was indeed alive. It is too easy and even arrogant to dismiss many dozens or hundreds of men as deceived or misled without evidence that they were anything of the sort, to assume that we 700 years later know better than they did. The reader may remain unconvinced that Edward II lived past 1327 and find the story of a former King of England living as a hermit in Italy too implausible, but there is enough evidence to at least consider the possibility that he was not murdered in 1327. Plenty of influential people at the time believed this. Even if we dismiss the Earl of Kent as stupid and gullible, and there is no reason to think he was, the Archbishop of York was not, the bishop and mayor of London were not, the Bishop of Vercelli and papal notary was not, Ingelram Berenger and William la Zouche were not. Taking all the pieces of evidence for the survival individually, one could make a case against them. Manuele Fieschi and perhaps even Pope John XXII were taken in by a clever impostor, or Fieschi was trying to blackmail Edward III in some way. The Earl of Kent, the Archbishop of York and their adherents were indulging in wishful thinking, or trying to incite a rebellion against Queen Isabella and Roger Mortimer's regime, or were fooled into thinking that Edward II was still alive as an excuse to arrest them for treason. The Archbishop of York sent a letter to the mayor of London on false information, which Donald, Earl of Mar and many others also believed. Lord Berkeley's words to the Parliament of November 1330 that he had not previously heard of Edward II's death were misinterpreted or wrongly recorded. William the Welshman was deluded or insane, or was William Ockley or some other person connected to Edward II. But when we put all the pieces together, we can build a strong case that perhaps Edward II did not die at Berkeley Castle in September 1327 after all. The wide range of chronicle stories about Edward II's death or murder, grief, red-hot poker, illness, suffocation and all the rest, show that none of them had the real story, and were going on assumption and rumours they had heard. None of the people involved talked about it publicly, so rumour was all they had.

It must be noted that no document so far even hints at Edward II being taken back to Italy after he had supposedly met his son in Germany in September 1338, or that he died in Italy. It is even possible that, having outlived his usefulness, he was killed once his keepers realised that his son Edward III would not allow himself to be manipulated by means of the continued existence of his father, and his body dumped somewhere. The meeting of Edward III and William le Galeys in Koblenz in early September 1338, if this really was the former King of England, is the last mention we have of Edward II. We also do not and cannot know for certain if Edward was deliberately kept alive in and after 1327 and taken to a secret location (presumably Corfe Castle) while a fake funeral was held for him in Gloucester; if this did happen, we do not know who was in on the fact that he was still alive; whether his wife Isabella knew or truly at this time thought he was dead; when his son Edward III found out; if other close members of his family such as his sisters Mary and Margaret and niece Eleanor Despenser ever did. We also cannot know who really was buried in Gloucester if Edward II was not. The Fieschi Letter says that it was the porter killed by Edward when escaping from Berkeley Castle, and this may be true, or it may simply be Edward II's later assumption or Manuele Fieschi's invention. There are so many questions which, frustratingly, we may never be able to answer.

Without a doubt, many people will read the present book and still come to the conclusion that Edward II died at Berkeley Castle in September 1327. This is absolutely fine; readers must make up their own minds on this topic, and there is ample evidence both for Edward's death in 1327 and his survival afterwards. What is not fine, and in fact is absurd, is for the three editors of an academic book published a few years ago to state that: 'It may be too much to hope that his [Seymour Phillips'] paper will put an end to speculation that the king survived his supposed murder in September 1327.'[3] It certainly is 'too much to hope' for. History, like any other academic discipline, thrives on debate, honest inquiry, engaging with the evidence and reaching new conclusions when the evidence requires it. It is not solely the preserve of scholars in ivory towers wishing to maintain a certain narrative upon which they have based much of their careers, and it is not anyone's business to try to close down debate and speculation. The debate about Edward II's murder or survival will continue.

AFTERWORD

BY IVAN FOWLER OF
THE AURAMALA PROJECT, ITALY

WHEN YOU'RE LOOKING FOR A NEEDLE IN A HAYSTACK, WHY NOT ASK THE HAY TO HELP YOU LOOK?

My name is Ivan Fowler, and I co-ordinate an initiative called the Auramala Project, run by the Cultural Association The World of Tels, based in Pavia, Italy. We want to solve the mystery of the fate of King Edward II of England. To do this, we are looking for two needles in two different haystacks.

The first haystack is: all the people in the world with English ancestors. The needle is a living descendant (or preferably two or three) in direct matrilineal line from Edward II's mother, Eleanor of Castile. The second haystack is: all the documents that survive from fourteenth-century Europe. The needle? Another document that can tip the balance of evidence either in favour of Edward II's death in Berkeley Castle or in favour of his survival.

This Afterword is a call to action, asking the general public to come forward, if they can, and help the research. The Auramala Project is a crowd-researching initiative, and you are all invited to lend a hand.

1. DNA and Genealogy: The 'Needle' That Might Be You

What constitutes hard proof

No matter what documents we find negating or corroborating the theory that Edward II survived, documentary evidence will never be enough. As Kathryn once quipped to me, we could find a selfie of Edward II at the hermitage of Sant'Alberto smiling and waving and saying he was still alive, and someone would still say it was photo-shopped. The only evidence that can really close this cold case for good is forensic: we need to DNA-test the remains said to be his, in order to see whether they really are or not. The best way to do this is by finding a direct living descendant of Edward II's mother, Eleanor of Castile, along the matrilineal line from mother to daughter down through the centuries. That person might be *you*. If you have any English ancestry at all, you are part of the haystack, and you might be the needle.

Finding the genetic 'needle': DNA typing and your family tree

Mitochondrial DNA is present in every cell of the body, remains unaltered from generation to generation, and is passed from mothers to all of their children, but is not passed on from fathers to *their* children. So, I, my brother and my sisters all carry our mother's mtDNA. But I and my brother have not passed it on to our children. My children have received my wife's mtDNA. But my sisters can pass on their mtDNA to their children, so any nieces or nephews I have from my sisters will carry our mother's mtDNA. If they are nieces, they will be able to pass it on themselves, and so on and so on. Therefore, by following the mother–daughter line down through the ages from Edward II's mother, Eleanor of Castile, we can isolate his mtDNA molecule, which he received from his mother but was not able to pass on to his children (who had the mtDNA of his wife, Isabella of France).

The good news is that, with a little genealogical research, any of us may discover that we are the carrier of the same mtDNA molecule as

Edward II, depending on our direct female-line ancestries. Once we have located the maternal descendants of the king's mother, we can compare their mtDNA molecule with that of the body purported to be that of Edward II in his tomb in Gloucester Cathedral. If they don't match, it means that is not Edward II's body, unless he was a changeling at birth (unlikely, given that he strongly resembled his father).

How likely is it that you may be a carrier of the special mtDNA molecule?

Surprisingly likely. Statistically, virtually all people of English descent are descended from Edward II, and therefore from his mother, as well as from every other person alive in England at the time who had children. Of course, being descended in the direct female line is rarer, but still there will be many more cases than you might think. You can find all the lines of descent we have so far uncovered, with the help of volunteer genealogists, on our website. If you are interested in genealogy, and have done any mapping of your own family tree, please take a look and see if any of the people listed on our website are in your family tree, and if they are, please get in touch with us!

Why do we need lots of people to participate in this project?

In part because it's exciting, and we want to share that excitement. In part because genealogists are human too, and make mistakes. We may well find that not all the people who think they descend in a mother–daughter line from Edward II's mother really do. If a mistake was made concerning the direct female lineage somewhere in their family tree, they will not have the same mtDNA as Edward II's mother. I would expect perhaps 5 to 10 per cent will find they have mtDNA molecules different to the others. If we were following the male line, it would be far higher though, again because, as the Romans used to say, *mater semper certa est, pater unquam* (the mother is always certain, the father, never). The other 90 to 95 per cent will all share one unique mtDNA molecule, which we will take to be Edward II's mother's, and therefore his. We compare that with the mtDNA extracted from the remains in Gloucester, and see what happens. What a big moment that will be when we get there!

Are we in the business of disturbing graves?

All of us in the Auramala Project wish to specify that we are not in the business of disturbing or desecrating graves. Indeed, to the authorities that will decide whether or not the final stage in the Project should go ahead, our intention is to propose a non-invasive approach. We wish to make use of technology and methods borrowed from non-invasive surgical techniques, such as laparoscopic surgery or 'keyhole' surgery. This would allow the necessary examinations to be undertaken with the minimal possible disturbance to the sanctity and physical state of the grave. It may well be possible to make use of existing microfissures in the tomb, that have opened up over the past seven centuries due to natural causes (changes in humidity, temperature, barometric pressure).

This is absolutely essential; principally, but not only, out of respect for the mortal remains of the dead (personally, I would be distraught to think of my own grave being disturbed in this way at some future date, and even more distraught if it were one of my ancestors' graves). The tomb of Edward II in Gloucester Cathedral is also one of the greatest examples of fourteenth-century sculpture in Great Britain, and no-one is more sensitive to the value of the conservation of artistic heritage than we are. Tombs were not made to be opened, and we would like to see this one remain closed.

2. THE DOCUMENTARY 'NEEDLE'

Meet the haystack: fourteenth-century documents

Curiously, it's not as big a haystack as it could be. By comparison with the modern world, the fourteenth century produced a tiny quantity of documents. A large proportion of the population was illiterate, printing had not been invented, and writing materials were costly. Of those documents that *were* created, a great many have been lost forever. Indeed, there are countless events that took place in the fourteenth century of which we know nothing. Countless people were born, lived and died and yet left no trace in documents whatsoever. Very few people are attested by more than one first-hand source, and most of those who are count among the highest-ranking individuals: kings, queens, dukes, popes, emperors, cardinals, bishops. So in reality, the haystack is vast, but nothing like as vast as the haystack that will probably confront historians investigating our own age, hundreds of years in the future.

The relatively small size of the haystack is part of the problem we face. Given the dearth of documents, in the study of medieval history we normally take a single, surviving, first-hand document as pretty good evidence that an event took place. So, in most cases, finding one is enough to convince historians that something happened; the chances are, a second document simply doesn't exist. Thousands of events accepted as fact by historians are attested by a single document. Here is just one example, which is close to home for me: the fact that in 1164 Emperor Frederick I, 'Barbarossa' invested Alberto Malaspina with the fief of Oramala (at the time spelled Auramala). One copy of the investiture has survived, and that's good enough for everyone.

If there is any doubt at all, historians look for corroboration from other documents. For example, we have only one copy of an extract of Manuele Fieschi's testament, telling us he died in Milan in the summer of 1348. We also have papal bulls sending him to Milan as papal legate in the spring of 1348, and other papal bulls in the autumn of 1348 assigning his possessions, benefices and bishopric to others because he had died. The corroborative documents do not say he died in Milan in the summer, but they allow for it to be true, and so there is no reason to doubt his testament. In a history book, one would simply write: Manuele Fieschi died in Milan in the summer of 1348, without bothering to insert a prudent 'probably' in the sentence.

The trouble with Edward II is: we have first-hand documents saying he died in Berkeley Castle on 21 September 1327, and corroborative documents backing them up, but at the same time we have first-hand documents saying he did not die, and corroborative documents backing them up, too. To compound matters, both versions come from reputable sources: the English Parliamentary rolls and the lord of Berkeley Castle both tell us he died, while a papal notary and an English archbishop both tell us he did not. There are not many cases in history where two such contrasting versions of the facts are backed up by first-hand documents written by such high-ranking men. It makes the whole affair fascinating, but frustrating: will a piece of evidence ever come up to tip the balance one way or another? *That* document is the needle in the haystack.

Crowd-sourcing: asking the haystack to help look for the needle

Up to now I have emphasised that the haystack is not really that huge. Now let's get to the fact that it is nevertheless big. Not hugely, immensely vast, but quite big enough, thank you. I doubt anyone has ever tried to estimate the number of documents produced in the fourteenth century that still survive. There are surely millions. So, you see, that's a pretty big haystack all the same. Now, readers will be thinking: can't you just narrow it down? Can't you just look at sources that are likely to prove useful, like archives in the places Edward II is said to have gone? Absolutely: that is precisely what the Auramala Project has been doing for the last five years. We have systematically examined documents from the places associated with Edward II's survival – the places mentioned in the Fieschi Letter. For logistical reasons (this is not our day job!) we have been limited to Italy, the south of France, England, and the published papal registers. So far, although we have found a lot of very useful information, we have not found the 'needle'. So, we are asking archivists, librarians, researchers and anyone else who might have access to or own documents from the fourteenth century anywhere to lend us a hand. Even if you live in Siberia, or Florida, or Zimbabwe, or wherever you may be. Ancient documents can literally turn up anywhere; you would be surprised. For example, letters addressed to Cardinal Luca Fieschi in the early 1300s were re-used to line the inside of a book cover after his death. That book ended up in a library in Prague, and historians discovered the letters there by pure chance hundreds of years later, when the book was being re-covered. One of those letters was sent from Auramala Castle in 1335, when Edward II may have been in the vicinities of the castle. This letter talks about agents of Luca Fieschi conducting secret business there at the time. Understandably, it is an enticing read.

Such documents can literally turn up anywhere, and there is no way of knowing where. This is why the only way forward for us, after having examined the 'most likely' places, is to ask people everywhere to help us look, by crowdsourcing the search, in the hopes of finding new evidence.

What kind of documents might the 'needle' be?

One document that would be extremely valuable is another sample of the writing of Manuele Fieschi to compare with the Fieschi Letter. Not all historians agree that the Fieschi Letter was, indeed, written by Manuele Fieschi. Haines, for example, has suggested that it was written by another person, or group of persons, and the name of Manuele Fieschi was affixed to make it seem more credible. Kathryn Warner has already discussed this theory in this book. We have looked everywhere for another document written by Manuele Fieschi, and found none. We have hundreds of documents about him, or written at his behest, but none written by him. If we were to find one, we could compare the style of the writing and the vocabulary with the Fieschi Letter to either confirm or deny that it was, indeed, written by him. Archivists and librarians and researchers out there: we are looking for a *manu propria* document signed Manuel de Flisco.

Why is this so important? As Kathryn Warner shows in this book, drawing upon the research of the Auramala Project, the real Manuele Fieschi was a far cry from the portrait that has been painted of him by many contemporary historians. Far from being a money-grabbing, scheming, blackmailing priest from the provinces, he was a high-ranking official of the papal court, in daily contact with the pope, privy to papal diplomatic correspondence with emperors, kings, princes and dukes, and who had literally hundreds of connections to noble families from

Portugal in the west to Cyprus in the east, from Sweden in the north to Sicily in the south. Above all, he had absolutely every means of checking whether or not the man he was talking to was Edward II. If the Fieschi Letter really was written by him, thanks to our research it would become extraordinarily difficult to explain away. Of course, people will still be able to claim that he was simply lying, but they would also have to explain why, and how on earth he thought he could get away with it, given his position.

Another document that might prove very useful is a *legatio*, a bequest to a church, monastery or other religious institution. A great many bequests were made in exchange for perpetual Masses to be said for the soul of a dead person. A *legatio* by any of the people you have read about in this book, to say Mass for the soul of Edward II, would help reveal when that person thought Edward II was dead, and possibly also places associated with him. For example, a bequest by a member of the Fieschi family to say Mass for his soul in one of the places listed in the Fieschi Letter would be, to say the least, tantalising. Since the letter mentions locations ranging from the Low Countries to France, Germany, Switzerland and Italy, there is quite a lot of room for this. But such documents from England, too, could be revealing. These bequests are also useful because they tend to be preserved, since they were useful to the religious institutions in order to explain how they acquired land, money and goods. A *legatio* mentioning Edward II in any context at all would be extremely useful to us.

Another kind of document that may tip the balance is a private letter from any one of the people mentioned in this book or addressed to any of the people mentioned in this book. As you know by now, the two most controversial, and useful, documents found to date are both letters, the Melton Letter and the Fieschi Letter. Another such find might be invaluable. As the collection of letters addressed to Luca Fieschi reminds us, any of these documents may literally turn up *anywhere*.

Since we just don't know exactly what kind of document may turn up, and where, I would say that if you have come across anything at all referring to the places or people mentioned in this book, and in particular mentioned in the Melton Letter and the Fieschi Letter, from the years 1327 to about 1350, we would be extremely interested in it.

If you look at our website, you will find complete lists of these people and places, and also lists of the archival material we have already examined, so that you don't go needlessly looking in places we have already looked. Although, if you do want to look there, it is welcome, because we might have missed something: we are only human.

JOIN US IN OUR QUEST

From Ivan: On behalf of all the people involved in the Auramala Project and in research into this historical mystery, Kathryn Warner and I wish to personally invite all readers to give thought to taking part in our research, in one way or another. It is a way to democratise the study of history, and bring our shared heritage back into our hands. Communication technologies have given lay people the chance to stop being mere readers of history books, and start help writing them instead. Why don't you seize that chance, and help us find King Edward II of England?

From Kathryn: This book is not intended to be the last word on Edward II's fate in and after 1327, but will, I hope, inspire further research and debate. Maybe one of you will find a document which will go some way to proving either that Edward died in 1327, or that he didn't. Finally, if you have any ideas or questions about anything you've read in the book, if there's anything that's occurred to you which I failed to mention, I'd love to hear from you. I'm always open to arguments, debates and theories on the matter, whatever side you happen to take, whether you believe passionately that Edward II was murdered in 1327 or whether you think he was alive years later in Italy or whether you're still on the fence. It's such a wonderful, rich debate and I would dearly love to hear your thoughts on the subject. Email me any time at edwardofcaernarfon@yahoo.com, or leave a comment on my Edward II Facebook page, https://www.facebook.com/EdwardofCaernarfon/, or my blog at https://www.edwardthesecond.blogspot.com. The Auramala Project's site is at https://theauramalaproject.wordpress.com/, and they would also be delighted to hear from you.

APPENDIX 1

THE FIESCHI LETTER

The Fieschi Letter of *c.* 1338, now in an archive in France.[1]

In the name of the Lord, Amen. That which I heard of the confession of your father I wrote by my own hand and therefore I took care to make it known to your highness. First he says that feeling England in subversion against him, afterwards owing to the threat of your mother, he withdrew from his family in the castle of the Earl Marshal by the sea, which is called Chepstow. Afterwards, driven by fear, he boarded a ship with lords Hugh Despenser and the Earl of Arundel and several others and made his way by sea to Glamorgan, and there he was captured, together with the said Lord Hugh and Master Robert Baldock; and they were captured by Lord Henry of Lancaster, and they led him to the castle of Kenilworth, and others were led elsewhere to various places; and there he lost the crown by the request of many. Afterwards, in consequence, you were crowned on the feast of Candlemas next following. Finally they sent him to the castle of Berkeley. Afterwards the servant who was keeping him, after some little time, said to your father: Lord, Sir Thomas Gurney and Sir Simon Bereford, knights, have come with the purpose of killing you. If it pleases, I shall give you my clothes, that you may better be able to escape. Then with the said clothes, as night was near, he went out of the prison; and when he had reached the last door without resistance, because he was not recognised, he found the porter sleeping, whom he immediately killed; and having got the keys of the door, he opened the door and went out, with his keeper who was keeping him. The said knights who had come to kill him, seeing that he had thus fled, fearing the indignation of the queen, even the danger to their persons, thought to put that aforesaid porter, his heart having been extracted, in a box, and maliciously presented to the queen the heart and body of the aforesaid porter as the body of your father, and as the body of the said king the said porter was buried in Gloucester. And after he had gone out of the prisons of the aforesaid castle, he was received in the castle of Corfe with his companion who was keeping him in the prisons by Sir Thomas, castellan of the said castle, the lord being unaware, Lord John Maltravers, lord of the said Thomas, in which castle he stayed secretly for a year and a half. Afterwards, having heard that the Earl of Kent, because he said he was alive, had been beheaded, he took a ship with his said keeper and with the consent and counsel of the said Thomas, who had received him, crossed into Ireland, where he stayed for nine months. Afterwards, fearing lest he be recognised there, having taken the habit of a hermit, he came back to England and landed at the port of Sandwich, and in the same habit crossed the sea to Sluys. Afterwards he turned his steps to Normandy and from Normandy, as many do, going through Languedoc, came to Avignon, where, having given a florin to a servant of the pope, sent by the said servant a document to Pope John, which pope had him called to him, and held him secretly and honourably for more than fifteen days. Finally, after various discussions, all things having been considered, permission having been received, he went to Paris, and from Paris to Brabant, from Brabant to Cologne so that out of devotion he might see The Three Kings, and leaving Cologne he crossed over Germany, that is to say, he headed for Milan in Lombardy, and from Milan he entered a certain hermitage of the castle (fief) of *Milascio*, in which hermitage he stayed for two years and a half; and because war came to the said castle, he moved to the castle of Cecima in another hermitage of the diocese of Pavia in Lombardy, and he was in this last hermitage for two years or thereabouts, always the recluse, doing penance and praying to God for you and other sinners.

In testimony of which I caused my seal to be affixed for the consideration of Your Highness. Your Manuele de Fieschi, notary the lord
pope, your devoted servant.

The Latin original:

*In nomine Domini amen. Ea que audivi ex confessione patris vestri manu mea
propria scripsci et propterea ad vestri dominacionem intimari curavi. Primo dicit
quod sentiens Angliam in subversione contra ipsum, propterea monitu matris
vestre, recessit a familia sua in castro Comitis Marescali supra mare, quod vocatur
Gesosta. Postea, timore ductus, ascendit barcham unam cum dominis Ugone
Dispensario et comiti Arundele et aliquibus aliis, et aplicuit in Glomorgam
supra mare, et ibi fuit captus, una cum domino dicto Ugone et magistro Roberto
de Baldoli; et fuerunt capti per dominum Henricum de Longo Castello, et
duxerunt ipsum in castro Chilongurda, et alii fuerunt alibi ad loca diversa; et
ibi perdidit coronam ad requisicionem multorum. Postea subsequenter fuistis
coronatus in proximiori festo sancte Marie de la Candelor. Ultimum miserunt
eum ad castrum de Berchele. Postea famulus qui custodiebat ipsum post aliqua
tempora, dixit patri vestro: Domine, dominus Thomas de Gornay et dominus
Symon Desberfort, milites, venerunt causa interficiendi vos. Si placet, dabo vobis
raubas meas, ut melius evadere possitis. Tunc cum dictis raubis, hora quasi notis,
exivit carcerem; et dum pervenisset usque ad ultimum ostium sine resistencia,
quia non cognoscebatur, invenit ostiarium dormientem, quem subito interfecit; et
receptis clavibus ostii, aperuit ostium et exivit, et custos suus qui eum custodiebat.
Videntes dicti milites, qui venerant ad interficiendum ipsum, quod sic recesserat,
dubitantes indignacionem regine, ymo periculum personarum, deliberarunt istum
predictum porterium, extracto sibi corde, ponere in una cufia, et cor et corpus
predicti porterii ut corpus patris vestri maliciose regine presentarunt, et ut corpus
regis dictus porterius in Glocesta fuit sepultus. Et postquam exivit carceres castri
antedicti, fuit receptatus in castro de Corf con socio suo qui custodiebat ipsum
in carceribus per dominum Thomam, castellanum dicti castri, ignorante domino
domino Johanne Maltraverse, domino dicti Thome, in quo castro secrete fuit per
annum cum dimidio. Postea, audito quod comes Cancii quia dixerat eum vivere,
fuerat decapitatus, ascendit unam navem cum dicto custode suo, et de voluntate et
consilio dicti Thome qui ipsum receptaverat, et transivit in Yrlandam, ubi fuit per*

.viiij. menses. Postea dubitans ne ibi cognosceretur, recepto habitu unius heremite, redivit in Angliam et aplicuit ad portum de Sandvic, et in eodem habitu trnsivit mare apud Sclusam. Postea diresit gressus suos in Normandia et de Normandia, ut in pluribus, transeundo per Linguam Octanam, venit Avinionem, ubi, dato uno floreno uni servienti pape, misit per dictum servientem unam cedulam pape Johanni, qui papa eum ad se vocari fecit, et ipsum secrete 30 tenuit honorifice ultra .xv. dies. Finaliter, post tractatus diversos, consideratis omnibus, recepta licencia, ivit Parisius et de Parisius in Braybantia, de Braybantia in Coloniam ut videret .iij. reges causa devocionis, et recedendo de Colonia per Alamania(m) transivit sive peresit Mediolanum in Lombardia(m), et de Mediolano intravit quoddam heremitorium castri Milasci, in quo heremitorio stetit per duos annos cum dimidio; et quia dicto castro guerra supervenit, mutavit se in castro Cecime, in alio heremitorio diocesis Papiensis in Lombardiam, et fuit in isto ultimo heremitorio per duos annos vel circa, semper inclusus, agendo penitenciam, et Deum pro vobis et aliis peccatoribus orando.

In quorum testimonium, sigillum, contemplacione vestre dominacionis, duxi apponendum. Vester Manuel de Flisco, domini pape notarius, devotus servitor vester.

APPENDIX 2

THE MELTON LETTER

The Melton Letter of 14 January (almost certainly 1330), with the statement that Edward II is alive in bold.[2]

William by the sufferance of God Archbishop of York, primate of England, to our dear valet Simon Swanland, citizen of London, greetings with the blessing of God and ours. Dear friend, we have heard from several of our confidants that we may reveal to you our secret business safely in all things. Wherefore we pray you, on the blessing of God and ours, that the thing we are sending to you remain secret, and that you do not reveal it to any man or woman in the world until we have spoken together. Please know that we have certain news of our liege lord Edward of Caernarfon, that **he is alive and in good physical health** and in a safe place by his own wish [or command], wherefore we are more joyous than we ever have been at this news we have heard. Wherefore we beg you as dearly as we trust in you that you procure for us a loan of two hundred pounds in gold, if you can have it brought secretly to the said lord from us for his comfort, and that you obtain two half cloths of different colours, a good cloth and intimate clothing and good fur of miniver [expensive fur from ermine or squirrel] for six garments, and three hoods, with miniver for finishing the hoods, and two coverlets of different colours of the largest size, with the hangings, and two belts and two bags, the best you can find for sale, and twenty ells of linen cloth dyed red, and ask for his cordovan [expensive Spanish leather] so that we will have six pairs of shoes and two pairs of boots, and have all the above-mentioned things packaged up in a bundle as mercers [cloth merchants] carry their goods. And we are sending you a horse and Brother William Cliff, bearer of these letters, to whom we wish you to deliver this same bundle, packaged up in the way stated above, and we will send you our bond of two hundred pounds, to be paid eight days after the Purification next coming [i.e. on 10 February, presumably 1330] at our manor of Cawood, and put the other things stated above in writing and you will be paid promptly.

Dear friend, please do these things at our request, for your great honour and profit, and ours, if it may please God. So many are the robberies on the road to our parts that we have been counselled to send you our letters [of protection] for doing these things, and that you should deliver to the bearer of these [letters] cloth for one robe and one fur, and include these in your account to us, and if he tells you that he has other expenses, deliver them to him and other things which he asks of you on our behalf and ensure that they are quickly delivered. And when it is delivered, set out yourself to us as soon as you can, to advise us how we will borrow a great sum of money for the said lord, as we wish that he may be helped as far as we and you are able to arrange. May God keep you. Written at our manor of Cawood on the day after Saint Hilary [i.e. 14 January].

The French original:

William par la soeffrance de dieu ercevesqe Deverwyk primat Dengleterre a nostre cher vallet Simond de Swaneslond citeseyn de Loundres saluz oue la benisoun de dieu et la nostre. Cher ami, nous auoms entendu par ascuns de notz privez qe nous vous purroms monstrer nostre prive conseil seurment en totes choses. Par qoi nous vous prioms sur la benisoun de dieu et la nostre qe ceste chose vous maundoms soit conseil, et qe vous ne le monstrez a nul homme ne femme du monde tant qe nous averoms parle ensemble. Voillez saver qe nous avome certeins noueles de nostre seignur lige Edward de Karnarvan qil est en vie et en bone sancte de corps en enseur leu a sa volonte demeign par quoi nous sumes plus ioyous qe unqes nous fumes des nouels qe nous oiames. Par quoi nous vous prioms si cherment com nous affioms en vous qe vous nous faire chevisance de CC li en or si vous les poetz aver pur esement et privement mener devers le dit seignur par nous et qe vous facez quere deux demi draps de divers colours, bon drap et prive vesture et bon pelur de meneveir pur vi garmentz et iii chaperons de meneveir pur perfourner les chaperons et deux couerlites de divers colours de la plus large assis oue les tapitz e ii seynturs et ii pouches des mellours qe vous sauerez trover avendre et xx alnes de drap linge de lak et demandez son cordwan et faites qe nous eioms vi peires de solers et ii peires de botes, et faites trusser les choses susdites en un fardel com les mercers menons lour mercerie, et nous vous mandoms un cheval et le frère Sire William de Clyf portour de cestes a qi nous voloms qe vous deliverez mesme cel fardel trusse en la manere susdite et nous vous maundoms nostre obligacion de CC li a paier oct iours apres la Purificacion prochein avenir a nostre manoir de Kawod et les autres choses susdites metez en escript et vous seriez prestement paiez.

Cestes choses cher ami voillez faire a nostre requeste pur vestre graunt honur et profit et le nostre, si dieu plest. Honi fet tant deroberies sur le chemyn devers noz parties qe nous avoms enconseil de vous maunder noz lettres a cestes choses faire deliverez al portour de cestes drap pur I robe et I forour et countez les en vestre accompte devers nous et sil eit [. . .]stir de dispenses deliverez ly et autres choses ce qil vous demaunde depar nous et faites qil soit hastiuementz delivres et quant it serra deliveres dressez vous devers nous aplus tot qe vous poetz pur nous ensenser coment nous cheviroms de grant somme dargent pur le dit seignur qe nous voloms qil soit ayde de quantqe nous et vous purroms cheuir a dieux qe gard. Escrit a nostre manoir de Kawod lendemayn de seint Hillaer.

APPENDIX 3

LORD BERKELEY'S TESTIMONY

Extract from Lord Berkeley's testimony to the November–December 1330 Parliament:[3]

Thomas of Berkeley, knight, came before the lord king in his full aforesaid Parliament, and spoke of this, that since the Lord Edward late king of England, the father of the present lord king, was lately delivered into the safekeeping of Thomas and of a certain John Maltravers to be kept in the castle of Thomas at Berkeley in the county of Gloucester, and was murdered and killed in the same castle in the keeping of Thomas and John, he wishes to acquit himself of the death of the same king, and says that he was never an accomplice, a helper or procurer in his death, nor did he ever know of his death until the present Parliament. And of this he is ready to acquit himself, as the king's court will consider.

And on this it was asked of him, that since he is lord of the aforesaid castle, and the same lord king was delivered into the keeping of Thomas and John to be kept safely, and they received and accepted the keeping of the king, how can he excuse himself, but that he should be answerable for the death of the king. And the aforesaid Thomas says that it is true that he is lord of the aforesaid castle, and that he together with John Maltravers received the keeping of the king to be kept safely as is said above. But he says that at the time when it is said that the lord king was murdered and killed, he was detained with such and so great an illness outside the aforesaid castle at Bradley that he remembers nothing of this … Whereupon he says that concerning the death of the lord king he is not guilty of helping, approving or procuring his death.

In the original Latin, as far as 'as the king's court will consider':

Thomas de Berkele miles venit coram domino rege in pleno Parliamento suo predicto, et allocutus de hoc, quod cum dominus Edwardus nuper rex Anglie, pater domini regis nunc, in custodia ipsius Thome et cujusdam Johannis Mautravers nuper extitit liberatus ad salvo custodiendum in castro ipsius Thome apud Berkele in comitatu Gloucestrie, et in eodem castro in custodia ipsorum Thome et Johannis murdratus extitit et interfectus, qualiter se velit de morte ipsius regis acquietare, dicit quod ipse nuncquam fuit consentiens, auxilians, seu procurans, ad mortem suam, nec unquam scivit de morte sua usque in presenti Parliamento isto. Et de hoc paratus est se acquietare, prout curia regis consideraverit.

APPENDIX 4

THE CONFESSION OF EDMUND OF WOODSTOCK

The confession of Edmund of Woodstock, Earl of Kent, made on 16 March 1330:[4]

This acknowledgement was made before Robert Howell, coroner of the king's household, and afterwards before the great men and peers of the land, at Winchester, on the sixteenth day of March, in the fourth year [of Edward III's reign, i.e. 1330]: That is, that Edmund, earl of Kent acknowledges that the pope charged him, on his blessing, that he should use his pains and diligence to deliver Edward, his brother, formerly king of England, and that thereto he would find his costs. And he said that a friar preacher of the convent of London came to him, at Kensington near London, and told him that he had raised up the devil [*avoit leve le deable*], who declared to him for certain that Edward, his brother, formerly king of England, was alive. And he said that the archbishop of York sent to him by a chaplain, Sir Aleyn, a letter of credence, which was: that he would aid him in the deliverance of his brother with five thousand pounds and moreover with as much as he had and as much as he could give. And he said that Sir Ingelram Berenger told him in London, from Sir William de la Zouche, that he would give as much as he could for the deliverance of his brother. And he said that Sir William Cliff came to him on the same message, by these signs that they rode together between Woking and Guildford, and he told him that he should avoid the town of Guildford by reason of his niece [Eleanor] Despenser who was in the same town of Guildford; and this same Sir William spoke to him of the alliance between Richard son of the earl of Arundel, and his [step]daughter★, and said moreover that this would be the greatest honour that ever befell him, and that he would aid him as much as he could to do this thing.

And he said that this same William came unto him from Hugh Despenser★★, who told him that he would be well pleased to be with him; for he said that he would be sure of the deliverance in short time. And he said that Sir William of Durham, clerk of his letters, and Brother Thomas of Bromfield were they who most abetted him and enticed him to do these things aforesaid. And he said that Sir Robert Taunton, from the archbishop of York, brought a message of these things aforesaid, and told him that he had ready five thousand pounds to do this business aforesaid, and this of the money of Sir Hugh Despenser★★★. And he said that this same Sir Robert and two friars preachers who are out of their [Dominican] order, of whom one is called Edmund Savage and the other John, were the chief brokers in this matter. And he said that Sir Fulk Fitzwarin came to him at Westminster and begged and enticed him to begin this thing, and encouraged him to do these things, and told him that this would be the greatest honour that ever befell him, and told him that he would aid him with body and heart and whatever he had. And he said that Sir Ingelram Berenger came to him from Sir John Pecche, that he was of this faction, and thereto would bestow body and heart and whatsoever he had. And he said that Sir Henry Beaumont and Sir Thomas Roscelyn talked to him in Paris, in the chamber of the duke of Brabant, that they were ready to come to England in aid of these things aforesaid; and that they enticed him to do these things; and that they would land towards the parts of Scotland, with countenance of Donald of Mar, and that he would aid them to uphold these things, and with all his strength. But the time of their coming is passed.

And he said that Sir Richard of Pontefract, confessor of the lady of Vescy★★★★, came to him at Kensington, at the coronation [of Queen Philippa on 18 February 1330], and afterwards at Arundel, from the archbishop of York, for these things aforesaid. And he said that a monk of Quarr and John Gymmynges, his cousin, had equipped a ship, a barge and a boat, to bring his brother and him to his castle of Arundel and from there wherever was ordained. And he said that of these things aforesaid he opened himself to Sir E[dward] of Monchiver [*recte* Monthermer] and George Percy. And he said that the letters which he sent to Sir Bogo Bayouse and to John Deveril, sealed with his seal, he sent them – the one letter written by the hand of his wife [Margaret Wake]. And he said that Ingelram Berenger, Malcolm Musard and John Gymmynges worked and took pains to do these things. And he said that Ingelram Berenger came unto him at Arundel, in his chamber above the chapel, and said that the bishop of London [Stephen Gravesend] would aid him in the deliverance of his brother with whatever he had. And these things he acknowledged to be true, and yields himself guilty that he has borne himself evilly for the undoing of his liege lord [Edward III] and of his crown, by countenance of these men aforesaid; and he wholly submits himself to the king's will, to come, in his shirt, to London, or in this city [Winchester], barefoot, or wherever the king shall appoint, with a rope around his neck, to do with him whatever shall please him.

*Isabella, eldest daughter of Hugh Despenser the Younger and the great-niece of Edward II and the Earl of Kent, who married the Earl of Arundel's son Richard Fitzalan in February 1321 when they were both children. William la Zouche married her widowed mother Eleanor Despenser née de Clare in early 1329.

**Eldest son and heir of Hugh Despenser the Younger, and William la Zouche's stepson, in prison in Bristol Castle; great-nephew of the Earl of Kent though only seven or eight years his junior.

***The identity of the Hugh Despenser mentioned here is unclear, or why Archbishop William Melton had so much of his money. Hugh Despenser the Elder and Younger were convicted of treason in 1326 and thus all their lands and their property were forfeit and should have gone to the Crown. It is also unclear why Edward II's and Kent's niece Eleanor Despenser, Hugh the Younger's widow and now married to William la Zouche, would have been so hostile to the Earl of Kent's plot that Kent was advised to avoid Guildford because she was there.

Eleanor had always been very close to Edward II, so much so that one chronicler thought they were having an incestuous affair, so it is hard to imagine that she would not have been happy to hear of his survival and of the plot to free him, especially as her new husband, her eldest son, her son-in-law Richard Fitzalan and her half-brother Edward de Monthermer were involved in it. Perhaps Kent was advised to avoid her so as not to incriminate her in the plot given that she spent much of Queen Isabella's regency in prison as it was, and was already in trouble in 1329–30 because she and la Zouche besieged Caerphilly Castle (her birthplace) in February–March 1329 in an attempt to gain control of it.

★★★★Isabella, sister of Henry, Lord Beaumont and Louis Beaumont, Bishop of Durham, and widow of John, Lord Vescy. She was a second cousin of Edward II and was also related to Queen Isabella, rather more distantly.

ABBREVIATIONS IN NOTES AND BIBLIOGRAPHY

AL:	*Annales Londonienses*
Anon:	*Anonimalle Chronicle*
AP:	*Annales Paulini*
CCR:	Calendar of Close Rolls
CCW:	Calendar of Chancery Warrants 1244–1326
CFR:	Calendar of Fine Rolls
CIM:	Calendar of Inquisitions Miscellaneous
CPL:	Calendar of Papal Letters Relating to Britain and Ireland 1305–41
CPR:	Calendar of Patent Rolls
Haines, Death:	Roy Martin Haines, *Death of a King*
Intrigue:	Ian Mortimer, *Medieval Intrigue: Decoding Royal Conspiracies*
Murimuth:	*Adae Murimuth Continuatio Chronicarum*
ODNB:	Oxford Dictionary of National Biography
Phillips:	Seymour Phillips, *Edward II*
PROME:	The Parliament Rolls of Medieval England
SAL MS:	Society of Antiquaries of London, Manuscript
TNA:	The National Archives (C: Chancery; DL: Duchy of Lancaster; E: Exchequer; KB: King's Bench; SC: Special Collections)
Vita:	*Vita Edwardi Secundi*
Warner:	Kathryn Warner, *Edward II: The Unconventional King*

NOTES

Introduction

1   Cuttino and Lynam, 'Where is Edward II?', 525, for the quotation. Desmond Seward's *The Devil's Brood*, published in 2014, and Robert Easton's 2013 *Royal Dates with Destiny* (which peculiarly gives the date of Edward's death as 20 February 1327, seven months too early) are just two of the many books published in the second decade of the twenty-first century which repeat the story.

2   Doherty, *Isabella and the Strange Death of Edward II* (2003); Weir, *Isabella, She-Wolf of France, Queen of England* (2005).

Chapter 1

1   There was also his youngest child Eleanor, born the year before his death, but she died as a child in 1311.

Chapter 2

1   Phillips, 98.

2   *CPR 1327–30*, 439; *The Household Book of Queen Isabella of England for the Fifth Regnal Year of Edward II*, ed. F. G. Blackley and G. Hermansen (Edmonton, 1971), 208.

3   Warner, *Isabella of France: The Rebel Queen*, 66–7.

4   *Household Book of Queen Isabella*, 219.

Chapter 3

1   Warner, 193–6.

2   Warner, *Isabella*, 189–96; *Edward II*, 198–203.

3   Warner, 168–9.

4   *Extraits d'une Chronique Anonyme intitulée Ancienne Chroniques de Flandre* in *Recueil des Historiens des Gaules et de France*, vol. 22, 425 note 4: *la royne … entra dans la chambre ou il estoit et s'agenoulla devant lui, et lui request que pour Dieu il vaulaist reffroidier son yre; main oncques le roy ne lui vault faire responce ne regarder sur elle.*

Chapter 4

1 *CPL*, 474; Warner, 191; Warner, *Isabella*, 179–80.
2 *CPL*, 253, 479.
3 SAL MS 122, 34; this definitely occurred in 1325, not 1326 as stated in Phillips, 545.
4 *CFR 1319–27*, 95, 101, 185.
5 *CPR 1327–30*, 51.
6 *Chronicle of Lanercost*, 258–9.
7 *AP*, 337.
8 *Anon*, 134.
9 *Murimuth*, 52: *fuit nimis delicate tractatus*.
10 *CCR 1327–30*, 77, 86.
11 *CPR 1317–21*, 364, 452; *CPR 1324–27*, 5; *CPR 1327–30*, 328; *CCR 1323–27*, 202–3, 554; *CFR 1319–27*, 85, 97, 280, 383; Haines, 'Sir Thomas Gurney, Regicide?', 53.
12 *AP*, 337; *Murimuth*, 52. Phillips, 543 note 130, citing *CIM 1308–48*, 286 (number 1166), notes that in January 1331 there was a room at Gloucester Castle called *Edwardes chaumbre* and a latrine opposite called *Kyngeswardrobe*, which might suggest that Edward stayed there, not at Llanthony Secunda.
13 *AP*, 333.
14 *Murimuth*, 52: *fuit usque Berkeley deductus secrete*.
15 Haines, 'Thomas Gurney, Regicide?' 55 note 62, citing Berkeley Castle Select Roll 39.
16 Galbraith, 'Extracts from the *Historia Aurea*', 216, and see Haines, 'Gurney, Regicide?', 55.
17 *Murimuth*, 52.
18 Phillips, 541.
19 Doherty, *Death*, 119–20.
20 Haines, 'Edwardus Redivivus', 70–1.
21 *ODNB* (grandfather); *CCR 1323–27*, 101, 120; *CPR 1321–42*, 168, 372, 378; *CPR 1327–30*, 100 (Despenser adherent); TNA SC 8/47/2308 (under-sheriff). Langland was the (presumably illegitimate) son of Rokele's son Eustace, known as Stacy, who was named after Rokele's own father: *CCR 1330–33*, 181.
22 *CCR 1323–27*, 169, 532 (witnessing Despenser grants); SC 8/98/4856 (petition).
23 Scott L. Waugh, 'For King, Country, and Patron: The Despensers and Local Administration 1321–1322', *The Journal of British Studies*, 22 (1983), 28, for Aylmer.
24 *CPR 1327–30*, 99.
25 *CPR 1327–30*, 74–99.
26 *CPR 1327–30*, 153.
27 TNA SC 1/29/64; Phillips, 542.
28 *Murimuth*, 52.

29 *Brut*, 253; Galbraith, 'Extracts', 216; *Recueil des Historiens*, 425 note 4.

30 *Lanercost*, 257.

31 *CCR 1327–30*, 212.

32 *CCR 1327–30*, 142, 157, 212; *CPR 1327–30*, 139, 180–1, 183, 191.

33 *CCR 1327–30*, 169, 187–8, 273, 278.

34 Tanqueray, 'Conspiracy of Thomas Dunheved', 119–20.

35 *CPR 1327–30*, 156–7.

36 *CPR 1327–30*, 95.

37 For Redmere, see TNA E 101/100/12, E 101/99/27; *CPR 1317–21*, 313; *CPR 1321–24*, 334; *CPR 1324–27*, 297; for Norton, TNA SC 8/6/286, SC 8/6/287, SC 8/114/5675, SC 8/3/150, SC 8/4/153; *CCW*, 274, 306; *CPR 1307–13*, 490; *CPR 1313–17*, 574–5.

38 *CPR 1327–30*, 99 (Dunheved), 156 (Norton and Redmere).

39 *CCR 1327–30*, 179.

40 *CCR 1327–30*, 232–3.

41 *CIM 1308–48*, 274–5.

42 TNA C 8/69/3444.

43 *CPR 1330–34*, 470.

44 TNA KB 27/272, membrane 2v.

45 *CCR 1330–33*, 178, 181.

46 *CCR 1333–37*, 712; *CFR 1337–47*, 43, 48.

47 *AP*, 337.

48 *Lanercost*, 259; *Anon*, 134.

49 *CCR 1327–30*, 146.

50 *CCR 1327–30*, 549. On 30 July 1329, Newgate was said to be 'so weak and threatened with ruin that the prisoners cannot be kept therein unless it be speedily repaired'. *CCR 1327–30*, 483. This gives some insight into how Dunheved was able to get out, and the order from the government to repair the prison may have been prompted by his escape.

51 *CCR 1327–30*, 158.

52 *CPR 1324–27*, 336.

53 *CCR 1327–30*, 182.

54 *CPR 1327–30*, 238, 242, 256, 272, 273.

55 Tout, 'Captivity and Death of Edward of Carnarvon', 165, 184–5: Shalford *conseilla qe le dit sire Rogier qil ordinast tiel remedie endroit des choses susdites qe le dit sire Rees ne nul autre Dengleterre ne de Gales aueroient matere de penser de sa deliueraunce.*

56 *CPR 1324–27*, 249.

57 *CPR 1321–24*, 77.

Chapter 5

1 Doherty, *Death*, 221.

2 TNA DL 10/253.

3 Cited in Haines, '*Edwardus Redivivus*', 85 note 98.

4   Tout, 'Captivity', 184. Shalford's letter was dated *le lundy procheyn apres la feste de la Natiuite nostre Dame, lan du regne nostre seignur le roi Edward qore est, qe Dieu gard, premer*, 'the Monday next after the feast of the Nativity of Our Lady, in the first year of the reign of our present lord king Edward, whom God protect', which is 14 September 1327 (the Nativity of the Virgin Mary is 8 September, which fell on a Tuesday in 1327).

5   Moore, 'Documents relating to the Death and Burial', 216–17, 223: *quo die idem Rex E. pater obiit apud Berkele*, 'the same day that King E. the father died at Berkeley'.

6   Phillips, 549 note 166.

7   *AP*, 337: *obiit rex Edwardus, qui cognominabatur de Carnarvan quia ibidem natus fuit, in castello de Berkele, ubi in custodia tenebatur*.

8   *Murimuth*, 53–4, 63.

9   Cited in Ian Mortimer's article 'Sermons of Sodomy' in *Reign of Edward II: New Perspectives*, ed. Dodd and Musson, 58.

10   *Anon*, 134: *Avint isint tost apres qe la roi eu maladist illueqes et murust le jour de seint Matheu le apostre devant le seint Michel, et fust enterre a Gloucestre en la veille de seint Thomas, quant il avoit regne xix annz, trois mois et deux semaines, de qi alme dieu ait merci amen*.

11   Cited in Phillips, 561: *enmaladist en le dit chastel de Berkelee grevousement de grant dolour et morust*.

12   Cited in Haines, 'Roger Mortimer's Scam', 146; Haines, '*Edwardus Redivivus*', 72; Mortimer, 'Sermons of Sodomy' in *Reign of Edward II*, 59, 60; Phillips, 561.

13   *Recueil des Historiens*, 427 (my translation).

14   *Lanercost*, 259.

15   Cited and translated in Tout, 'Captivity', 166.

16   *Scalacronica*, ed. Maxwell, 74; ed. Stevenson, 152.

17   *Croniques de London*, 58; Phillips 561 and note 236, citing the Wigmore chronicle: *quicquid aliter pacis mundi ablocuntur morte naturali moriebatur*.

18   Cited in Phillips, 562–3.

19   Brereton, *Froissart*, 43. Froissart calls Edward Despenser *messire Edouwart le Espensier*. Some months later, on 6 January 1367, Froissart was in Bordeaux when Edward II's great-grandson Richard II was born there.

20   *Brut*, 253 (modernised spelling).

21   Translated and cited in Haines, *Death of a King*, 49.

22   Galbraith, 'Extracts', 217 (my translation).

23   Mortimer, *Perfect King*, 484 note 16.

24   Antonia Gransden, *Historical Writing in England II: c.1307 to the Early Sixteenth Century* (London, 1982), 43.

Chapter 6

1   For all the preceding, *Intrigue*, 67–8.

2   Moore, 'Documents', 220, suggests that the 'secret' embalming 'shows almost conclusively that there was good reason to conceal a crime'.

3 Haines, 'Edwardus Redivivus', 73.
4 F.D. Blackley, 'Isabella of France, Queen of England (1308–1358) and the Late Medieval Cult of the Dead', *Canadian Journal of History*, 14 (1980), 26.
5 Moore, 'Documents', 217, 226.
6 Beaukaire's name appears twenty-first on a list of twenty-seven *servientes ad arma* in Edward III's household on 24 June 1328: *Calendar of Memoranda Rolls (Exchequer) Michaelmas 1326–Michaelmas 1327*, 375.
7 *CPR 1327–30*, 37–9.
8 *Intrigue*, 66 and 100 note 32.
9 *Murimuth*, 53–4: *Et licet multi abbates, priores, milites, burgenses de Bristollia et Gloucestria ad videndum corpus suum integrum fuissent vocati, et tale superficialiter conspexissent*. Both Bristol and Gloucester are about 20 miles from Berkeley, in opposite directions.
10 Haines, 'Roger Mortimer's Scam', 146 note 43. He also states, p. 145, that 'superficially' means that the men 'could not inspect it [the body] very closely'. This may be true but is also speculation; Murimuth does not say that.
11 King, 'Death of Edward II Revisited', 5, 20.
12 Moore, 'Documents', 223.
13 Haines, 'Edwardus Redivivus', 72.
14 *CCR 1327–30*, 228.
15 Moore, 'Documents', 217, 225–6.
16 Moore, 217, 225.
17 Moore, 216.
18 W.M. Ormrod, 'The Personal Religion of Edward III', *Speculum*, 64 (1989), 870 note 120, citing TNA E 101/383/2.
19 Ralph E. Giesey, *The Royal Funeral Ceremony in Renaissance France* (Geneva, 1960), 82.
20 Moore, 'Documents', 221–2, for all the details in this paragraph.
21 Frances A. Underhill, *For Her Good Estate: The Life of Elizabeth de Burgh* (1999), 40–1; *CCR 1330–33*, 132.
22 Moore, 'Documents', 218.

Chapter 7

1 *PROME*, November 1330 Parliament.
2 *PROME*, November 1330 Parliament.
3 Tout, 'Captivity', 185: *Sur quey le dit sire Rogier monstra la dite lettre a Willame Docleye, et lui comaunda de porter la dite lettre a Bercleye*.
4 *CCR 1330–33*, 165.
5 As translated by the editors of *PROME*.
6 For more discussion on this point, see below, p. 123, 617.
7 John Smyth, *Lives of the Berkeleys*, vol. 1, 296–7. Smyth, a servant at Berkeley Castle for decades, wrote a most valuable account of the history of the family between 1616 and 1640. Many of the original documents he read no longer exist.

8   *CPR 1334–38*, 398.
9   W.M. Ormrod, *Edward III* (London and New Haven, 2011), 123 and 617.
10 *CCR 1330–33*, 315–16, 322, 324–5.
11 Galbraith, 'Extracts', 217.
12 *CCR 1330–33*, 322; *CPR 1330–34*, 121, 148; Haines, *Death of a King*, 91; Haines, 'Gurney, Regicide?', 59.
13 *CCR 1330–33*, 316, 322.
14 For the full story of Gurney's capture, see Hunter, 'On the Measures Taken', 278–86; Haines, *Death of a King*, 90–5; Haines, 'Gurney, Regicide?', 59–61.
15 *CCR 1330–33*, 575–6; *Foedera 1327–44*, 839; Hunter, 'Measures Taken', 282.

Chapter 8

1   *Calendar of the Plea and Memoranda Rolls of the City of London: volume 1: 1323–64* (1926), 72.
2   *CCR 1327–30*, 531.
3   *CPR 1327–30*, 373.
4   *CPR 1327–30*, 379, 385, 391, 397, 415.
5   *CPR 1327–30*, 396; Ormrod, *Edward III*, 82–3, 612.
6   Andy King, 'Death of Edward II Revisited', 9; *Intrigue*, 161.
7   *CPL*, 308; King, 'Revisited', 9 note 42.
8   *The Brut or the Chronicles of England*, ed. Brie, 263.
9   Phillips, 549 note 166.
10 G. O. Sayles, *Select Cases in the Court of the King's Bench under Edward III* (Selden Society, 76, 1957), 43. The Latin original says that Edward II *fuit superstes et in plena vita in prisona castri de Corfe*.
11 Sayles, *Select Cases*, 43–4.
12 *Foedera 1327–44*, 775.
13 Sayles, *Select Cases*, 44.
14 *Intrigue*, 161.
15 For Swanland as mayor and his family connection to Melton, see *Calendar of Letter-Books of London 1314–37*, 77; *Croniques de London*, 11; Gwyn A. Williams, *Medieval London* (2013), 131.
16 The letter is cited in full in English translation and the French original in Appendix 2.
17 Frederick Devon, *Issues of the Exchequer* (London, 1837), 133; SAL MS 122, 41; *Calendar of Memoranda Rolls Michaelmas 1326–Michaelmas 1327*, 374, 378.
18 Bloom, 'Simon de Swanland and Edward II', 2; Warner, 218.
19 *CPR 1321–24*, 189, 301, 324; *CPR 1327–30*, 25; Warner, 'Adherents of Edmund of Woodstock', 794 note 88.
20 Bloom, 'Swanland and Edward II', 1–2.
21 *Perfect King*, 77, 451 note 56.
22 Haines, 'Sumptuous Apparel for a Royal Prisoner', 892.
23 Melton's letter is only briefly mentioned in one footnote, 571 note 297, where Phillips states that it 'confirms that Melton had been led to believe

that Edward was still alive in 1330 but provides no evidence that this was the case'. One wonders what evidence could be provided in a letter beyond the archbishop's statement that Edward 'is alive and in good physical health' and his request for clothes and money for him.

24 *AL*, 249–51.
25 For example, in 1324 he defended and protected Adam Orleton, Bishop of Hereford, against Edward's persecution of him.
26 *Lanercost*, 217; *Vita*, 139.
27 *ODNB*, 'William Melton'.
28 *Brut*, 263; *AP*, 349.
29 *CCR 1330–33*, 132; *CPR 1327–30*, 557.
30 For an account of the timing of Kent's plot, see Ian Mortimer's 'Plot of the Earl of Kent 1328–30' in his *Medieval Intrigue*, and for an account of Kent's fellow conspirators and their backgrounds, see my article 'Adherents of Edmund of Woodstock'.
31 *Brut*, 263.
32 *Lanercost*, 264–5.
33 *Murimuth*, 255–6; *Intrigue*, 83, 86.
34 Haines, '*Edwardus Redivivus*', 75.
35 Haines, '*Edwardus Redivivus*', 75, 84 note 80 gives the story; *Murimuth*, 60; and see *AP*, 349.
36 *CPR 1327–30*, 125.
37 *Murimuth*, 52; *Brut*, 253.
38 *Intrigue*, 75 and 102 note 67; Haines, '*Edwardus Redivivus*', 71, both citing Berkeley Castle Muniment Select Rolls 39–40; King, 'Revisited', 10, citing TNA E 371/85 membrane 14, points out that Maltravers was appointed constable of Corfe Castle on 17 November 1326.
39 *Brut*, 265 (modernised spelling).
40 *CCR 1330–33*, 151. The other 'late enemies' included Hugh Despenser father and son and Edmund Fitzalan, Earl of Arundel, all executed in 1326.
41 See also below, in the section 'Arguments For and Against'.
42 *Brut*, 267.

Chapter 9

1 *CPR 1327–30*, 556–7, 571.
2 *CCR 1330–33*, 24.
3 *CCR 1330–33*, 24.
4 *CCR 1330–33*, 131. The counties were Surrey, Sussex, Hampshire, Bedfordshire, Buckinghamshire, Shropshire, Staffordshire, Nottinghamshire, Derbyshire, Essex, Hertfordshire, Gloucestershire, Herefordshire, Cambridgeshire, Northamptonshire, Suffolk and Norfolk.
5 *CPR 1327–30*, 557; *CCR 1330–33*, 132.
6 *CCR 1330–33*, 51.
7 Sayles, *Select Cases*, 44–5.

8   *CCR 1288–96*, 226; Martyn Lawrence, 'Power, Ambition and Political Rehabilitation: The Despensers, *c*.1281–1400' (Univ. of York DPhil thesis, 2005), 209.
9   *PROME*, January 1316 Parliament.
10 *CPR 1327–30*, 14; *CCR 1323–27*, 624.
11 *CFR 1307–19*, 201, 204, 208; *CFR 1319–27*, 21, 67, 130, 202; C. Moor, *Knights of Edward I* (1929), vol. 1, 81–2.
12 *Murimuth*, 255–6; *CFR 1327–37*, 169.
13 *CCR 1327–30*, 526, 555.
14 *CPR 1327–30*, 360, 375.
15 *Murimuth*, 256.
16 *Murimuth*, 255–6; *CFR 1327–37*, 181.
17 *Murimuth*, 255.
18 *CPR 1301–07*, 382.
19 For Musard and his career, see Warner, 'Adherents', 795.
20 *CPR 1327–30*, 326; *CFR 1327–37*, 43.
21 *CPR 1327–30*, 216–17; *CCR 1327–30*, 182.
22 *CPR 1317–21*, 584; *CPR 1321–24*, 203.
23 Warner, 'Adherents', 792–5.
24 *CCR 1327–30*, 195.
25 *CPR 1327–30*, 548–9, 557.
26 *CFR 1327–37*, 168–9, 175; *CPR 1327–30*, 557.
27 *Murimuth*, 256.
28 *CCR 1323–27*, 647–8, 652.
29 *CCR 1330–30*, 14.
30 *CPR 1317–21*, 419, 435; *CPR 1321–24*, 66.
31 *CPR 1317–21*, 278.
32 *CPR 1307–13*, 203, 325.
33 *CPR 1327–30*, 557.
34 *CPR 1327–30*, 529; *CCR 1330–33*, 63, 157; *CFR 1327–37*, 173.
35 *CFR 1327–37*, 122, 134, 162, 164, 171 (Caerphilly); *CCR 1330–3*, 38 (adhesion).
36 *CCR 1330–3*, 42–3; *CFR 1327–37*, 169.
37 *CPR 1327–30*, 571.
38 King, 'Revisited', 14–15; *AP*, 349.
39 *CPR 1327–30*, 459, 477; *CCR 1327–30*, 583–5; *Foedera 1327–44*, 774–5.
40 Kathleen Edwards, ed., *The Registers of Roger Martival, Bishop of Salisbury, 1315–1330*, 93; W. H. Dixon and J. Raine, *Fasti Eboracenses: Lives of the Archbishops of York*, vol. 1 (London, 1863), 429.
41 *Murimuth*, 255. There are no references to a man named Aleyn or Alan being arrested or having his goods seized because of adherence to Kent between March and August 1330, as many dozens of men were.
42 *Murimuth*, 256.
43 *CFR 1319–27*, 324, 330; *CFR 1327–37*, 44; *CCR 1327–30*, 190, 541; *CPL 1305–41*, 261, is a reference to Wyvill as Isabella's secretary in July 1327. On

26 October 1326, when Edward of Windsor was appointed keeper of the realm because Edward II had 'left' England when he sailed from Chepstow, Robert Wyvill had custody of the privy seal, an indication of how close he was to Isabella at that time; *CCR 1323–27*, 655.

44 *CFR 1327–37*, 432; *Calendar of Inquisitions Post Mortem 1336–46*, 198; TNA SC 6/978/30, C 143/227/15.
45 *CCR 1330–33*, 175.
46 *CPL 1305–41*, 359.
47 *CCR 1330–33*, 156.
48 *CPL 1305–41*, 297.
49 Phillips, 570 note 289; *Murimuth*, 255–6.
50 Hunter, 'Measures Taken', 283.
51 *Foedera 1327–44*, 843.
52 *CPR 1330–34*, 201.
53 *CPR 1330–34*, 144.
54 *CCR 1330–33*, 165. Two other men were ordered to be arrested as well: an adherent of Roger Mortimer called John Wyard, and John de Exonia (i.e. of Exeter), formerly constable of Wallingford Castle. Wyard was found and arrested before 12 January 1331, but was immediately pardoned for adherence to Mortimer: *CPR 1330–34*, 47, 53.
55 *CPR 1330–34*, 106; *CCR 1330–33*, 584.
56 *CPR 1330–34*, 18.
57 *CPR 1330–34*, 535.
58 *CPR 1334–38*, 88, 111–12.
59 *CPR 1340–43*, 378; *CPR 1343–5*, 173, 535, 541–2; *CPR 1345–8*, 532.
60 Phillips, '"Edward II" in Italy', 210.
61 *CCR 1330–33*, 175.
62 *Brut*, 264.
63 *CCR 1330–33*, 147.
64 *CPR 1327–30*, 544, 563, 570–2.
65 *CCR 1330–33*, 151.
66 *CPR 1327–30*, 544.
67 Haines, *Edward II*, 212, 233; Haines, *Death of a King*, 115.
68 *CCR 1330–33*, 24, 43; *CFR 1327–37*, 185.
69 *CPR 1330–34*, 20; *CCR 1330–33*, 74–7, 79, 81.
70 *PROME*, November 1330 Parliament.
71 Haines, 'Scam', 152–3.
72 *PROME*.
73 *Foedera 1327–44*, 783–4; *CPL 1305–41*, 499.

Chapter 10

1 See pp. 173, 178–83, 240–2 for more information.
2 Translation by the Auramala Project, used with kind permission; the full text is in the Appendix in English translation and the Latin original.

3 Geoffrey le Baker's *Chronicon*, translated by David Preest (2012), 22; Baker suggests that Edward was trying to reach Lundy Island in the Bristol Channel, which belonged to Hugh Despenser. Giovanni Vallani, *Nuova Cronica* (Fondazione Pietro Bembo, Ugo Guanda Editore in Parma, 1991), Libro Ottavo; *Recueil des Historiens*, vol. 22, 425 note 4: *Le roy Edouard, qui sur la mer estoit, ne scavoit que faire.*

4 SAL MS 122, 90.

5 Phillips, 591.

6 *Recueil des Historiens*, 424.

7 As noted by King, 'Revisited', 19 note 97.

8 *AP*, 311, which states *castrum fregerunt et occiso custode evaserunt*; *CPR 1327–30*, 42, 125: pardon to Walkfare in March 1327 for the escape and for the death of le Foulere.

9 Dixon and Raine, *Fasti Eboracenses*, vol. 1, 435–6.

10 King, 'Revisited', 10, citing TNA E 37185, membrane 14.

11 *CFR 1327–37*, 211.

12 *CPR 1327–30*, 557.

13 *CPR 1327–30*, 448; *CPR 1330–34*, 119; *CCR 1330–33*, 294. Two of Richard de Burgh's children, John and Maud, married Edward's niece and nephew Elizabeth and Gilbert de Clare in 1308, and a third, Eleanor de Burgh, had been one of Edward's companions before he became king. Elizabeth de Clare was the mother of William, Earl of Ulster. Edward arranged the future marriage of Eleanor de Burgh's son John Multon to Piers Gaveston's daughter Joan in 1317. Another de Burgh daughter, Elizabeth, married Robert Bruce in 1302; she was imprisoned by both Edward I and Edward II in and after 1306, but they treated her much better than Bruce's sisters, because of who her father was.

14 *CCR 1330–33*, 294.

15 Derek Vincent Stern, *A Hertfordshire Demesne of Westminster Abbey: Profits, Productivity and Weather* (2000), 94.

16 Vale, *The Princely Court*, 129–30.

17 *CPR 1307–13*, 76; Sarah Hopper, *To be a Pilgrim: The Medieval Pilgrimage Experience* (Stroud, 2002), 95; Père Jean Rocacher, *Rocamadour: Un Prêtre Raconte la Roche Mariale* (Paris, 1999), 22.

18 I am grateful to Elena Corbellini of the Auramala Project for this information.

19 https://theauramalaproject.wordpress.com/2016/05/23/the-hunt-for-the-king-35-mapping-the-fieschi-power-network/

20 Edward's only other surviving sister Mary the nun died at Amesbury Priory in May 1332. His other living sibling was Thomas of Brotherton, Earl of Norfolk, the elder of his two half-brothers, who lived until August 1338, but the two men had never been close. Thomas had not joined his brother the Earl of Kent's plot to free Edward in 1329–30, perhaps because he had married his son and heir to one of Roger Mortimer's daughters and thus felt tied to Mortimer and Isabella's regime (or perhaps because he did not believe Edward was alive).

21 Thank you to Ivan Fowler of the Auramala Project for the information.

22 J.R.S. Phillips, 'Edward II and the Prophets', in *England in the Fourteenth Century: Proceedings of the 1985 Harlaxton Symposium*, ed. W.M. Ormrod (Woodbridge, 1986), 196–8; T.A. Sandquist, 'The Holy Oil of St Thomas of Canterbury', in *Essays in Medieval History Presented to Bertie Wilkinson*, ed. T.A. Sandquist and M.R. Powicke (Toronto, 1969), 330–44. In the late 1390s, Edward's great-grandson Richard II found the holy oil locked in a chest in the Tower of London, though it is not entirely clear whether it had been in England for all the ninety years since 1308.

23 Mortimer, *Perfect King*, 20–1, 442 note 14; Ormrod, *Edward III*, 98; the *Brut* discusses the prophecy and Edward II's characterisation as a goat, 243.

24 Rupert Taylor, *The Political Prophecy in England* (New York, 1911), 48–52 and Appendix 1. I am grateful to Ivan Fowler for the reference.

25 Michael Prestwich, *Edward I* (London, 1988), 113.

26 Froissart, *Chronicles*, 165.

27 Hopper, *To be a Pilgrim*, 95.

28 Nadine Deutscher, *Der Schrein der Heiligen Drei Könige im Kölner Dom* (2011), 6ff.

29 Ormrod, 'Personal Religion of Edward III', 856.

30 Leonard Korth, *Köln im Mittelalter* (1888), 16–17, 61.

31 Klaus Jacobi, *Meister Eckhart in Köln: Lebensstationen-Redesituationen* (1999), 211.

32 Haines, *Death of a King*, 111; Haines, *Edward II*, 231; Cuttino and Lynam, 'Where is Edward II?', 542. The Duchy of Guelders now covers the territory of the modern Dutch province of Gelderland and part of the modern German state of North Rhine Westphalia; the Duchy of Jülich nowadays lies partly also in North Rhine Westphalia and partly in the Limburg province of the Netherlands, and is sometimes called Juliers, its French name.

33 Vale, *Princely Court*, 238, 311, 313.

34 Haines, *Death of a King*, 111.

35 Eleanor's itinerary is in Vale, *Princely Court*, 311.

36 Blake R. Beattie, *Angelus Pacis: The Legation of Cardinal Giovanni Gaetano Orsini 1326–1334* (2007), 8.

37 Sophia Menache, *Clement V* (Cambridge, 1998) 166–7.

38 Bruno Gebhardt, *Handbuch der deutschen Geschichte: Frühzeit und Mittelalter*, Band 1 (Stuttgart, 1970), 526, for Balduin's 1323 visit to Paris. Blanche de Valois, half-sister of the future King Philip VI of France and aunt of Edward III's queen Philippa (although she was a few years younger than Philippa), was the first of the four wives of the emperor Charles IV, who was baptised Wenzel but changed his name in honour of his uncle Charles IV of France.

39 Wolfgang Schmid, 'Vom Rheinland nach Böhmen' in *Die Goldene Bulle: Politik, Wahrnehmung, Rezeption*, vol. 1 (Berlin, 2009), 434.

40 Walter Woodburn Hyde, 'The Alpine Passes in Nature and History', *The Scientific Monthly*, 45.4 (1937), 325.

41 Hyde, 'Alpine Passes', 325–6.

42 Information from Ivan Fowler.

43 Deutscher, *Schrein*, 5.

44 Hyde, 'Alpine Passes', 325, 328. Frederick Barbarossa ('Redbeard') was Edward III's great-great-great-great-great-grandfather via Edward's mother Isabella, but was not an ancestor of Edward II.

45 *CCR 1318–23*, 363; *CCR 1323–27*, 353.

46 Thanks to Ivan Fowler for the information.

47 The present mayor and dignitaries of the town, in conversation with Ivan Fowler, also do not believe that Edward was ever there.

48 Ian Mortimer made this identification: *Perfect King*, 414; *Intrigue*, 198, 200. Seymour Phillips agrees that Mulazzo is the most likely identification: *Edward II*, 586. Stefano Castagneto, a member of the Auramala Project, thinks that an 'I' in a name is unlikely, phonetically speaking, to turn into a 'U' over time, but this may simply be a scribal error; it is very easy to write an 'I' instead of a 'U'. Ivan Fowler of the Auramala Project has seen modern-day archivists write Mulazzo as 'Milazzo' by mistake, and this error could certainly have been made as well by their fourteenth-century predecessors.

49 *Intrigue*, 198, 200.

50 Thank you to Ivan Fowler for the information; https://theauramalaproject. wordpress.com/2013/12/18/the-hunt-for-the-king-6-a-mysterious-castle/; see also *Intrigue*, 226 note 106.

51 *CPR 1313–17*, 340; the family tree is in *Intrigue*, 215–16.

52 *CCR 1313–18*, 589. Essentially, Carlo Fieschi was chosen as lord of the city of Genoa, and as it was an important port, this was an extremely eminent position. Another of Luca and Carlo's brothers, Federico Fieschi, was appointed 'to be of the king's household forever' in August 1317: *CPR 1317–21*, 10.

53 Information from https://theauramalaproject.wordpress.com/2014/01/22/ the–hunt–for–the–king–8–the–countryside–wreckers–and–the–king/

54 *Intrigue*, 196; *Perfect King*, 413.

55 Phillips, 586 note 43.

Chapter 11

1 On this point I disagree with Cuttino and Lyman's otherwise very helpful timeline in their article 'Where is Edward II?', 540–3: they say that Edward probably reached Melazzo (i.e. *Milascio*, though this is surely the wrong identification) in *c*. June/July 1331. This seems impossibly fast for Edward to have completed his two journeys through France, to Brabant, Cologne and over the Alps to Italy.

2 Hopper, *To be a Pilgrim*, 98–9; https://www.peterrobins.co.uk/itineraries/ map.html?itin=usk.

3 https://www.peterrobins.co.uk/itineraries/map.html?itin=usk

4 https://www.peterrobins.co.uk/itineraries/emo.html

5 https://www.peterrobins.co.uk/itineraries/map.html?itin=tournay

6   *Scalacronica*, 70.
7   'Edward III, his Father and the Fieschi', and 'Edward and the Moneylenders', 175–257.
8   *Intrigue*, 196ff.
9   *Intrigue*, 209; https://theauramalaproject.wordpress.com/2014/01/30/debating-our-research-with-ian-mortimer/
10   As suggested to the author by Ivan Fowler.
11   *Intrigue*, 215–17, for the Fieschi family tree. Manuele Fieschi was the great-grandson of Opizzo Fieschi, Count of Lavagna, whose brother Sinibaldo was Pope Innocent IV. Tedisio, another of Opizzo's brothers, was the grandfather of Luca Fieschi and the father of Ottobuono, Pope Adrian V.
12   *CCW*, 117.
13   *CPR 1292–1301*, 608.
14   Hilda Johnstone, *Letters of Edward, Prince of Wales 1304–05* (Cambridge, 1931), 54.
15   Phillips, 'Italy', 218–19 note 49.
16   *Intrigue*, 190, 223 note 52.
17   *Intrigue*, 190, 222–3 note 48, citing Brumisan's letter in *Foedera 1272–1307*, 559. The letter begins *Illustri & magnifico domino Ydoardo, Dei gratia excellenti Regi Anglorum, Brumisan uxor Ugolini de Flisco comitis Lavaniae, ejus consanguinea & ancilla*, 'To the illustrious and magnificent Lord Edward, by the grace of God excellent King of England, Brumisan, wife of Ugo Fieschi, Count of Lavagna, his kinswoman and servant.' Later in the letter she refers to *patrem meum, bonae memoriae, dominum Jacobum de Cateto*, 'my father of good memory, Lord Giacomo del Carretto'. Brumisan added that she knew Edward I had always 'tenderly loved' Giacomo and his other relatives from the house of Savoy. Thank you to Ivan Fowler for the translation.
18   The genealogist Kevin McKenzie, in a personal communication with the author, has expressed his belief that Cardinal Luca Fieschi's mother Leonora or Lionetta was indeed a daughter of Giacomo del Carretto and Caterina da Marano. Del Carretto's daughter Brumisan, who addressed Edward I as her kinsman in 1278, married Ugo Fieschi, brother of Cardinal Luca's father Niccolo. If the Leonora/Lionetta who married Niccolo was Brumisan's sister, this would mean two Carretto sisters marrying two Fieschi brothers. Luca Fieschi's first cousin Andriola Fieschi, daughter of his father Niccolo's brother Federico, married Antonio del Carretto, brother of Brumisan and perhaps of Leonora/Lionetta. Brumisan Fieschi née del Carretto appears in no Italian record and her existence is only known because of her letter to Edward I in 1278, and thus it is certainly possible that she had a sister Leonora/Lionetta who also appears in no Italian records which identify her family background.
19   *CPL 1305–41*, 187, 310, 322, 359.
20   As suggested by Doherty, *Death*, 212, who calls it a 'clever piece of blackmail' and suggests Fieschi was trying to wheedle favours out of Edward III by writing it.

21 Percivalle's father Guglielmo and Manuele's father Andrea were brothers: *Intrigue*, 217. Percivalle was appointed Bishop of Brescia in 1317 and Bishop of Tortona in 1325. Information that he was with Luca in England comes from Mario Traxino of the Auramala Project, an expert on the Fieschi family.

22 Jean's mother was Marguerite Duèse, sister of John XXII, born Jacques Duèse.

23 Edward II gave Laudun a pair of silver dishes and a silver-gilt basin, 'chased and enamelled, with ewer', worth £7 10s when Laudun left England on 17 May 1321: Thomas Stapleton, 'A Brief Summary of the Wardrobe Accounts of the tenth, eleventh, and fourteenth years of King Edward the Second', *Archaeologia*, 26 (1836), 334. For Laudun as an envoy to England in 1324 and again in 1326, see *CPL 1305–41*, 455, 462–4, 473, 478; *CPR 1324–7*, 269; *CCR 1323–7*, 563–4.

24 *CPR 1307–13*, 278.

25 Guillaume Mollat, *Jean XXII (1316–1334): Lettres Communes analysées d'Après les registres dits d'Avignon et du Vatican* (Paris, 1877), vol. 4, nos. 46811 and 46812: thank you to Ivan Fowler for the references.

26 *CPL 1305–41*, 8, 201, 294, 310, 327–8 (death); *CIM 1308–48*, 333–4; *CCW*, 320, 560.

27 For example, the monastery of Sant'Andrea di Borzone, the Fieschi 'family monastery', had another dependency in the diocese of Piacenza, Santa Maria di Taro. Manuele Fieschi was executor to the appointment of the prior in 1336. Three members of Luca Fieschi's household held prebends in the diocese of Piacenza, Manuele Fieschi was executor to another four prebends in the diocese, and other members of Luca's household were executors for another six prebends in the diocese, totalling fourteen papal letters linking Luca's household with the diocese, one of the dioceses with the highest number of links to the Fieschi family. Thank you to Ivan Fowler for this information.

28 *Intrigue*, 187–8; https://theauramalaproject.wordpress.com/2015/04/01/the-hunt-for-the-king-reply-post-who-was-afraid-of-edward-ii/

29 Archives départmentales de l'Hérault, series G/1123, folio 86r; Cartulaire de Maguelone, Register A; see Phillips, 'Italy', 214–15.

30 https://theauramalaproject.wordpress.com/2015/11/01/the-hunt-for-the-king-24-the-fieschi-letter-was-part-of-bishop-arnauld-de-verdales-personal-archive/; Phillips, 583 note 33.

31 For an overview of Italian scholarship on the Fieschi Letter, see Phillips, 'Italy', 216–18.

32 Benedict XII's orders to Verdale include the following: 'We [the pope] will write two letters to Him [Ludwig] of the same form contained in the attached document enclosed with the present documents, and We desire that firstly you present Him the letter marked "A" on the back, and having received from Him an answer about that for which we sent you, and about the substance of that which We told you in person and then later in letters,

without any transgression observed in anything, then, presenting him the other letter marked "B" on the back, you shall obtain from him, if you can, an answer concerning its contents.' *Close Letters, Vatican Register 134, no cccxciv [414 verso]* cited in https://theauramalaproject.wordpress.com/2014/04/16/the-hunt-for-the-king-9-pope-benedict-xiis-letter-to-his-legate-arnauld-de-verdale-at-the-court-of-emperor-louis-de-bavaria-january-1339/.

33 The theory is the Auramala Project's; see https://theauramalaproject.wordpress.com/?s=verdale for their many fascinating posts on the subject.

34 Ormrod, *Edward III*, 248; https://theauramalaproject.wordpress.com/2015/04/01/the-hunt-for-the-king-reply-post-who-was-afraid-of-edward-ii/.

35 Cited in https://theauramalaproject.wordpress.com/2015/11/08/the-hunt-for-the-king-25-back-to-the-verdale-hypothesis-with-new-evidence/

36 As suggested by Elena Corbellini of the Auramala Project.

37 Phillips, 584 note 33. The King of Aragon from November 1327 until his death in January 1336 was Alfonso IV, son of Cardinal Luca Fieschi's claimed relative Jaime II, then Alfonso's 16-year-old son Pedro IV, who ruled Aragon for more than half a century until his death in 1387. Pedro was betrothed to Edward II's youngest child Joan of the Tower in 1325, though the marriage never took place.

38 Phillips, 592.

39 King, 'Revisited', 20.

Chapter 12

1 Phillips, 'Italy', 213 note 24.

2 Mortimer, *Perfect King*, 151; Ormrod, *Edward III*, 201.

3 Ormrod, *Edward III*, 618, for Edward's itinerary.

4 Peter Schmid, 'Bayerns Blick nach Westen: Ludwig der Bayer und König Eduard III' in *Bayern mitten in Europa: vom Frühmittelalter bis ins 20. Jahrhundert*, ed. Alois Schmid and Katharina Weigand (2005), 82–3.

5 *Wardrobe Book of William de Norwell*, 212, 214. The first (undated) entry says: *Francisco Lumbard servienti domini regis ad arma pro tot denariis per ipsum solutis pro expensis Willelmi le Galeys qui asserit se patrem domini regis nunc nuper arestati apud Coloniam et per ipsum Franciscum apud regem sic ducti usque ud Confluenciam per manus proprias, 25s 6d*; 'To Franciscus Lumbard, sergeant-at-arms of the lord king, for that amount of money spent by him on the expenses of William le Galeys who asserts that he is the father of the present lord king, recently arrested at Cologne and led to the king by the said Franciscus at Koblenz by his own hands, 25s 6d.' The second: *Francekino Forcet' pro denariis per ipsum receptis pro expensis Willelmi Galeys in custodia sua existentis quia nominavit se regem Angliae patrem regis nunc videlicit per tres septimanas mense Octobris dicto anno xii per manus proprias ibidem xviii die Octobris, 13s 6d*; 'To Francekino Forcet[i?] for the money received by him for the expenses of William le Galeys remaining in his custody, because he called himself King

of England, father of the present king, namely for three weeks in the month of October of the said twelfth year [of Edward III's reign, i.e. 1338] by his own hands on this 18th day of December, 13s 6d.' I am grateful to Kevin McKenzie for visiting The National Archives in Kew and looking at and photographing the original document, E 36/203, and to Paul Dryburgh of The National Archives for his advice. The words 'for three weeks in the month of October of the said twelfth year' were written in superscript above the text, i.e. a clerk added the words later, presumably because he had forgotten to include them; this is not uncommon in the document.

6   For example, *CPR 1301–07*, 532.
7   *Calendar of Memoranda Rolls Michaelmas 1326–Michaelmas 1327*, 375.
8   *CPR 1345–48*, 428.
9   *Perfect King*, 464 note 53; *CCR 1313–18*, 570; *CCR 1330–33*, 121 etc.
10 *Calendar of Memoranda Rolls Michaelmas 1326–Michaelmas 1327*, 379.
11 *Norwell*, 214, for Athelard, *de armaturis et aliis hernesiis regis ibidem arestatis et de ibidem venire faciendo usque Andewarpiam*; thank you to Ivan Fowler for bringing this entry to my attention. Ian Mortimer has also pointed out that *arestare* does not simply mean 'arrest' in the modern sense, but in the fourteenth century had a wider application: sailors could be 'arrested' to work on ships, or carpenters and masons were 'arrested' to work on a royal building, for example. *Greatest Traitor*, 260, *Intrigue*, 180, and see also Phillips, 'Italy' 222 and note 71, and *Edward II*, 594.
12 *Intrigue*, 181, for Norwell serving Edward II since 1313.
13 *Norwell*, 207.
14 Rudolf, count palatine of the Rhine, was the son of Emperor Ludwig's older brother Rudolf 'the Stammerer', Duke of Bavaria. Ludwig of Brandenburg was the emperor's son with his first wife Beatrix of Silesia. Ludwig the emperor and Duke Rudolf of Saxony-Wittenberg were both grandsons of Rudolf von Habsburg, King of Germany (d. 1291), and nephews of Albrecht I von Habsburg, the King of Germany who died in 1308 and was buried in Speyer Cathedral.
15 Schmid, 'Bayerns Blick nach Westen', 83.
16 *Perfect King*, 148–9.
17 Schmid, 'Bayerns Blick', 81.
18 *Intrigue*, 202–6; Phillips, 594–5.
19 *Intrigue*, 180–1, and 221 note 26.
20 Thank you to Kevin McKenzie for suggesting and discussing this point with Ivan Fowler and myself.
21 Ormrod, *Edward III*, 203.
22 *Intrigue*, 311–13. Margaret 'the Maid' was the daughter of Erik II of Norway and the granddaughter and heir via her mother of Alexander III of Scotland, who married Edward I's sister Margaret of England. She was thus the first cousin once removed of Edward of Caernarfon, who was betrothed to her in 1289 when he was 5 and she 6.

23 Pierre Chaplais, *Piers Gaveston: Edward II's Adoptive Brother* (1994), 111–12.
24 *Edward III*, 123.
25 See Phillips, 585, for an overview.
26 Haines, '*Edwardus Redivivus*', 79–80; Haines, *Edward II*, 237–8.
27 Doherty, *Death*, 207–13.
28 *Greatest Traitor*, 259–60.
29 Phillips, 'Italy', 220; *Edward II*, 589, 592–3.
30 King, 'Revisited', 19.
31 *Perfect King*, 201.
32 *CPR 1340–43*, 333, 355–6.
33 *Perfect King*, 201.

Part IV

1   Mortimer, 'Sermons of Sodomy', originally published in *Reign of Edward II*, reprinted in *Intrigue*, 45ff.
2   Mary Saaler, *Edward II 1307–1327* (London, 1997), 140; Ivan Fowler has also independently suggested this point to the author.
3   The expression *per cautelam* cannot mean that Edward was killed 'as a precaution', which would be *causae cautelae*. *Per cautelam* with the meaning 'by a trick' or 'by trickery' is medieval, not classical, Latin (thanks to Ivan Fowler).
4   'King Edward II: A Mysterious Death', *Medieval Murder Mysteries*, shown on the Yesterday channel in the UK on Tuesday 17 November 2015.
5   Chaplais, *Piers Gaveston*, 112–13.
6   Chronicler Geoffrey le Baker claimed decades later that Edward II was forced to abdicate his throne to his son in early 1327 by being threatened that if he did not do so voluntarily, a person not of royal birth would succeed him as king instead. This has often been understood by later commentators to be a reference to Roger Mortimer, though Baker does not say this, and there is no other confirmation of this story. It is impossible that any of the English lords and bishops, or indeed Queen Isabella, in 1327 would have recognised anyone but Edward III as king, with his younger brother John of Eltham and Edward II's half-brothers the earls of Norfolk and Kent after him in the succession, and the notion that they would ever have chosen Mortimer as the crowned and anointed King of England is nonsense. Mortimer had no possible claim to the throne and was only distantly related to Edward II and Edward III. There is also a modern idea, based solely on a statement by the chronicler Jean Froissart (born *c*.1337), that Isabella was pregnant with Mortimer's child at the time of their downfall in 1330, a child whom Edward III would have seen as dangerous to his occupation of the throne. Edward III's claim to the English throne came via his father Edward II, not Isabella, and an illegitimate half-sibling born to his mother and her lover years after Edward II's death, although certainly embarrassing, would not have threatened the young king's position

in any way. There is no reason to think that Isabella ever did give birth to Mortimer's child, and no confirmation of Froissart's claim that she was pregnant in 1330.

7 See my book *Isabella of France: The Rebel Queen* for a longer discussion of Edward and Isabella's relationship.

8 Tommaso di Carpegna Falconieri, *The Man Who Believed He Was King of France: A True Medieval Tale* (2009); Charles Wood, 'Where is John the Posthumous? Or, Mahaut of Artois Settles her Royal Debts', in *Documenting the Past: Essays Presented to George Peddy Cuttino*, ed. Jeffrey Hamilton and Patricia Bradley (1989), 99–117.

9 Michael Evans, *The Death of Kings: Royal Deaths in Medieval England* (London, 2003), 156–7.

10 Jonathan Sumption, 'Plotting the Past', *The Guardian*, 5 April 2003.

11 Hamilton, 'Uncertain Death', 1272; Haines, *Edward II*, 212; Doherty, *Death*, 147–8 (two quotations); Tout, 'Captivity', 173; Jonathan Sumption, 'Plotting the Past', *The Guardian*, 5 April 2003; Haines, 'Scam', 149; Haines, *Death of a King*, 113; Phillips, 567 note 274, agrees that regarding Kent as 'stupid and gullible' is 'probably a fair assessment'.

12 *Intrigue*, 83.

13 See also *Intrigue*, 83–4.

14 See Linda E. Mitchell, *Portraits of Medieval Women: Family, Marriage, and Politics in England 1225–1350* (2003), 101–4, who praises Beaumont and Vescy's (and especially Vescy's) grasp of political intrigue, and comments on how astutely they read the signs and managed to switch their loyalties at the right time, on several occasions.

15 *Murimuth*, 60.

16 McKisack, *The Fourteenth Century 1307–1399*, 100.

17 Haines, 'Sumptuous Apparel', 892.

18 Haines, 'Scam', 150.

19 Haines, 'Scam', 151; Phillips, 571 note 297.

20 Haines, *Edward II*, 212, 233; Haines, 'Sumptuous Apparel', 891.

21 Haines, 'Scam', 150.

22 King, 'Revisited', 20.

23 King, 'Revisited', 20.

24 Warner, 'Adherents', 781; King, 'Revisited', 7.

25 *CCR 1330–33*, 17–18, 52.

26 Haines, *Death of a King*, 113.

27 King, 'Revisited', 13.

28 King, 13–14, and for the 'sting' remark.

29 King, 13.

30 *Brut*, 267.

31 *Intrigue*, 88; King, 'Revisited', 12.

32 Haines, *Death of a King*, 78; Haines, 'Gurney, Regicide?', 57; Phillips, 580.

33 David Carpenter, 'Where is Edward II?', *London Review of Books*, 7 June 2007, 32–4, cited in Mortimer, *Intrigue*, 124–5. See King, 'Revisited', 16; Phillips, 579–80; Hamilton, 'Uncertain Death', 1271.

34 *PROME*; and see Seymour Phillips' comment in his *Edward II*, 579 note 18, that when he co-translated *PROME*, his 'intention there was to avoid over-interpretation of the text' and that he was aware it was open to different meanings.

35 Quintus at www.thelatintranslator.com, now sadly defunct.

36 Haines, *Edward II*, 221.

37 https://theauramalaproject.wordpress.com/2014/11/08/the-hunt-for-the-king-19-exploding-a-myth-about-the-fieschi-letter/

38 In his *Cronica Nuova*, Libro Undecimo.

39 Phillips, 592–3.

40 Phillips, 592.

41 Phillips, 591–2.

42 *Perfect King*, 152–4; see also *Intrigue*, 178–82.

43 Doherty, *Death*, 213–4.

44 Phillips, 'Italy' 224–6; *Edward II*, 596–8.

45 Phillips, 594.

46 In J.S. Hamilton's review of my book *Edward II: The Unconventional King* in *The Medieval Review*, number 15.06.34, 2015; https://scholarworks.iu.edu/journals/index.php/tmr/article/view/19272/25396 .

Conclusion

1 I owe this point to Ivan Fowler.

2 Edward ordered Gurney to be questioned 'concerning the sedition and conspiracy [to kill Edward II] aforesaid and the assent, instigation and procuration made concerning it, and by whom and in what manner they were made, and to cause his confession to be put into writing by a notary public'.

3 *Thirteenth Century England X*, ed. Michael Prestwich, Richard Britnell and Robin Frame (2005), viii, about Phillips' article '"Edward II" in Italy'.

Appendices

1 The original Latin text and English translation are taken from the Auramala Project and used here with their kind permission; for more information, see https://theauramalaproject.wordpress.com/the-fieschi-letter/

2 Original text from Warwickshire County Record Office, CR 136/C2027, printed in Haines, 'Sumptuous Apparel', 893–4, and my translation from the French (a slightly different translation appears in Mortimer, *Medieval Intrigue*, 154–5).

3 Taken from *PROME*, November 1330 Parliament, 57.

4 E. M. Thompson, *Adae Murimuth Continuatio Chronicarum*, 253–7; French in the original; my translation differs somewhat from the printed translation.

SELECT BIBLIOGRAPHY

Note: This is an intentionally short bibliography which cites only sources, articles and books directly relevant to Edward II's death or survival. For a longer one, see my *Edward II: The Unconventional King*, and for an exhaustive bibliography of Edward's life, death, reign and era, see Seymour Phillips' *Edward II*.

PRIMARY SOURCES

Adae Murimuth Continuatio Chronicarum, ed. E. M. Thompson (London: Eyre and Spottiswoode, 1889)

Annales Londonienses 1195–1330, in W. Stubbs, ed., *Chronicles of the Reigns of Edward I and Edward II*, vol. 1, 76 (London: Rolls Series, 1882)

Annales Paulini 1307–1340, in Stubbs, *Chronicles*, vol. 1

The Anonimalle Chronicle 1307 to 1334, from Brotherton Collection MS 29, ed. W. R. Childs and J. Taylor (Yorkshire Archaeological Society Record Series 147, 1991)

Archives départmentales de l'Hérault, series G/1123, folio 86r (Fieschi Letter)

The Brut or the Chronicles of England, part 1, ed. F. W. D. Brie (London: Early English Text Society, 1906)

Calendar of the Close Rolls, 6 vols., 1307–33 (London: HMSO, 1898–1906)

Calendar of Entries in the Papal Registers Relating to Great Britain and Ireland: Papal Letters, vol. 2, 1305–1341, ed. W.H. Bliss (London: Eyre and Spottiswoode for HMSO, 1895)

Calendar of the Fine Rolls, 3 vols., 1307–1337 (London: HMSO, 1911–13)

Calendar of the Patent Rolls, 7 vols., 1307–1334 (London: HMSO, 1891–1903)

Calendar of Memoranda Rolls (Exchequer): Michaelmas 1326–Michaelmas 1327 (London: HMSO, 1968)

Croniques de London depuis l'an 44 Hen. III jusqu'à l'an 17 Edw. III, ed. G. J. Aungier (London: Camden Society, 1844)

Flores Historiarum, ed. H.R. Luard, vol. 3 (London: Eyre and Spottiswoode for HMSO, 1890)

Froissart: Chronicles, ed. Geoffrey Brereton (London: Penguin, 1978)

Galbraith, V. H., 'Extracts from the *Historia Aurea* and a French "Brut"', *English Historical Review*, 43 (1928)

The Chronicle of Geoffrey le Baker of Swinbrook, trans. David Preest (Woodbridge: Boydell and Brewer, 2012)

Chronicon Galfridi le Baker de Swynebroke, ed. E. M. Thompson (Oxford: Clarendon Press, 1889)

Foedera, Conventiones, Litterae et Cujuscunque Generis Acta Publica, vol. 2.1, 1307–1327, and vol. 2.2, 1327–1344 (London: Thomas Rymer, 1818)

Gesta Edwardi de Carnarvon Auctore Canonico Bridlingtoniensi, in W. Stubbs, ed., *Chronicles of the Reigns of Edward I and Edward II*, vol. 2, 76 (London: Rolls Series, 1883)

Hallam, Elizabeth, *The Itinerary of Edward II and His Household, 1307–1327* (London: List and Index Society, 1984)

The Chronicle of Lanercost 1272–1346, ed. Herbert Maxwell (Glasgow: James Maclehose and Sons, 1913)

Le Livere de Reis de Britanie e le Livere de Reis de Engletere, ed. John Glover (London: Longman, Green, 1865)

The National Archives: Chancery, Duchy of Lancaster, Exchequer, King's Bench and Special Collection records

The Parliament Rolls of Medieval England, ed. Chris Given-Wilson et al., CD-ROM edition (Scholarly Editions, 2005)

Polychronicon Ranulphi Higden, monachi Cestrensis, vol. 8, ed. J. R. Lumby (London: Longman, Green, 1865)

Recueil des Historiens des Gaules et de la France, vol. 22: *Contenant la troisième livraison des monuments des règnes de Philippe le Bel, de Louis X, de Philippe V et de Charles IV, depuis MCCXXVI jusqu'en MCCCXXVIII*, ed. M. M. de Wailly and Delisle (Paris: Victor Palmé 1840)

Scalacronica: The Reigns of Edward I, Edward II and Edward III as Recorded by Sir Thomas Gray of Heton, knight, ed. Herbert Maxwell (Glasgow: James Maclehose and Sons, 1907)

Scalacronica: By Sir Thomas Gray of Heton, knight. A Chronicle of England and Scotland From A. D. MLXVI to A. D. MCCCLXII, ed. J. Stevenson (Edinburgh: Maitland Club, 1836)

Society of Antiquaries of London MS 122 (Edward's chamber account of 1325–26)

Vita Edwardi Secundi Monachi Cuiusdam Malmesberiensis, ed. N. Denholm-Young (London: Thomas Nelson and Sons, 1957)

The Wardrobe Book of William de Norwell: 12 July 1338 to 27 May 1340, ed. Mary Lyon et al. (Brussels: Palais des Académies, 1983)

Warwickshire County Record Office, CR 136/C2027 (William Melton's letter of January 1330)

SECONDARY SOURCES

Bloom, J. Harvey, 'Simon de Swanland and King Edward II', *Notes and Queries*, 11th series, 4 (1911)

Burden, Joel, 'Re-Writing a Rite of Passage: The Peculiar Funeral of Edward II', in *Rites of Passage*, ed. N. F. McDonald and W. M. Ormrod (Woodbridge: Boydell and Brewer, 2004)

Childs, W. R., 'Welcome, My Brother: Edward II, John of Powderham and the Chronicles, 1318', in I. Wood and G. A. Loud, eds., *Church and Chronicle in the Middle Ages: Essays Presented to John Taylor* (London and Rio Grande: Hambledon Press, 1991)

Cuttino, G. P. and Lyman, T. W., 'Where is Edward II?', *English Historical Review*, 53 (1978)

Dodd, Gwilym and Musson, Anthony, eds., *The Reign of Edward II: New Perspectives* (York: York Medieval Press, 2006)

Doherty, Paul, *Isabella and the Strange Death of Edward II* (London: Constable and Robinson, 2003)

Fowler, Ivan, *Auramala: The King Lives* (Pavia: The World of TELS, 2013). A thoroughly revised Italian edition of the novel, *Edward: Il Mistero del Re di Auramala*, was published by Piemme in June 2016, and the English version is eagerly anticipated.

Haines, Roy Martin, 'Edwardus Redivivus', *Transactions of the Bristol and Gloucestershire Archaeological Society* (1996)

Haines, Roy Martin, *Death of a King* (Lancaster: Scotforth Books, 2002)

Haines, Roy Martin, *King Edward II: His Life, His Reign, and Its Aftermath, 1284–1330* (Montreal: MacGill-Queen's University Press, 2003)

Haines, Roy Martin, 'Sir Thomas Gurney of Englishcombe, Regicide?', *Somerset Archaeological and Natural History*, 147 (2004)

Haines, Roy Martin, 'Roger Mortimer's Scam', *Transactions of the Bristol and Gloucestershire Archaeological Society*, 126 (2008)

Haines, Roy Martin, 'Sumptuous Apparel for a Royal Prisoner: Archbishop Melton's Letter, 14 January 1330', *English Historical Review*, 124 (2009)

Hamilton, J. S., 'The Uncertain Death of Edward II', *History Compass*, 6, 5 (2008)

Hunter, Joseph, 'On the Measures Taken for the Apprehension of Sir Thomas de Gournay, One of the Murderers of Edward II', *Archaeologia*, 27 (1838)

Johnstone, Hilda, *Letters of Edward, Prince of Wales 1304–5* (Cambridge: Roxburghe Club, 1931)

King, Andy, 'The Death of Edward II Revisited', in *Fourteenth Century England IX*, ed. James Bothwell and Gwilym Dodd (Woodbridge: Boydell Press, 2016)

Moore, S. A., 'Documents relating to the Death and Burial of Edward II', *Archaeologia*, 50 (1887)

Mortimer, Ian, *The Greatest Traitor: The Life of Sir Roger Mortimer, Ruler of England 1327 to 1330* (London: Pimlico, 2003)

Mortimer, Ian, 'The Death of Edward II in Berkeley Castle', *English Historical Review*, 489 (2005) (reprinted in his *Medieval Intrigue*)

Mortimer, Ian, 'Sermons of Sodomy: A Reconsideration of Edward II's Sodomitical Reputation', in *The Reign of Edward II: New Perspectives*, ed. Dodd and Musson (reprinted in his *Medieval Intrigue*)

Mortimer, Ian, *The Perfect King: The Life of Edward III* (London: Vintage, 2006)

Mortimer, Ian, *Medieval Intrigue: Decoding Royal Conspiracies* (London: Continuum, 2010)

Perry, R., *Edward the Second: Suddenly, at Berkeley* (Wotton-under-Edge: Ivy House Books, 1988)

Phillips, J. R. S[eymour], '"Edward II" in Italy: English and Welsh Political Exiles and Fugitives in Continental Europe, 1322–1364', in *Thirteenth Century England X*, ed. Michael Prestwich, Richard Britnell and Robin Frame (Woodbridge: Boydell Press, 2005)

Phillips, Seymour, *Edward II* (New Haven and London: Yale University Press, 2010)

Saaler, Mary, *Edward II 1307–1327* (London: Rubicon, 1997)

Tanqueray, Frédéric J., 'The Conspiracy of Thomas Dunheved, 1327', *English Historical Review*, 31 (1916)

Tout, T.F., 'The Captivity and Death of Edward of Carnarvon', *Collected Papers of T.F. Tout*, vol. 3 (Manchester: Manchester University Press, 1934)

Vale, Malcolm, *The Princely Court: Medieval Courts and Culture in North-West Europe* (Oxford: Oxford University Press, 2001)

Valente, Claire, 'The Deposition and Abdication of Edward II', *English Historical Review*, 113 (1998)

Warner, Kathryn, 'The Adherents of Edmund of Woodstock, Earl of Kent, in March 1330', *English Historical Review*, 126 (2011)

Warner, Kathryn, *Edward II: The Unconventional King* (Stroud: Amberley, 2014)

Warner, Kathryn, *Isabella of France: The Rebel Queen* (Stroud: Amberley, 2016)

ONLINE SOURCES

My blog edwardthesecond.blogspot.com contains many hundreds of
  articles about Edward II, his life, family and reign, including many
  about his death or survival, linked in the sidebar under 'Aftermath
  of Edward's Reign'
My friends at the Auramala Project run a fantastic blog at https://
  theauramalaproject.wordpress.com/, full of information and original research about Edward II's possible survival in Italy
Ian Mortimer's website has two must-read articles about Edward II's
  fate, in addition to all his printed material on the subject: http://
  www.ianmortimer.com/essays/inconvenientfact.pdf and http://
  www.ianmortimer.com/essays/uncertainties.htm

INDEX

If you enjoyed this book, you may also be interested in...

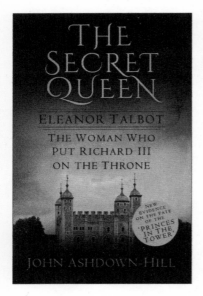

The Secret Queen

JOHN ASHDOWN-HILL

978 0 7509 6846 1

When Edward IV died in 1483, the Yorkist succession was called into question by doubts about the legitimacy of his sons (the 'Princes in the Tower'). The crown therefore passed to Edward IV's undoubtedly legitimate younger brother, Richard, Duke of Gloucester. But Richard, too, found himself entangled in the web of uncertainly, since those who believed in the legitimacy of Edward IV's children viewed Richard III's own accession with suspicion. From the day that Edward IV married Eleanor, or pretended to do so, the House of York, previously so secure in its bloodline, confronted a contentious and uncertain future. John Ashdown-Hill argues that Eleanor Talbot was married to Edward IV, and that therefore Edward's subsequent union with Elizabeth Widville was bigamous, making her children illegitimate. In his quest to reveal the truth about Eleanor, he also uncovers fascinating new evidence that sheds fresh light on one of the greatest historical mysteries of all time – the identity of the 'bones in the urn' in Westminster Abbey, believed for centuries to be the remains of the 'Princes in the Tower'.

The destination for history
www.thehistorypress.co.uk